THE
BARTENDER'S
MANIFESTO

⁂ THE ⁂
BARTENDER'S
MANIFESTO

HOW TO THINK, DRINK & CREATE
COCKTAILS LIKE A PRO

TOBY MALONEY
& THE BARTENDERS OF THE VIOLET HOUR
WITH EMMA JANZEN

PHOTOGRAPHS BY ZACHARY JAMES JOHNSTON
ILLUSTRATIONS BY ZISSOU TASSEFF-ELENKOFF

CLARKSON POTTER/PUBLISHERS
NEW YORK

CONTENTS

At the violet hour, when the eyes and back
Turn upward from the desk, when the human engine waits
Like a taxi throbbing waiting . . .
At the violet hour, the evening hour that strives
Homeward, and brings the sailor home from sea . . .

—T. S. ELIOT, "THE WASTE LAND"

Welcome to The Violet Hour. My name is Toby Maloney. I'm a bartender and I fucking love my job.

For reasons I can't begin to understand, not everyone respects the title of bartender. For most of my career, people thought bartending was a stopgap, something one did while waiting for their life to really start. But in those golden days that we bartenders dream about, the tavern was the focus of the town and the bartender was at its center. That person was thought of highly for all the things they could do—recount jokes, introduce new friends, and listen to tales of woe with furrowed brow. They knew when to say something, when to hold back. Their skills were not limited to knowledge of beverage recipes, but encompassed charisma, character, and empathy. We bartenders still hearken back to the days when Jerry Thomas wore diamond pins and threw fire for an awed audience because we know there is so much more to the profession than just slinging drinks.

I tend the bar, I keep the bar; I keep things moving, I keep people satisfied. Not just for an evening, but for the many fruitful evenings in guests' lives. On the nights it goes well, there is nothing else like it. Patrons sit gobsmacked and the air is afire with adulation, adrenaline, and Angostura. The chit and clack of the impact printer sets the pace, the mechanical hare just ahead of us greyhounds. Simple movements seem choreographed. The impromptu cocktail creation is just as good as you imagined it. You're in sync with the other bartender, ducking just when their sledgehammer shaker is coming down, slipping straws and garnishes in passing drinks, requesting a bottle from the back bar with a nod.

Working a shift in a cocktail bar is like a ten-hour squash game in a dirty submarine* being battered against a rocky shoal. But it is worth every bruise and cut and pair of sticky boots, because when someone sips from that frosty glass and shivers or closes their eyes or curls their toes, I feel it, too. There is a heady

---

* Or racket ball in a dirty submarine, as the other Toby, Toby Cecchini, describes it in his book, *Cosmopolitian: A Bartender's Life.*

combination of physicality, creativity, study, showing off, and camaraderie that keeps me coming back for more.

I've been in the service industry since I was eleven. I started as an underwater ceramic engineer,* but I've also cooked and prep-cooked, been a busboy and waited tables, worked the door, coat-checked, managed, bar-managed, and general-managed. I've owned bars and sold bars and ordered drinks in more bars than I can remember. I arrived in Chicago in the early '90s road weary and broke. I bartended and worked in kitchens so I could have the flexibility to fuck off to Southeast Asia for hot weather, spicy food, and frigid beer every winter. Then I moved to New York City and lucked into the cocktail game early, earning my chops in venerable cocktail meccas like Milk & Honey, Flatiron, Freemans, and Pegu Club.

In the spring of 2007, I moved back to Chicago to open a cocktail bar across the street from Wicker Park, where at that time you were more likely to get mugged than get organic kale at a farmers' market. I partnered with One Off Hospitality, a group that included Terry Alexander, Peter Garfield, and Donnie Madia, who had some of my favorite bars and restaurants under their umbrella.† There were many late nights assembling a place that would prove to be unlike any other in the city. A few days before opening, we went to one of the neighborhood's finest dives, Phyllis' Musical Inn, to vote on a name. We all tossed our ideas into a wet beer pitcher, pulled out streaky slips of paper, and read them out loud. "The Violet Hour" won by a nose over "Mother's Ruin."

"The Violet Hour" comes from the T. S. Eliot poem "The Waste Land" and from *The Hour,* a book by Bernard DeVoto. In his charming-yet-somewhat-curmudgeonly look at the art of imbibing, DeVoto described his perfect martini as 3.7 to 1, strained with a perforated, not coiled, strainer, and added that it must be consumed in an urban, not rural, setting. He was particular and persnickety, some of which we wanted to bring with us, some not so much. Either way, we did bring a very specific vision to the City of Broad Shoulders, and that pioneering cocktail bar ended up being exactly the seismic paradigm change we thought it would be.

Chicago hadn't seen anything like it before. The Violet Hour was massive, warehouse-size, like five times the physical size of Milk & Honey. Together with inventive architect and interior designer Thomas Schlesser, we turned the space into a surreal wonderland, a dark utopia the color of a frozen lake with flickering candlelight and a huge back bar. And the curtains—the curtains! Made of thick, weighted velvet, they suggested an opulence and a grandeur the city's cocktail scene

---

* Dishwasher.
† Plus Jason Cott of Alchemy Consulting.

hadn't offered in decades. A huge bonus was how the fireplace glowed on the far wall, promising succor with a come-hither wink on freezing winter nights.

We hired a staff that had never touched a jigger before, people who had not once set foot behind a bar. We took that menagerie of artists and dreamers and shaped them into crackerjacks of Hospitality, gave them the tools to be artisans and technicians of cocktails, and let them loose to aim for the stars. They showed up early and stayed late. Most of them could have made a lot more money at a more casual joint down the street (and worked fewer hours doing it), but they stayed here because it was a place where they were encouraged to grow and play and lead.

At first most people thought we were pretentious as all get-out. Probably because we were ostentatious as fuck. During service, our staff wore ties, vests, or vintage dresses—unthinkable attire, considering the casual nature of Wicker Park. We didn't allow cell phone conversations or take reservations. We didn't sling light beer or neon "martinis" in garish V-shaped glasses. We filled our back bar with spirits that were considered esoteric at the time, like Campari and Jamaican rum—not the usual suspects like Ketel One and Johnnie Walker. There were bowls of fresh berries, fragrant bouquets of mint, and a kaleidoscope of citrus on the bar instead of lowbrow plastic flip trays with nuclear-red cherries and green olives languishing in fetid brine. We wanted people to shake off familiar drinking routines and try something new, a task that sometimes felt like trying to push a boulder up a damn hill.

Secondly, we had rules. Yes, actual rules, printed out, framed, and hung in the front vestibule and in the bathrooms. We got the idea from Milk & Honey—a place where the inimitable Sasha Petraske put the utmost importance on making sure everybody felt comfortable. At Milk & Honey, the rules meant there was always a place to sit, the music played at a volume that allowed you to talk to your tablemates without yelling, and people from all walks of life treated each other with respect. We wanted to create a similarly welcoming atmosphere at The Violet Hour—no one wedging themselves between you and the person you were talking to, vying for the bartender's attention by waving a twenty-dollar bill, then

spilling their drink in your lap as they try to get it off the bar. No roving packs of dubious dudes hitting on every woman, playing the odds, annoying the whole room. What we wanted to create (and what Milk & Honey did so well) was, in a word, civilized.

By 2007, bars in New York City were well on the path to widespread cocktail acceptance, but here in Chicago, we were still on the front lines. I understand why people thought we were suspender-wearing, fedora-crowned jerkfaces. There was this pervasive notion at the time that all bars were the same, that they should cater to everyone, on every occasion, where you settled in with your usual and guzzled it without much thought. I *love* a good dive bar, beer bar, wine bar, or punk rock bar. I like shots of Jäger washed down with a Schlitz, with Ministry loud on the juke. But I didn't want those bars to be the only options the world had to offer. I wanted to create a place for cocktails, a place that *added* to the conversation instead of simply contributing to the existing hullabaloo.

It ended up working. The Violet Hour became a go-to spot for folks who wanted to do a deep dive into the world of cocktails. Or a place to take one's folks when they were in town, as well as a killer destination for a third date. Now folks come from far and wide to drink our cocktails and nobody bats an eye at our lack of vodka. How did it work out this way? I think it comes down to one simple truth: Enthusiasm and pretension cannot share the same air. If you are excited about something and work hard to bring it into the world with bright eyes and bubbly fervor, it will resonate with others.

The Violet Hour was to be a place where every staff member had passion, curiosity, and enthusiasm for their work. We wanted to cultivate an environment where bartending was taken as a serious profession. By that, I didn't mean that it *had* to be a career for every single person we hired, but we did want it to be more than just a job. A place where the bartenders wouldn't simply follow a checklist of best practices, but instead learn the ins and outs of drink making in a way that spoke to their interests and strengths so they could then fly free with the support to explore and improvise, invent and create. We encouraged everyone to find their niche, to read as much as they could about things like cocktail history and science, and to look for ideas everywhere. Everyone, from the door guys to the servers to the barbacks and bartenders, showed up to work every day with a genuine eagerness to learn and share their passion with others.

We also worked damn hard to create an organoleptic experience—that is, one that would stimulate all the senses. We start with the obvious five: sight, smell, sound, taste, and touch. The candlelight and dapper outfits, the smell of mint bouquets, sweet strawberries, and sunny citrus, all cut fresh for service. The cacophony of tin shakers smashing ice and liquid together, the soft murmur of the room and clinking glasses. The texture of the cocktail, the weight of the glass, and the padding of the comfy barstools—all these things come together to build a complete experience. Together, they are often more powerful when you don't notice them. When you orchestrate all of the elements correctly, it fucks with another sense: the sense of time—you can spend hours at The Violet Hour in the blink of an eye.

Of course, we also made damn good drinks. I believe this happened as a by-product of our enthusiasm, and because we approached drink making with a focus on ingenuity over the nebulous concept of "authenticity." When I first started in the "craft cocktail" scene, it was all about the classics. When and where was such and such made, by whom, with exactly what. This was interesting, and we benefited greatly from the approach as booze companies responded by bringing back lost and forgotten ingredients like Old Tom gin and crème de violette. Suddenly, we were able to make drinks like the Martinez and Aviation the way they used to be made. But instead of just re-presenting those drinks to our guests, we decided to use classic cocktails as a *launchpad* for creation, taking what's good about the past and embracing the present at the same time. Interpretation over rote repetition. Ingenuity over authenticity.

Looking back, I don't think we've changed all that much since the early days. We're a little more laid-back with the rules, and our music may be a bit louder, but for the most part we've worked really hard to maintain that original magic. That passion. That inherent need to create an all-encompassing *experience* for the people who walk through our curtains. Even through a global pandemic, we managed to keep the home fires burning. Which is, I suppose, how you have this tome in your hands right now . . .

This is the violet hour, the hour of hush and wonder, when the affections glow and valor is reborn, when the shadows deepen along the edge of the forest and we believe that, if we watch carefully, at any moment we may see the unicorn.

— BERNARD DEVOTO, *THE HOUR*

HOW TO USE
THIS BOOK

This is not a cocktail book that sits on your coffee table and gets nonchalantly regarded by friends and family while they wait for you to bring them a drink. It's a detailed look at the inner workings of what we do every night; an inked version of the lesson-by-lesson guide we use to teach bartenders the ins and outs of cocktail making and bartending, The Violet Hour Way. In short, it's a manifesto! A loudspeaker declaration of our motives, moves, intentions, and point of view. Every bit and bob that we think makes our approach specific to *us*.

In these pages, we won't simply tell you how 1 + 1 = 3—we'll teach you how to *think* like a bartender, how to *drink* like a bartender, and how to *create* cocktails like a bartender. By the end, you should be able to see the forest for the trees, because we'll look at everything and how it intertwines with everything else to create a beautiful orchestration of drink making and bartending. No detail is too small or insignificant. We'll teach you how to build upon the century-old canon of cocktails that millions of bartenders before you have worked to perfect. We'll also teach you how to nail technique, and how to deliver a memorable experience for the thirsty people on the receiving end of your liquid inventions.

The book starts with the mechanics of cocktail making in part one, where we set sail into formidable waters by tapping into the nuances of good technique. In part two, we dive into the murky territories of philosophy, followed by part three, where we explain how to flesh out a basic spec into something complex and phenomenally delicious. In part four, we explore what it means to bartend and how to find your personal style, finishing with part five, a big cannonball splash into the spirit of creativity with a workshop on how to transform the spark of an idea into a composed recipe.

This book is *not* Cocktails 101. The first thing we do with new bartenders is give them a list of required reading to build a foundation of knowledge before starting The Violet Hour school. If you don't yet know the difference between a Hawthorne strainer and a julep strainer, or a rhum, a rum, and a ron, or a Corpse Reviver and a Suffering Bastard, then go pick up a copy of Meehan's or Morgenthaler's bar books,* Martin Cate's *Smuggler's Cove,* and Gary Regan's *The Joy of Mixology.* Then come back and see us. We're skipping a lot of the basics because they have already been covered so brilliantly by the folks above.

There are recipes, too, yes! But this book is less about making *our* cocktails verbatim than it is about learning how to *think* and *create* the way The Violet Hour

---

* That is, *Meehan's Bartender Manual* by Jim Meehan and *The Bar Book* by Jeffrey Morgenthaler.

✳ FIND YOUR OWN PATH ✳

Here are a few routes we suggest taking to change your experience of reading this book, depending on your level of familiarity with mixing cocktails and bartending. Pick your path and follow the circuit. It will make all the difference.

| HOME BARTENDERS AND COCKTAIL NERDS START AT BALANCE (PAGE 20) | PROFESSIONAL BARTENDERS START AT INSPIRATION (PAGE 126) | CHEFS START AT INSPIRATION (PAGE 126) | SOMMELIERS AND CICERONES START AT RITUAL (PAGE 246) | DISTILLERS START AT BALANCE (PAGE 20) |

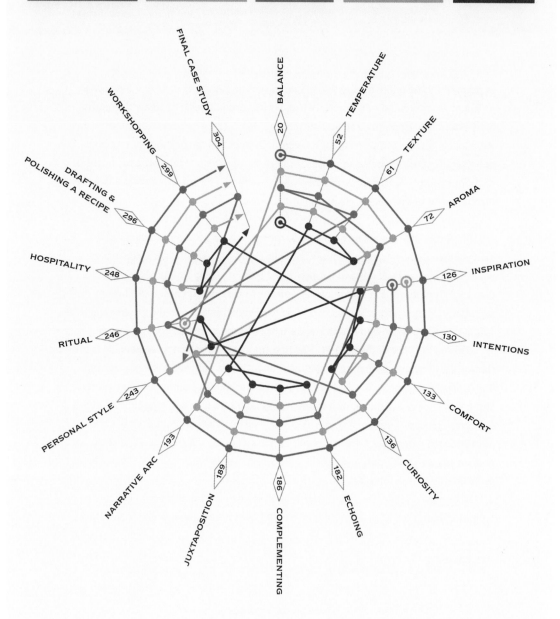

bartenders do. If you can make a drink exactly as it's written in this book, right now, with the prescribed brands, house-made syrups, and obscure bitters, that's awesome! Do it! But if you don't have all the ingredients on hand, we're offering the tools and techniques to look at a recipe and be able to make something that has the same spirit. You might end up with a drink that tastes totally different from what's sketched on the page—that's the fun part. Whatever you end up making should still be compelling, satisfying, and memorable, and that's what matters.

Use the recipes as homework. Mark them up, write in the margins! There are shaken drinks and stirred drinks, summer and winter drinks, drinks with whiskey and tequila and gin and beyond. In all situations, there is a key on the recipe page that you can use to find more info on shaking and stirring, syrups, glossary terms, techniques, garnish pictures, and the types of ice you will need.

We've written out the recipes using a template we created in-house. Every cocktail we have ever made was written down using this template. When broken down like this, you can see how each technique, philosophy, and flourish relates to the other parts of the cocktail. You can also see Balance even if the pillars of the Triptych (page 32) are split and jiggled six ways from Sunday. It makes analyzing a drink simple addition instead of an overly complicated wormhole. The spec should be read from top to bottom so you can visualize how the cocktail looks and tastes, but as you will see in the mixing instructions, drinks should be built in the reverse order, with the cheapest ingredients (or those you don't want to make mistakes with) going into the mix first, and the expensive ones coming into play last.

In the recipes, you'll also see that we take the exhaustive approach of explaining thought processes, tips, and tricks in the mixing instructions. I'd love to make some grandiose infomercial claim that the path to a perfect cocktail is as easy as shake/stir/strain, but that's a bullshit description for something much more complicated, like giving the instructions "combine lemon juice, egg yolk, and butter" and expecting someone to make Hollandaise. The nuance, the attention to technique, the attention to detail—the journey—that is as important as the destination. Start with a glance at the mise en place before you move on to the spec, and read the mixing instructions *before* you pick up a bottle to get your head straight before you start pouring.

Every cocktail bar has its own approach. This is ours. There are theories in here that you'll like and others that you'll roll your eyes at and call me an ass for including. Read to the end anyway, and if you still disagree with everything, come to The Violet Hour some night and let's argue about it, have a couple of drinks, and discuss some more. This whole bartending thing is a long and winding road—the journey, arm out the window playing with the warm breeze, is something everyone can enjoy.

COCKTAIL MECHANICS

EXECUTING TECHNICALLY SOUND COCKTAILS.

I'm going to fill you in on the secret to creating and mixing cocktails at the James Beard level. It's quite simple. All it takes is paying attention to every single little seemingly inconsequential fucking detail in every one of your drinks, every time. That's why high-level bartending is so difficult. It demands the energy to care, to avoid the shortcut, to take the extra second to make a drink better. There's no magic to the whole thing. It's just really hard work.

When I begin teaching the ins and outs of the industry to bartenders, I always bring up the story of Harlan Howard, a prodigious Nashville songwriter from the '50s and '60s who penned more than 4,000 songs and was inducted TWICE into the Songwriters Hall of Fame. He coined a phrase that would resonate with musicians of all stripes for generations to come when he claimed that country music is simply "three chords and the truth." Meaning: The best songs are ones that are so simple there is nowhere to hide. In the case of cocktails, the truth is technique. *Cocktails are just three ingredients and the truth!*

Inherent in this philosophy is that, like any good chef will tell you, before you do literally anything else, you need to understand your ingredients inside and out—what their characteristics are, how those shift depending on the day or season, and how they work in tandem with others. Then you need to learn the right techniques to get your drink across the finish line in a way that results in something delicious. This is the "when to sauté versus when to roast" part of the equation.

These simple tenets get a lot more complicated when you start to look at every little tiny fucking detail of drink making. This is because, like the butterfly effect, everything that goes into a cocktail—from the ice, the juice, and the proof of the booze to the sweeteners, garnishes, and final aromatics—will affect everything else. To maintain harmony in the glass, you can't change one thing without shifting another, so it's important to understand every single ingredient and technique and how it impacts the ones surrounding it. Three ingredients, and THE GODDAMN TRUTH!!

Once you understand this and put in Malcolm Gladwell's 10,000 study and practice hours, you'll get to the point where you can pick up any bottle of booze, sweetener, and ancillary ingredient and whip up something delicious intuitively. You'll have the right instincts, flexibility, and foundation of knowledge to make leaps and bounds in the heat of the moment. You'll be able to *think* and *drink* like a bartender, mix up recipes from a spec,* and create something drinkable on the fly.

In the Mechanics section, we kick-start the process by looking at cocktails through the lenses of Balance, Temperature, Texture, and Aroma. These are the building blocks of a good cocktail, and they demand specific and practiced techniques to get right. These concepts are intricately intertwined. They are also *perilously* intertwined. If your Texture is out of whack, it's often because you screwed the pooch concerning Balance or Temperature. More often than not, if you've got one of the mechanics wrong, you probably have at least two, maybe three wrong, and there is no Aroma that can save a drink that has been built with poor materials and crappy craftsmanship. That's why you have to read all the sections and consider how they weave together in order to get a bird's-eye view of cocktail technique. As you go through the first four lessons, keep the axiom "three ingredients and the truth" at the forefront of your mind.

---

* Refers to the ingredients and measurements but not the mixing instructions.

✦ BALANCE ✦

When I think about Balance, I think about my friend and favorite chef Monique King. I met her while shucking oysters, waiting tables, and bartending at Soul Kitchen in Wicker Park, at the intersection of North, Damen, and Milwaukee (known to locals as "The Crotch").

One of the stars of the menu was a pecan-crusted catfish, coated in Dijon mustard, dredged in cornmeal and ground pecans, sautéed, and then topped with a lemon butter pan sauce. I've had lemon with seafood a million times, but the way the sharp mustard and bright lemon juice balanced out the fatty pecans and sweet, round cornmeal makes me drool as I sit here and write this twenty-five years later.

Monique knew exactly how to strike the right Balance between fat, acid, bitterness, and sweetness—a skill that divides good chefs from great ones and mediocre dishes from excellent ones. It's also one of the most important things a bartender can do to make cocktails that don't suck. There must be equilibrium between booze, acid, sugar, bitter, strong, subtle, rich, and it doesn't just happen magically when you combine ingredients according to a spec.

When you set out to make a drink—even one you've mixed a dozen times already—you have to consider the character and behavior of every ingredient, nail your jiggering and mixing techniques, recall what good Balance tastes like, and then diagnose problems and fix them when they arise. Balance isn't just one singular and unchanging target to hit. It shifts and evolves at the mercy of room temperature, glassware, ice quality, ancillary water content, and the fickle habits of the drinker. You have to take all of that into consideration and devise a plan of attack for making a drink that will taste good at the first, middle, and last sip. That's how you create a cocktail that is enjoyable from start to finish—a cocktail that is precisely and *holistically* Balanced.

UNDERSTANDING
YOUR INGREDIENTS

In this section we'll first look at the most common elements used to make cocktails—the booze, sugar, citrus, and bitters—individually and in painstaking detail. Later, we'll talk about how to combine all four via the magic of shaking and stirring. Read this lesson start to finish, as each section builds upon the others. In the end you should be able to make Balanced drinks with consistency.

BOOZE

When you're learning a sport like soccer, you need to learn how to pass and shoot the ball so you don't have to think about it when you're under pressure. The bartender's primary tool is booze. That is why at The Violet Hour, we highly recommend that our bartenders have tasted every bottle behind the bar, understand the properties of each, and have at least one cool fact to whip out when needed.

---

* SHIFTY *

HOW TO TASTE: THE BRIEF VERSION

You should definitely learn how to dissect and discuss the flavors of different whiskeys, rums, gins, etc., so you have a sense of what they taste like. If you haven't done this before, pick up a copy of F. Paul Pacult's *Kindred Spirits* for the long version. Here is that advice distilled.

1. Pour it into a glass.

2. Smell before you sip.

3. Gently roll the spirit around in your mouth. Spit.

4. Repeat step three, considering Aroma.

5. Sip, spit (or not), sip again.

When tasting spirits or cocktails, we are not just looking for the *flavor* of what is in your mouth. I consider flavor the *least* important thing about cocktail making! If you're working with good shit—that is, high-quality spirits, a menagerie of syrups and bitters, fresh citrus for juice and garnish—the drink *better* fucking taste good because the flavor in all those things has been given to you by dozens of hardworking people, from the distiller to the coworker who made the syrups to Mother Nature herself. You just have to combine all those things in the right ratios and not fall on your face while doing it.

Instead, we taste and evaluate for other reasons. The first is the level of alcohol in the spirit. Its alcohol by volume (ABV) is the primary factor that will determine how you approach mixing and what other ingredients should star in the show that is your cocktail. Pay attention to how much the spirits "burn"—i.e., how they attack the taste buds when you sip them. Do this often, and you should eventually be able to get a sense for what is high- or low-proof based on how it sizzles on your palate. Make a good habit of bookmarking the proof of whatever booze you are using in your brain every time you grab a bottle to mix.

Next, one of the more valuable skills we teach is how to properly *describe* what you are tasting. Evocative descriptions help cement memories! I was tasting tequila one day with the formidable nose of Joaquín Simó.* He took a whiff and a taste of a reposado and said, paraphrased, "This is reminiscent of the cotton candy at the fair my family used to go to; the cart had a diesel motor chugging away a couple of feet from it, so when you started eating, you got this combination of pink cloud candy, vanilla, fuel, and oil flavors. This tequila tastes like that, but in a beautiful way." When he said that, I was transported to that very time and place. It helped me find a way to remember that flavor profile forever.

We aim to find descriptions for all three stages of tasting: the attack,† mid-palate,‡ and finish.§ Think about this process as more like looking at clouds and seeing shapes like a bunny or a dragon, and less like picking up the flavors of garlic and basil in a marinara. Your subjective palate is going to latch onto things that will be different from what everybody else detects. We all have different likes and

We didn't have the same standard set of wine-world descriptions for things. We created a language as we went, and Toby would always appreciate it when you came back with some weird-ass shit. Like Amaro Sibilla—I would always say it reminded me of figs, with a lingering finish of Catholicism, because there was an incense element to it that felt kind of churchy. We talked about drinks based on how they made us feel.

—NANDINI KHAUND,
2007–2015

---

* Of Death & Co and Pouring Ribbons fame.
† The first impression of a smell, aroma, taste, or flavor profile.
‡ The center of the tasting experience. This is where you pull out the most tasting notes.
§ How the flavor of a distillate or cocktail behaves after you swallow it.

dislikes, flavor memories, and backgrounds. This is what makes drinking and creating cocktails intriguing and a source of never-ending gratification and fun.

When you taste, ask yourself about what you're tasting: What's your first impression? What does this taste remind you of? Can you associate it with a memory? Take the first flavor idea that comes to mind and then push it three steps further. For example: The Pedro Ximénez sherry you're tasting has notes of dried fruit. Cool. What kind? Apricots or cherries? Brown raisins or golden raisins? Have those fruit notes been dried in the sun or in a dark larder with herbs hanging from the rafters? Did they end up in a jammy compote or in a pie baked with granola? Get weird! "Walking past a pallet of hydrangeas at the garden center" will stick in your brain tendrils much longer than "floral" will. There is no wrong answer in any of this, except not digging deep enough.

✦ *An Example:*

Spirit: Rhum agricole.

Fact: Made with fresh-pressed sugarcane in Martinique.

Scratching the surface: Tastes grassy.

Digging deeper: Tastes like the chlorophyll from the stem of a fresh-cut flower.

Hitting pay dirt: Tastes grassy and chlorophyll-y but in an after-it-rains-mud-on-the-ground situation; maybe the mud is clay; some cooked petrol notes and cake batter flavors in there, too.

To further this education, I like to identify a spirit in each category that I judge all other spirits against. A touchstone, if you will. In life, everything is judged against something else: good and evil, joy and misery, juniper-y gin and citrus-forward gin. Yes, the quality of the spirit matters in this conversation, and life is too short to drink from the well, so what I really mean is evaluating spirits on their inherent characteristics and noticing how they compare to others, not if one is "better" than another. I have a touchstone brand for every spirit: my quintessential bourbon, rye, tequila, pear brandy, and beyond. The gin I judge all others against is Beefeater. I know Beefeater, I love Beefeater. So when I taste another gin I think, "Oh cool, this gin is a bit less juniper-y, more citrusy, with some unusual botanicals and a lower proof." From there, I can play around with how to use it in a drink that will highlight those unique qualities.

You can do that with every spirit, as well as having a "mind print" of liqueurs so when you taste something new, you can relate it to something you already know. "This French alpine liqueur is more like Bénédictine than Chartreuse, but it has the texture of high-octane génépy." Like Albert Einstein said, in relativity, we set the stage for creativity. Or something like that.

Go out and do this with every distillate you can get your hands on. Build that arsenal of spirits knowledge in your brain. Keep a tasting journal! Revisit stuff you already "know" to see if your palate has changed, because that happens, too. Once you have an encyclopedia's worth of tasting notes and trivia points in your head, the process of creating a cocktail becomes easier. And finding ways to Balance ingredients in a drink becomes even more simple. You don't have to fumble around trying to figure out how a rye differs from a bourbon because you put in the practice hours and now your bicycle kick comes naturally.

SYRUPS

Sugar has a bad reputation in cocktails, probably thanks to the overly sweetened drinks of the '70s through the early aughts. Today, many people perceive sweetness as trashy and unsophisticated, but sugar is a critical element in every cocktail because it makes booze more palatable and Balances the acid in a drink made with citrus juice. No decent drink is made without some form of sugar.*

There are many different types of sweeteners you can bring to a cocktail, and each one will have a different level of sweetness, or Brix,† as the scientists like to say. Some bartenders might argue with this, but the exact Brix isn't really important— having a general understanding of a syrup's level of sweetness and how that relates to others is. I have a sweetness scale of 1 to 10 in my head, and as my central point of navigation, I've assigned simple syrup (1:1) a volume of 5, right smack in the middle. Everything else, I taste and drop onto that scale in relation to simple, so when I'm mixing up a drink or creating one, I have that information to draw on and can adjust my booze, acid, or bitters accordingly.

Every syrup also has characteristics that go beyond "sweet." For example, grenadine is sweeter than simple syrup, but is also hella tart, so it hovers around a 7.25. Chartreuse is really complex and Campari is wicked bitter, but both are also sticky sweet (and that monk juice is boozy as all tarnation), so those land on the scale at 2.7 and 4.1, respectively. You can't just swap out the ratio of simple or Demerara syrup for fruit syrups or liqueurs because they are all much more complex than mere sucrose and water. And, as with all things, this is very subjective, so you need to figure out how all these things read on your palate and not simply memorize how they land on mine.

---

* Seriously, the Pink Gin and Gin Rickey are more self-flagellation than cocktail.
† A measurement in degrees, taken by hydrometer; the sugar content of a solution at a given temperature in water or alcohol.

⇒ KNOW YOUR SWEETENERS ⇐

Every sweetener should be evaluated *in relation* to others so you can figure out how to achieve balance when combining with booze, acid, and bitters. I use a scale of 1 to 10 to rank the relative sweetness of syrups at the bar. This is what works for me. Find out what works for you! And remember that liqueurs, amari, and spirits also have inherent sugar, so their sweetness needs to be considered in relation to your other sweetening agents when constructing a drink.

3.75

MAPLE SYRUP

THIS IS NEVER AS SWEET AS I THINK IT'S GOING TO BE, 3.75

One of America's oldest sweetening agents, and the most popular go-to before cane sugar became ubiquitous and cheap in the end of the nineteenth century, maple syrup is made from tree sap and brings a lovely, super subtle, earthy flavor to cocktails. Use Grade A Dark, Very Dark, or Grade B— the darker and more robust versions have a viscosity and flavor that shines even when matched with high-proof spirits.

4.75

HONEY SYRUP

WE DO 3 HONEY TO 1 WATER, SO THIS IS A 4.75 FOR ME

The oldest source of natural sweetness available to man (thanks, bees!), honey contributes flavor and a rich warming consistency to drinks. But the hefty weight and extreme sticky viscosity means it can be difficult to incorporate in its unadulterated state, which is why we always dilute honey into a syrup for ease of use. I like three parts honey to one part water, which is just enough to make it pourable while maintaining thickness.

5

SIMPLE SYRUP

5, THE SYRUP ON WHICH EVERY OTHER SYRUP IS COMPARED

Typically made from either cane sugar or beet sugar, the bags of generic table sugar you find at the grocery store are used to make 1:1 simple syrup—the most famous workhorse sweetener of them all. Thanks to the rigorous processing methods used to refine sugar into this finely ground, snow-white state (we'll spare you the gory details), table sugar has almost no flavor or aroma whatsoever, which is why it's perfect for pairing with unaged spirits—the way it plumps up the body and flavor of a drink while not altering the characteristics of the booze or other ingredients in the glass is truly remarkable.

6

COMMERCIAL CANE SYRUP

THIS IS A SOLID 6

Sometimes we use Petite Canne Sugar Cane Syrup from Martinique, as it is a Textural middle ground between simple and Demerara. This syrup is best utilized on a beach in Martinique when the Agricole is flowing freely. For a Ti' Punch it's a necessity.

6.5

DEMERARA SYRUP

I WANT IT TO BE A 7.5 LOGICALLY, BUT IT'S A 6.5

Demerara and white table sugar both come from sugarcane. White sugar is refined within an inch of its life, though, while Dem is the raw-ish version that comes from the first pressing of cane, so it has a more robust texture and sweetness. We primarily use a Demerara syrup when making cocktails with aged spirits, because the flavor and aromas match perfectly.

6.75

BROWN SUGAR

DON'T OVERPACK THE MEASURING CUP, AND IT SHOULD BE CLOSE TO DEMERARA, 6.75

Sucrose crystals coated with a layer of molasses have great moist granules. The soft and chewy state of the sugar reads as thicker than Dem and simple before you even transform it into a syrup, which means it has more heftiness than both aforementioned options when syrup-ified. It's great at smoothing out sharp bitterness and rough spice qualities in a drink.

7.25

GRENADINE

LOTSA WAYS TO MAKE THIS, GO FOR A 7.25

A sweetener whose cocktail history dates back to the mid-1800s, true grenadine is simply pomegranate juice mixed with syrup. Many bars use only cooked or only fresh pomegranate juice for their house grenadine, a choice that swings from a syrup made up of only the bass notes of a timpani drum (cooked pom) or jangly like a hi-hat (only fresh). At TVH we blend fresh juice with reduced juice to merge the tart, astringent, grippy characteristics of the former with the darker, fatter, and more earthy qualities from the latter. Sheer opulence emerges from the reduced portion, and the brightness of the fresh juice lightens that rich essence up to a palatable Balance. Together, the two versions of pomegranate combine in a way that is over-the-top awesome, especially when combined with dry spirits like applejack, rye, and blanco tequila, where you need that extra dense syrup to create a glamorous mouthfeel.

For more on syrups, go to page 311.

Another important point: One of the most potentially counterintuitive and totally mind-blowing things I've learned about sweeteners during the course of writing this book is that 2:1 syrups are not twice as sweet as 1:1 syrups. YEP. The Brix of 1:1 simple syrup is 48%; the Brix of 2:1 Demerara syrup is 64%. So yes, Demerara is sweeter, but not twice as much. Remember this when you're choosing which one to use in a drink.

Nobody wants to make a drink that's "too sweet." We've all had that cocktail that made our molars sing an aria. I get that. So the goal with sugar in a cocktail is to find the . . . sweet spot, where drinks are sublime without being a dentist's gold mine. Like a chef salting a dish within three grains of being too salty, you want to get to the tipping point where one more drop of syrup would make the drink too sweet, because that is how to create a luxe Texture. Most of the time you need to just push until your palate screams stop—between a few drops and a sixteenth of an ounce. An amount that wouldn't change your morning venti coffee can make your cocktail creation killer.

CITRUS

The acid you get from a lemon, grapefruit, or lime brings sunshine into your glass and, more important, a contrast to booze and sugar. Like a dollop of yogurt on a leg of braised lamb, or a splash of Crystal on a heaping bowl of gumbo, a sour wouldn't be a sour without the mouthwatering addition of acidity. To make the best cocktail you can, your citrus juice needs to be fresh as fuck.

That sounds easier than it is, because citrus and its delectable juice can be a huge wild card, with quality and acidity levels differing from region to region, season to season, month to month, hour to hour, and when it's cold versus at room temperature. From the minute the juice hits the air, it starts to oxidize. At The Violet Hour we say citrus juice is at its best between the stages of "squeezed à la minute" up to twelve hours. We did our fair share of experiments and decided this is the measure that works best for our program.

Some bartenders (thank you for doing this, Dave Arnold!*) have put forward the theory that four-hour-old juice is best for cocktails, as its acidic qualities have had plenty of time to mellow, shaving off the characteristics that read as too sharp and letting the oils that made their way from the peel into the juice during squeezing disperse. For me this is mostly splitting hairs. I've had many cocktails made with juice squeezed à la minute that were amazing, and I'm not sure if I could have possibly enjoyed them more if the juice had "breathed" for a couple of hours. So, this is one of those nerd-out-if-you-please or don't-worry-and-don't-bother kind of situation that's best left up to your discretion. Do tests yourself to find what works for your palate.

---

* Check out his book *Liquid Intelligence* for all your drink science needs.

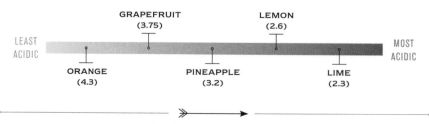

GRAPEFRUIT
(3.75)

LEMON
(2.6)

LEAST
ACIDIC

MOST
ACIDIC

ORANGE
(4.3)

PINEAPPLE
(3.2)

LIME
(2.3)

PH SCALE (BALLPARK ACIDITY)

The point here is to always taste your citrus before putting it into a cocktail. I've heard horror stories of bars using four-day-old juice, which must taste as fetid as the fermenting condiment you forgot about in the back of the fridge. Generally speaking, you can tell when lime juice is *too* old because it will look dusky, smell and taste acrid—not sour, but *acrid,* like battery acid or a blown fuse instead of citrus—as it oxidizes. Knowing the quality of your citrus juice before you start mixing is important, because if it lands on the tart or sweet side, you have that intel to adjust your spec accordingly: if it's on the acidic side, you might have to add more sugar to achieve Balance, or vice versa.

AROMATIC BITTERS

Defined by a cacophony of herbs, spices, and other botanicals, bitters like Angostura and Peychaud's—plus the wild world of new-school options like Bittercube, Bittermens, Bitter Truth, Scrappy's, and so on—are called "non-potable" specifically because they are intended to be used as a flavoring element, not consumed solo.[*] Like the atmospheric sound in a film, bitters are background support, adding complexity and filling the gaps that exist between sweet, sour, and boozy.

Despite the tiny quantities in which they are used, bitters can have an enormous impact on a drink. Even one dash too far can screw up your Balance, and most commercial bitters come with dasher tops that are notoriously inconsistent in their measurements, throwing out too much or not enough depending on how full or empty the bottle is. When we opened The Violet Hour, we put everything in dropper bottles calibrated to dispense specific measurements with precise consistency for this reason. After a while, we decided that opening and closing them was too time-consuming, so now we use both styles; we've trained folks well enough on the foibles of the dasher bottle that we store some of the more frequently used bitters like Angostura and Peychaud's in them so they can be grabbed quickly.

---

[*] Sometimes we use aromatic bitters as the base of a drink—there is nothing quite like a half ounce of Angostura or Peychaud's bitters to turn a cocktail up to 11—but not very often, because it's fucking expensive.

The esoteric bitters we store in the dropper bottles since they aren't used often. If the bar is full, those few seconds add up and can make a big difference in a guest's experience.

My rule of thumb when working with bitters is to always add them to the mixing vessel first. Getting into this habit ensures you'll always remember them (believe me, when you're in the weeds, it's easy to forget a dash of this or that), and if you end up dashing too much because the bottle is almost empty, you can toss what's in the glass or shaker without having to leave precious booze and other ingredients behind as well.

POTABLE BITTERS

Also colloquially referred to as "bitters," Italian amari like Campari, Fernet-Branca, Aperol, and Cynar and their international comrades (mostly from France) like Salers and Suze are typically a neutral base spirit macerated with herbs, citrus peels, roots, barks, and spices and then sweetened into a liqueur. The proof is much lower than that of aromatic seasoning bitters—usually anywhere from 16% to 35% ABV—which means they work splendidly as a modifier in cocktails.

At The Violet Hour, we classify these "bitters" into two groups: aperitif and digestif. Both are decidedly different in terms of proof, complexity, and level of bitterness, as well as sugar content. For me, the biggest difference, in general, is just what the group names suggest: food. An aperitif is low-proof because your stomach is empty, and has a bitterness that is often tempered with other things, like vermouth and gin in a Negroni, or soda and Prosecco in an Aperol spritz. Aperitifs get your stomach ready for a meal, kind of like stretching before a race. When working with aperitifs, make a mental note of the proof on the bottle and then have a sip and focus on how sweet it is. Many have a surprising undercurrent of sweetness beneath their bitter attack, so you will have to dial back the amount of syrup you are adding to a drink to compensate for this.

A digestif is much boozier and more bitter, which is also how I like my friends and coworkers. Good for times when your palate is a bit fatigued after eating and you have a full stomach. Fernet, Cynar, Rabarbaro, or Hungary's unique Unicum, neat,[*] is going to be what you need. But because of this extreme volume of bitterness (and sometimes a surprising amount of sweetness, too), they can be a flavor bully when paired with other ingredients, so it's wise to keep an eye on their intensity of flavor and proof so you can adjust for Balance.

---

[*] *Neat* means spirits that are served at room temperature or cold right from the bottle, both undiluted by shaking or stirring.

THE TRIPTYCH

Now we get into the actual theory of how to put booze, citrus, and sugar together via a system I've dubbed "the Triptych"—a reference to when three panels of a painting stand alone in their own right, each with its own meaning, and how when they come together, they collectively mean something else, something more interesting.

In my experience, the *vast majority* of cocktails are made from templates that have an inherent balance between three ingredients, or categories of ingredients, which are then tempered and massaged by dilution to create a drink. In sours, it's spirit, citrus, and sugar. In stirred drinks, it's almost always booze, sweetener, and garnish. Even in drinks like the Manhattan and Negroni you can break the respective components into these categories.

Of course, it's more complicated than it sounds, because the three pillars of the Triptych are constantly in motion. If you nudge one measurement, the others will be affected. You cannot up the amount of booze in your drink without adjusting the other two components. But even in light of that, I like this system because it makes it easier to find a path toward Balance. In every cocktail, we're working to Balance booze with sugar and a third component (acid or brightness or bitterness). Three ingredients and the truth!

As many bartenders know, most modern recipes are just variations on a small handful of originals, like the sour, the Old-Fashioned, the martini, the Manhattan, and beyond, which is why we recommend memorizing them—worst case, you can whip out a margarita or Manhattan at a moment's notice without referencing a recipe, but best case, you can use them as a fresh foundation to create from by using substitutions. We call these templates the Mother Drinks as a cheeky nod to Gary Regan's system of "cocktail families," as put forth in his groundbreaking 2003 guide *The Joy of Mixology*.

The point to understanding the Mother Drinks is that looking at Balance in this way should help you manage to find it no matter if you're looking at a flip, a sour, a smash, or anything (or everything) in between. Finding your Balance, and the measurements, ratios, and templates that speak to you will take some trial and error. But once you have these standards you will be able to substitute any ingredient and still make a delightful cocktail.

> *You don't need a refined palate to know when a cocktail is not balanced. Always keeping the Triptych in mind when creating new cocktails felt like my safety net.*
>
> —JIM TROUTMAN, 2008–2020

THE MOTHER DRINKS

These are the five Mother Drinks we use as templates for creation at The Violet Hour. I think of them as similar to Escoffier's five mother sauces. Just as the famous French chef identified the cornerstones for almost every sauce to follow when he named hollandaise, béchamel, velouté, sauce tomate, and espagnole, there are only a few main cocktails that every bartender needs to open the door for invention to follow.

With Escoffier's sauces, the idea is that each one serves as a sort of primed canvas for creating other sauces. Take a hollandaise and add tarragon and you get a béarnaise. An espagnole with tomatoes, onions, peppers, and herbs is Sauce Africaine. The Mother Drinks work in a similar way, showing the simplicity of how most modern cocktails are just variations on the originals made with new ingredients added or tweaked with substitutions. Take a sour and use a liqueur instead of simple syrup and you get the Daisy. Dress your Vieux Carré with a split-base of vermouth, apple brandy instead of Cognac, and walnut bitters instead of Ango and you have something familiar but shiny and new. When you understand the framework of the Manhattan, you can create variations on the fly using almost any combo of base spirit, bitters, and vermouth.

Use these five cocktail templates as a starting point for creation, a framework that holds up your inspirations and intentions, the chassis that is built out with good technique and painted with flavor. Use them often, use them wisely, and your notebook will start to fill with clever recipes.

THE SOUR

Sours have been around since before Professor Jerry Thomas's time, but in 1862 he defined them as spirit, sugar, water, and a quarter of lemon (i.e., citrus). That model still stands steadfast today—a template so simple and sturdy you can build new and different cocktails from it: the daiquiri, the Dark and Stormy, Amaretto Sour, New York Sour, Brandy Crusta, Long Island Iced Tea—the list goes on and on.

Our house spec for the sour looks like this because the Balance sits right on my palate. The spirit stands out just enough while being matched by equal parts sugar and acid. Maybe you like your sours on the dry side, or sweeter. Tinker with those measurements and write 'em down so you can test it out with every sort of sour you can think of.

2.0 OZ. . . . . . SPIRIT

.75 OZ. . . . . . CITRUS

.75 OZ. . . . . . SIMPLE SYRUP

THE OLD-FASHIONED

In 1806, the first time the word "cocktail" was defined in print, the Old-Fashioned was called "a stimulating liquor composed of any kind, sugar, water, and bitters." Dead simple in its assembly. In the Old-Fashioned, the three points to Balance are booze (spirit and bitters), sweetener (syrup), and for me the Old-Fashioned *must* have a citrus oil garnish ("acid") to be complete. A glass of booze and sweetener is not a cocktail because it's missing that third point of contrast. The aromatic garnish, almost always a citrus peel in the case of Old-Fashioned-style drinks, adds the bright, sharp, acidic part of the cocktail's personality that sours already inherently have in the body of the cocktail. It's the fresh-cut parsley on top of lasagna or onion and cilantro on a barbacoa taco. It simply must be present.

> 2.0 OZ......SPIRIT
>
> .25 OZ......DEMERARA SYRUP
>
> 3 DASHES...AROMATIC BITTERS
>
> CITRUS PEEL, EXPRESSED AND INSERTED

THE MARTINI/MANHATTAN

With other stirred cocktails like the Martini/Manhattan, Negroni, and Vieux Carré, you have to dig a little deeper to find the three points of Balance. My friend Otis likes to say that every cocktail ingredient has a degree of relative sweetness and acidity hidden below the obvious attributes, and I agree with him on this. Vermouth has booze, sweetness, and acidity. Cream has low-key acidity and sweetness. French aperitifs have all three as well, which is why they pair so well with vermouth. Almost no ingredient is only one thing. Look for the overlap and for ways to group multiple ingredients together in these situations. One example is the Martini/Manhattan template. Just as Helen of Troy had a face that launched a thousand ships, these drinks have launched a million cocktails. They are only slightly more complicated than the Old-Fashioned in that instead of sugar, we use vermouth, which has both sweetness and proof.

> 2.0 OZ.....SPIRIT
>
> 1.0 OZ.....VERMOUTH
>
> 2 DASHES...BITTERS
>
> CITRUS PEEL, EXPRESSED FOR A MARTINI
>
> CITRUS PEEL, EXPRESSED PLUS LUXARDO CHERRY
>
> FOR A MANHATTAN

THE VIEUX CARRÉ

The Vieux Carré is the love child of the Manhattan and an improved Old-Fashioned, conceived in the sultry heat of New Orleans. It is more complex than both of those because it has more ingredients! Two bitters make this drink deep, more like a gumbo than a clam chowder. If you want to stick really close to the classic, it's two spirits sharing the bill, plus vermouth, liqueur, two types of bitters, and two garnishes. The garnish you express with *last* will be key, because it will have the most prominent Aroma. I like expressing the orange peel before the lemon peel when it's hot outside, and reverse that order when it is cold.

```
1.0 OZ......SPIRIT
1.0 OZ......SPIRIT
1.0 OZ......VERMOUTH
.25 OZ......LIQUEUR
2 DASHES...BITTERS
2 DASHES...BITTERS
2 .........CITRUS PEELS, EXPRESSED
           AND INSERTED, IF THE DRINK IS SERVED
           ON THE ROCKS; DISCARDED IF SERVED UP
```

THE NEGRONI

When describing the Negroni, I always retell the tall tale of the cowboy count, Count Negroni, who one day, in a flash of genius, asked his loyal barista to make him an Americano (the cocktail not the coffee) but to sub out that pesky soda water for gin. Did it happen this way? Who knows? Who cares? Most of the time, the Negroni is billed as equal parts. You see ours is not. I find that most equal-parts drinks are not in balance, skewing to the sweet or boring, a lazy way to remember the drink's proportions. Instead, I looked at the Triptych and found a more palatable Balance between each panel. The classic Negroni usually has an orange slice as garnish, but that does nothing for the Aroma and therefore doesn't help boost the Triptych, so we use a big orange peel, expressed over the top of the drink, to help Balance out the richness inside.

```
1.5 OZ......SPIRIT
1.0 OZ......VERMOUTH
.75 OZ......APERITIF OR DIGESTIF
3 DASHES...BITTERS
CITRUS PEEL, EXPRESSED AND INSERTED
```

JIGGERING

I learned to bartend by free pouring. In the clubs, a lightning-fast Cosmo or apple martini was of the utmost importance, so there was no time to do it any other way. But when mixing high-end cocktails with razor-thin ratios, like 99 percent of the ones we serve at The Violet Hour, you need to be precise, because a quarter ounce too much can ruin a drink. Jiggering gives you more control, which is why we jigger everything. If you're reading this book, you probably already know how to do this, so we're going to skip to next-level thoughts on measuring properly, the practices we think are somewhat unique to The Violet Hour.

Stacking

Sometimes we combine more than one ingredient in a jigger at the same time to make sure the overall measurement does not exceed the volume of the two measured separately. This is to minimize errors. For example, if you have a cocktail that calls for half an ounce of liqueur plus half an ounce of simple syrup—both with inherent sweetness—you

would stack them in the 1-ounce side of your jigger to ensure that precisely one ounce of sweetener goes into the drink. If you were to pour both the liqueur and the syrup independently, you could accidentally over-pour each by a scant .125 ounce, in which case there is now a sneaky full .25 ounce of extra sweetness in your drink, making your balance FUBAR.* You can also do this with citrus, amari, or booze, if you wish, if there are two similar ingredients going into the cocktail.

Fat vs. Skinny

Most times, finding Balance among the three pillars of the Triptych is as easy as finding your preferred ratio, measuring precisely, then shaking or stirring correctly. BUT NOT ALWAYS. Which is why you should always straw taste everything you're going to mix into your drink *before you mix it* to get a sense of your ingredients and how they're going to come together in the glass. Sometimes your lime is too acidic, your muddling strawberries too sweet, or the only whiskey you have on hand is high-proof instead of the standard 80. If any one of these things is not what your recipe calls for, you might have to tweak one of the other elements by a teeeeeny-tiiiiiiny skosh of liquid to make it align correctly.

That's why we also use designations of "fat" and "skinny," indicated by a + or − next to the amount, to identify when to slightly over- or underpour a measurement

---

* Fucked Up Beyond All Repair.

(usually by creating a positive or negative meniscus in the jigger) in a recipe.* This is equivalent to the cookbook instruction "season to taste."

> ✦ *An Example:* Say we're making a classic Sidecar, and because I tasted my ingredients before mixing, I know my lemon juice is running on the tart side today—I will pour the curaçao straight at three-quarters and fat pour the Demerara syrup (to smooth out the rough edges) to shimmy everything into the right Balance.

2.0 OZ. . . . . . **COGNAC**		2.0 OZ. . . . . . **COGNAC**
.75 OZ. . . . . . **DRY CURAÇAO**	TO: ⟶	.75 OZ. . . . . . **DRY CURAÇAO**
.75 OZ. . . . . . **LEMON JUICE**		.75 OZ. . . . . . **LEMON JUICE**
.25 OZ. . . . . . **DEMERARA SYRUP**		.25+ OZ. . . . . **DEMERARA SYRUP**

You still have only 1 ounce (albeit a healthy ounce) of sweetener in the drink as a whole, but the ratio between the syrup and the liqueur has been tweaked slightly to help soften the acidic qualities of the lemon juice. This is a game of eighths and sixteenths—a few drops one way or the other changes the cocktail!

UNDERSTANDING BULLIES

Some ingredients have so much going on that they will completely and totally dominate a drink, and often in a bad way. It's nigh on impossible to make a Balanced cocktail with two ounces of St-Germain (a flower bomb) or Ardbeg (a trench of smoke and ash). Just like you wouldn't add two full ounces of fish sauce to a Thai curry, you're not going to anchor a vodka cocktail with three-quarters of an ounce of crème de violette, or pit too much maraschino liqueur against a demure spirit like pisco. We call these spirits and liqueurs bullies: ingredients so loud and audacious that they will affect a cocktail exponentially by volume.

I'm not saying bullies are a bad thing you should never use. I love fish sauce! But I pay very close attention to how much I add, and even then, I usually skimp a little knowing I can add another dash at the end. The same

---

* Just remember that a "fat" pour is the only time you will ever pour a positive meniscus when mixing a drink.

* SHIFTY *

COMMON BULLIES

Absinthe

Amari

High-proof liquors

Herbal liqueurs

Hyper-smoky Scotch

Floral liqueurs

Flower hydrosols
(rose water and orange
flower water)

thing goes for bullies in drinks: Know how to make them work in a cocktail, and they can be wonderful vehicles of flavor. You just need to negotiate with them a little. Here are some tactics we use when building and creating cocktails:

+ *Start low:* Start by adding less than what the spec calls for (skinny!) and then scale up later, should the flavor not be bold enough.

+ *Split the base:* Dial back the full measurement and merge the bad boy with an ingredient that is more demure. For example: If you have a super-smoky mezcal in your margarita, instead of using two full ounces, split it half and half with a blanco tequila.

+ *Use it as a rinse:* Swirl the bully around the interior of the glass instead of using it in the body of the cocktail. This brings all the wonderful Aromas of the spirit to the experience in a way that eases its way into the conversation instead of kicking down the door. This also layers the Aroma when there is a garnish involved, like we do in the Sazerac, where the absinthe is being supported with a spritz of lemon oil. Make sure there is some water or ice in the glass if the proof is high.

Splitting a drink's base is kind of like cooking—if you make a pesto, you don't want to use 100% basil and aggressive olive oil in the same recipe because it'll be overpowering. Use other flavors that complement and Balance out that bold note. There is a push and pull to flavors to see where they'd end up together. You want it to be Balanced but not a slap in the face.

—STEPHEN COLE, 2007–2011

WATER CONTENT

Now you should have an understanding of the primary ingredients used to make a cocktail, and how you have to look at each one and how it relates to the others in order to start a journey toward Balance. You know your booze and its character, your citrus quality, how much sweetness your syrup has, the attitude of your bitters and amari, and you have a general sense for how each element has all of these things at the same time: inherent sweetness, acidity, bitterness, and proof, where applicable. Next is where the magic happens. Where a glass of ingredients becomes a cocktail. The last pillar of Balance we explore is water content.

The only rule of cocktails, with no exception, is that there can be no cocktail without water content. Water is the invisible ingredient and the most important ingredient, as it makes up the vast majority of your cocktail.* It is what fuses all the disparate components and transforms them into something that reads as unified and singular, what opens up the flavors of your ingredients, calms the alcohol content, and unites the citrus with the sugar and the bitters. It is what makes a cocktail a *cocktail.* The glue of every drink. We bartenders also call water content "dilution," so I'll use the terms interchangeably here.

Water comes into play at three stages during the mixing process: the inherent water content in your booze, liqueurs, and vermouth (proof), the inherent water content in other ingredients like syrups and juices, the way ice melts when (and how) you shake or stir, and the water that might be in the glass already, like ice, soda, beer, sparkling wine, or ice cubes. Each one is just as important as the others because it will inform exactly how you should shake, stir, or swizzle a drink to make sure it stays Balanced at the first, middle, and last sips. We'll go into each of these in detail in this section, but first, a few general rules about shaking, stirring, and swizzling that apply to every drink you aim to make.

SHAKING, STIRRING, SWIZZLING

The first question I get all the time, from newbies and enthusiastic drinkers alike, is when to shake versus when to stir a drink. Taken at face value, it's easy: Shake drinks that have citrus, cream, or eggs. Stir ones that only have booze, bitters, liqueurs, fortified wines, and other sweeteners. This is primarily for Textural reasons, which we'll get into more later. The second question people always ask is *how* to shake or stir. Everyone's physical maneuvers will differ. Find what works best for your body. Listen to what the ice is telling you. Feel the temperature of the vessel, and practice, practice, practice!

---

* Other bartenders who are more math-savvy than I have extrapolated that the diluted ice that lands in your final cocktail can be up to 50 to 100 percent of the drink.

On Shaker Tins

When I started bartending in the clubs back in the '90s, everyone used a Boston shaker, with the metal bottom and pint glass. These were clunky, heavy beasts, brutal on a body that had to shake a swimming pool's worth of Surfers on Acid every night. The glass seemed to suck up all the flavors, it would take ages to rinse out all the residual taste from whatever tequila or sambuca had previously been inside, and, most important, once they were hot from cleaning, they held on to that heat for-fucking-ever.

So I went down to the Bowery and found the WinCo brand big tins and carried those around until I found a "cheater" tin that would ride as high as possible when combined.* This often took hours upon hours, and I would finish the afternoon dusty, sweaty, and parched beyond reasonability, with numerous cuts on my hands from separating hundreds of tins. But it was worth it. Having metal on metal was a boon.

It sucked how they had a smaller capacity, but what made up for that was how the metal tins washed out fast and chilled quickly—to get them cold, you just tossed them in your well, gave them a spin, and they were good to go. Tin-on-tin also makes shaking more intuitive. The tough metal makes it a tactile experience, where every cell of your fingertips can sense the Temperature shifts and every tiny sensor in your ear can hear the sound of the ice fracturing and backfiring as it goes through a spin cycle. You don't have to stretch the imagination to envision exactly what is going on inside the shaker. Instead, you can rely on muscle memory and animal instinct, because there is only the thinnest barrier between you and the contents moving around inside.

I carried my shakers in a violin case, an idea stolen from the Chicago mob, who carried their tommy guns (nicknamed the "Chicago typewriter") in violin cases. That with the stingy brim and the double-breasted chalk-striped overcoat on top of a three-piece suit, and I felt like an original gangster. I took the tin-on-tin with me to Milk & Honey, and it has since been adopted by bars the world over for its durability, practicality, and ability to conduct a chill like literally no other shaker situation out there. At The Violet Hour we use Koriko tins specifically since they are well constructed and, at 28 and 18 ounces, have a volume that can make a Ramos or two sours comfortably.

HOW LONG (AND WITH HOW MUCH INTENSITY) TO SHAKE AND STIR

This is where water and the mechanics of dilution come into play. Where you learn to adjust your process based on the specific recipe you are staring down. It's where things get tricky, because every drink demands a different approach based on its

---

* I also used milkshake tins because the big tin would cap the milkshake tin and you could make five Cosmos or Appletinis in that setup.

starting proof, how the drink will evolve over time once it hits the glass, and what liquids are waiting patiently in the serving vessel. There is no one-size-fits-all recommendation!

Proof

Every bottle of alcohol has both proof (literally a percentage of alcohol) and water. For example, in that lovely bonded whiskey that is 100 proof (50% ABV), there is 50 percent water. In that cheeky, delightful vermouth, there is almost 80 percent water, because the ABV is usually around 20%. Consider the full build of your drink and make a rough estimate of the ratio of booze to water before you start getting it cold, because that is one of the many factors that should go into how much dilution you need to add during the mixing process, which will in turn inform how long (and with how much force) you shake or stir the drink.

In short: The higher the proof of your build, the more dilution it will need to soften and click together into Balance as a drinkable drink. Kinda like when you add water or ice to a dram of Scotch or nip of bourbon to make it more palatable. The amount of dilution you add to a spirit will be different based on whether you are pouring something fiery and cask-strength or something that's a more even-keeled 80 proof, right? The same thing goes for cocktails.

If you have good ice in your tin, you're not trying to destroy the ice, you're controlling it, spinning it around like clothes in a laundry machine to bust chips off the cubes, which will turn into water right away to cool down and dilute the drink. If you have the right shaker, a professional metal tin, you can feel it getting cold. Then frost will appear, and that means the ice is melting into the drink and it's good to go.

—ANDREW MACKEY, 2007–2020

- ✦ *An Example:* Mix up two gimlets. Same specs. Five ice cubes in each shaker.*
  Make one with navy-proof gin, and the other with your favorite standard-proof
  bottle. Shake them both for the same amount of time. Taste the standard-proof
  one. If you shook it long enough, it should be delicately Balanced, like the
  surface of a lake during a quiet day, uniform and calm with no ripples breaking
  up its meditative Zen. The one with the overproof gin will taste sharper, more
  gin-forward, with white-capped peaks of juniper-spiked booze interrupting the
  flow. If you do this exercise and can't tell the difference between the two right
  away, hang in there! It can be subtle. Practice makes perfect and repetition will
  help calibrate your palate.

- ✦ *Another Example:* Try this same exercise with a stirred drink like an Old-
  Fashioned. Build two versions: one with cask-strength whiskey (usually 120 to
  130 proof) and one with regular old 80 proof. Fill your mixing glasses three-
  quarters of the way with ice and start stirring. Stir for the same amount of time
  and then taste. The unbalanced one might have a prickle of bitters poking its
  head above the noise, since it hasn't had the chance to sink into the booze by
  way of water content. How much longer do you have to stir the high-proof one
  before it tastes just as balanced as the other? The answer might surprise you.

How the Cocktail Is Served

If you are serving a drink over ice, or over ice and soda, beer, sparkling wine, etc., the
drink will *gain dilution* after it is shaken or stirred and added to said ice or ice and
bubbly component. I like to put it this way: Ice "cooks" a cocktail by adding water as
it melts. The longer it sits on ice, the more "cooked," or thin and watery, it will get.
(In addition to this, the rate at which ice melts is dictated by its surface area, so a
cocktail served on crushed ice will fall out of Balance much faster than one served on
cubes. Hold this in your brain for a bit and we'll explore the full minutiae of the point
in the Temperature chapter, page 52.)

As bartenders, you have to shake, stir, or swizzle in a way that your drink will
taste right *over the entire course of its life*, not just in that snapshot of a first sip. You
need to consider how a cocktail is going to "rest" in the glass, much like cooking
a steak or whole roast bird. Abe Vucekovich has another apt metaphor where he
describes it in terms of how a flower blooms. With drinks served on ice, you want to
stir them to the point where the flower just begins to open, because as it sits

---

* Or pick a number that feels best to you. We use five, and we use five *every time* to ensure consistency.
  You can build a habit and start to shake intuitively when you always have the same number of cubes
  in the tin.

on the rocks, it will continue to marinate and "blossom," depending on the rate of consumption and the temperature of the ice. If the drink is served up, you want that flower to be in full bloom, perfectly diluted, for the first sip. That is why Balance can be hard to nail. It's not a single bull's-eye to hit in every situation. You have to be a psychic and envision the future of the cocktail, then calculate your shake or stir accordingly.

✦ *An Example:* A Negroni can be served either up or on the rocks, right? When served up, it will warm over time, but the dilution will not change because there is no ice in the glass. With an up drink, you have to stir or shake the shit out of it, so it's perfectly cold and masterfully diluted when it hits the coupe. To see what I mean, mix a Negroni that you intend to serve in a coupe without ice. Stir it suuuuper briefly and then strain into the glass. Taste it right away, then taste it again in 5 minutes. Notice how it has changed and decide whether the drink was pleasing from first sip to last. Prepare another Negroni, but this time stir it for three or four times the amount of time you stirred the first one so the drink has more dilution. In theory, this one will taste better than your first attempt on the first sip, middle sip, and last sip. Is that the case for you?

If the Negroni is going to be served over ice, that is a totally different evolution (we call this "Narrative Arc," which is explained in greater detail in its own lesson later). As the drink sits on those rocks in the glass, the ice will melt, adding more dilution over time. In this scenario, you need to stir or shake a little less before straining so there's room for the flavors to hold up as the ice melts. Dive into the same experiment: Stir one Negroni ever so quickly and strain it onto the ice cubes in your glass. Taste the first sip and leave it for a few minutes before trying the drink again. Do it again with a Negroni that you have stirred for longer. Pay attention to the way the cocktail changes with both levels of water content from the stirring process and decide what works best for you (or the person you are giving the drink to).

Shaking a drink is like cooking on top of a stove. An open flame, a little more aggressive energy transfer to break ingredients like citrus and eggs apart and put them back together to fully incorporate. Stirring is like putting your cocktail in the oven, letting all the things marinate in and of themselves with an even, constant, and gentle energy transfer.

—ABE VUCEKOVICH, 2015–PRESENT

Narrative Arc also depends on the person drinking the cocktail—and this is where the real next-level bartending comes into play. If your guest just stepped in off the street on a particularly brutal hot and humid Chicago summer day, that first daiquiri should be served up, with full dilution, because you know it'll be gulped down quickly and you want it to taste perfect in that moment. But if you're at home and want to turn on *Love Island* or *The Great British Bake Off* and nurse your Old-Fashioned over the course of a whole episode, you'd stir maybe only briefly because you know the drink will mellow over a large ice cube as you enjoy the show.

It's like playing soccer. Sometimes you make a pass "into space," kicking a ball toward nothing because you know one of your teammates is running to that spot and will get there at the same time as the ball. That's how I picture the imbiber and the last sip of a cocktail interacting. Knowing how fast your teammate runs (i.e., how fast the drinker drinks) should inform the pace you put on the ball (i.e., how much chill and dilution you need to inject into that drink before it is served).

TYPES OF SHAKES AND STIRS

At The Violet Hour, we teach bartenders to customize their shake or stir based on how the drink will be served. Here we outline the different types of shakes and stirs, listed from longest and hardest to the quickest and more gentle. These are *general* methods that are all determined in relation to one another, so read all of them first to see the big picture. And remember, if you change the proof of your base spirit, you might have to increase the amount of dilution time accordingly.

GOAL: *A shaken drink served up, like a gimlet or a Bee's Knees*
METHOD: **COUPE SHAKE**

The longest and hardest of all the shakes. The drink will not dilute any more in the glass because it is served up, without ice, so you need enough water content for the drink to taste Balanced before you strain it. Shake until you hear the ice starting to wear down in the corners. Then shake a little longer—it should still sound like the Blue Line flying on the straightaway between Harlem and Cumberland. When it starts sounding like a bus slogging through the slush of Damen two warm days after a blizzard, it's time to stop. It should look relatively lively inside, and when you taste the drink, it should taste pitch-perfect. If it's not—if you didn't consider your proof so something feels askew—shake more.

GOAL: *A shaken drink served on a single large chunk or a few cubes, like a margarita or a Mexican Firing Squad*

METHOD: ROCKS SHAKE

Cocktails served on the rocks will gain more dilution once they hit the ice in the glass. Shake for less time than you would for the coupe shake. The second straw taste before you strain should reveal a cocktail that is a little on the boozy side, *almost* totally Balanced, but not quite. If we had to put it into percentages, you're aiming for 80 percent Balance instead of the 100 percent a coupe shake demands. The first sip of the drink will still taste good, by the middle it will start sinking into glory, and the last drops will still taste Balanced.

GOAL: *A shaken drink served on rocks and carbonated liquid, like a Tom Collins or a Dark and Stormy*

METHOD: COLLINS SHAKE

These cocktails have a lot of water content in the glass, between the ice and carbonated liquid, so this is a very short shake. Use three ice cubes (five will add too much dilution) and shake just to combine the components and give them a quick chill—let's call it 15 percent of a coupe shake. On the second straw taste, the drink should taste even more boozy, bold, and sweet than it would if you were to apply a rocks shake. Once it lands in the glass, the drink will mingle with the soda or ginger beer or whatever, which immediately smooths out the rough edges and dries the cocktail out. It will taste vibrant and bold on the first few sips, then perfectly Balanced somewhere in the middle, and still end with full structural integrity.

GOAL: *A shaken drink served on crushed ice, like a mai tai or a Bramble*

METHOD: WHIP SHAKE

To maintain Balance with crushed ice drinks, you need the cocktail to absorb only the tiniest amount of water during the shaking process because it will dilute rapidly and with gusto as it sits on a large amount of crushed ice in the glass. Add about 2 ounces of crushed ice to the tin and give it the lightest, most featherweight flutter of a shake—just enough to make sure the ingredients are incorporated and chilled so they won't melt the ice in the glass too much. When you straw taste, it should come off like a slightly chilled version of the ingredients. Nothing more and nothing less. By the time the drinker fiddles with their straw and takes the first sip, all the vibrant flavors will shine throughout the duration of the drink.

GOAL: *A stirred drink served up, like a martini or a Manhattan or a Sazerac*

METHOD: COUPE STIR

The Balance of a drink served up (or down, i.e., chilled and served in a chilled

Old-Fashioned glass, like a Sazerac) is laid bare for all to see because there will be no more dilution influencing the Balance of the drink once it hits the glass. Stir with vim and vigor (but not so much you disrupt that silky Texture), straw tasting early and often, until the drink is diluted to the point that it can be consumed without any additional tweaking. It should hit your palate like a too-cold white wine: not boozy or burning, but happily frosted and frigid.

GOAL: *A stirred drink served on a single rock or chunk of ice, like a Vieux Carré or a Negroni*
METHOD: **CHUNK STIR**

This style and the following rocks stir are almost the exact same thing, for all intents and purposes. We make the slight differentiation because every tiny detail matters. When you serve a drink over large rocks, spheres, or chunks, the ice melts slowly and evenly into the cocktail over a long period of time. Stir until the drink appears to be just a handful of rotations away from being perfect. Slightly shorter than a coupe stir, but longer than a rocks stir.

GOAL: *A stirred drink served on a few rocks, like a Vieux Carré, an Old-Fashioned, or a Negroni*
METHOD: **ROCKS STIR**

For stirred drinks that will hit a few cubes of ice in the glass, stop stirring when the drink is starting to click into harmony but still seems quite boozy. That's because the drink will gain a big blast of dilution from the cubes it lands upon in the glass—they offer a larger amount of surface area than chunks do, which means they will melt even faster, adding a lot of water in a short period of time. Really do the math on your proof with this stir, because an Old-Fashioned will have a wildly different ABV than a Negroni, and a Negroni will have a proof that differs from that of the Vieux Carré. In relation to the other types of stir, make this the shortest stir you can, and you'll stay gold.

Swizzling

The only mixing method that shares its name with the style of the cocktail itself, swizzling is just a fast, exuberant stir with a specialized tool, used when you have a crushed ice drink that you want to get cold, diluted, and texturized really fast. Kinda like throwing battered chicken into a deep fryer, crushed ice cooks drinks with fervor!

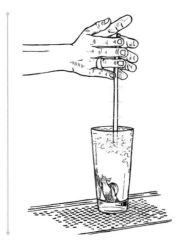

STRAW TASTING:
HOW TO ANALYZE AND ADJUST

Even if you've made hundreds of daiquiris in your lifetime, there's always a chance that one of a million tiny things will happen in the heat of the moment that throws off your optimal Balance. That's why we teach bartenders to always analyze and adjust every single drink before it is served to a guest. This is how we put out consistent cocktails every night. The ingredients and the way they come together are constantly being judged and adjusted as needed, so the final drink of the night tastes just as good as the first one, no matter whether your lime juice is super tart or your whiskey is higher proof than the one you had yesterday. We do this via two straw tastes during the mixing process.

STRAW TASTE #1: The first taste is to make sure you haven't forgotten any ingredients. Do it after all the ingredients are combined in the shaker tin or mixing glass, but before the ice and techniques come into play. When you're juggling eight drink orders and someone asks you for the closest taco joint, it's easy to forget a dash of this or a half ounce of that. The drink will usually taste brash, coarse, hot, and sweet because you haven't softened anything with water content yet. Get a sense for how much sweetness and acidity might be involved and speculate on whether that might need to shift on your second taste. Flag those characteristics in your brain.

STRAW TASTE #2: The pivotal straw taste. The make-or-break. Contemplate how the drink has evolved so far and decide whether it needs adjusting in this moment, based on how it will be served later. Do this after you've shaken, swizzled, or stirred your cocktail. You are looking at everything going on in the cocktail to see if it all collides correctly: the Balance, Texture, and Temperature. If one is off-kilter, chances are the others will be, too, but in most cases the solution will be relatively simple.

We'll go into detail on how to evaluate Texture and Temperature in those respective lessons. For now, just look at the Balance and ask yourself: Have I added enough dilution to this drink so that it will taste Balanced at the first sip, the middle sip, and the last sip? If not, shake or stir longer. Is there a good Balance between booze, sugar, and acid (or other ingredients involved)? No? You might have to bump up the sugar a little or add a touch more acid to bring everything into alignment. You can tell if a drink is overdiluted because it will start delicious but end like a sad trombone, like a ghost of its former self. Kind of like a hard seltzer.

By doing these three simple things—taste, analyze, and adjust—you will make your drinks decidedly better immediately. Get into that habit early. Indulge in that Sisyphean moment of walking down the hill and contemplating. Take an extra beat to make the cocktail as good as you can!

GOOD STRAINING ETIQUETTE

We almost always strain our cocktails to keep ice chips and bits of flotsam and jetsam out of the drink. There are a few ways to go about this, plus one exception to the rule:

SHAKEN DRINKS: We use a Hawthorne strainer, the type with the coil, because that serpentine web of metal is best for keeping unwanted broken ice chips or floaty things like pieces of mint or cucumber at bay. Strain with the gate* closed as tight as possible. Bring the almost-empty tin down quickly and abruptly when you strain, stopping just above the surface of the drink. It should be a short, fast, vertical movement.

> *When to Double Strain:* We pass a shaken drink out of the tin through a regular strainer plus a fine strainer (aka double strain) in every instance where the guest's lips come in contact with the cocktail directly. So: coupe drinks, rocks drinks with no straw, and laybacks. This removes unwanted particles and keeps egg whites denser (in drinks where eggs are in play). You usually have a wide-open gate when double straining because the fine strainer will catch what the first strainer allows through. Hold the double strainer above the glass and tap the strainer with the bottom of the shaker to get the last drops out, not the other way around. If you hold the shaker still and tap the strainer against it, it's much messier.

STIRRED DRINKS: We use a julep strainer, the type with the larger holes, because stirred drinks often don't have miscellaneous ice chips or herbs that would otherwise weasel their way into the glass. Hold the strainer so the convex shape of the glass is positioned like a dome or an upside-down spoon. Make sure you have enough ice in the mixing glass that the strainer sits high and makes solid contact with the part of the glass the liquid is cascading from.

---

* The part of the strainer that the liquid flows through. There is a little metal flap that protrudes and is manipulated by the index finger, to open or close the gate.

ROLLING: The one situation when we don't strain is called "rolling," which is when you shake and then roll the drink, with all the bits and ice, into the glass. Some bars call this a "dirty dump." This is used almost exclusively for drinks that we whip shake and serve over crushed ice, like the Briarpatch (page 86). You don't need to strain in this instance because you have crushed ice in both the tin and the glass. The exception: You would strain a cocktail that is whip shaken if it was going into a glass with any other type of ice or no ice, to avoid floating ice chips.

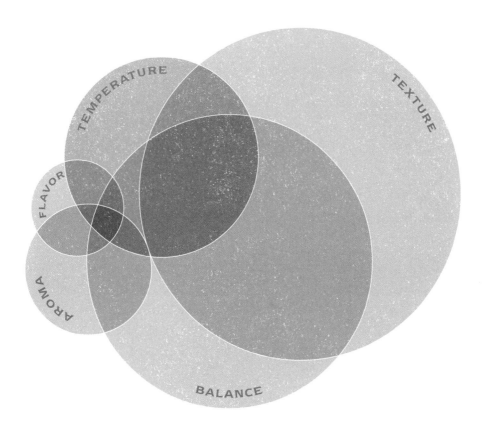

ASPECTS OF A COCKTAIL

How the mechanics relate to each other:
1. The size of the circle denotes how important that aspect is to a cocktail.
2. How much the circles overlap shows how interconnected those
aspects are. Note that Aroma/flavor doesn't affect Texture.
3. The diagram shows, from left to right, how a cocktail is experienced.

⚒ ∙ TEMPERATURE ∙ ⚒

Back in the mid-1800s, one of the first sources of commercially harvested ice was Henry D. Thoreau's bathtub, Walden Pond. During the summer, while "sucking out all the marrow of life" at the New England sanctuary, the author skinny-dipped* in waters that would later freeze, be cut into blocks, and get shipped all over the world.

These enormous blocks of ice ended up in the libations of the wealthy and famous at the behest of the Boston "Ice King," Frederic Tudor. Because ice was evanescent and rare and expensive, the upper classes got it first, before it became something everyone wanted. Soon hundreds of tons were shipped around the world to places like Calcutta, Martinique, and New Orleans.

This obsession with really cold water is, in my opinion, one of the reasons the cocktail is a uniquely American invention. Commercial ice cubes got their start in America, and ever since, we Americans have been rabid for the stuff. This American quirk is why Temperature is an absolutely critical component to making cocktails that don't suck. Everybody knows that a cold cocktail is a good cocktail. A barely chilled one, not so much.

There are a lot of factors that go into getting Temperature right in cocktails. You must consider the ingredients (booze and other liquids), the ice you're using (both during fabrication and where the drink lands), the method of energy you will apply (shake, stir, or swizzle), plus the glassware you're serving the drink in, because each individual cog in the system will make a significant impact on the outcome. When drinks aren't the right Temperature, they are simply not worth one's time, so let's make the most of this lesson.

---

* Well, okay, maybe he didn't skinny-dip. The nude speculation is unadulterated conjecture on the part
of the author. Never let the truth get in the way of a good story!

ICE

Ice is an ingredient in and of itself, the primary catalyst to make sure your booze, sugar, and other ancillary ingredients chill and dilute in a way that makes them come together and taste delicious. The quality of the ice, the size and shape, Temperature, and the way you use it all determine the outcome of how cold your drink will get. That is why we put painstaking care into our ice program, employing perfectly clear shapes made in a Clinebell by Just Ice, numerous Hoshizaki machines, and an ice crusher that looks like it could be the star of a Stephen King novel.

Let's start with a brief lesson on how ice dilutes and chills. There are plenty of science-nerd bartenders (and I mean that with nothing but love and respect) who have done an incredible job of breaking down this science to the very smallest details. Here's the nutshell version: To get ice to melt, you have to warm up the outermost layer of the cube. You do this by putting ice into liquids that are warmer than the ice is and adding energy (via shaking or stirring), which forces the Temperature of the ice to rise and its shell to melt. As the ice melts, it contributes chill to the surrounding liquids. Also inherent in this process is the fact that the melted water sinks into the drink, which is why Dave Arnold famously says, "There is no chilling without dilution. There is no dilution without chilling." The two go hand in hand.

QUALITY

To get the best results from your cocktail ice, you need to make sure it is the right quality. We define quality ice as ice that is flavorless. Because the melting water lands in the drink, it is of the utmost importance that it doesn't influence the flavor in a negative way. For this reason, we use only filtered water for making ice.

"Quality" also means clear ice, but when we first opened The Violet Hour, there were no fancy ice companies selling clear ice to bars, or machines that made huge blocks of ice, so we had to improvise. Our "ice program" was as lo-fi as you get: Freeze some water in a big-ass hotel pan and chip it down to size. No band saws or chain saws, no cool hoists or cutting rooms, just a glove, a sharp implement, and the stout heart of a warrior. We've come a long way since those early days, and now our ice disappears like a ninja when it sidles up to liquid in the glass.

OPTIMAL CHILL

The other important thing is to have ice that is the right temperature for the task at hand. By nature of being frozen water, all ice freezes at 32°F. But it can also be colder, specifically reaching the Temperature of the inside of your freezer. Our ice at the bar starts off much frostier (–4°F) than what you would use straight out of your freezer at home (mine is a comparatively balmy 10°F). This is important because the temperature of your ice will influence how long it takes to dilute when shaken, stirred, or swizzled. The colder the ice, the longer it'll take to melt, and vice versa.

Specifically, we have ice that is slightly tempered* for shaking and stirring, and ice that is super fucking cold for serving drinks over. For the former, bringing frozen cubes up to 32°F or so is optimal for mixing. Anything dramatically colder than that isn't ideal, for a few reasons. First, when you toss room-temperature liquid on ice that's too cold, the ice can pop, fracture, and shatter, which fundamentally changes the surface area of the cubes. This gets in the way of developing a consistent shake or stir. Second, ice that is *too* cold will not melt fast enough to bring the right amount of dilution to a cocktail.

This is a huge point, and one I've hardly seen made anywhere else: When you don't bring your mixing cubes up to 32°F before shaking or stirring, by the time the tin feels cold to the touch and you think the drink is ready to strain, it almost never has enough water content (dilution) for all the ingredients to align in proper Balance. This tiny detail often means you won't get the best Temperature or Texture, either. It'll be a wash. That's why you must, *must* temper your mixing cubes before sending them off to war in the shaker tin or mixing glass. I now add 1 to 1½ ounces of cold water to my shaker when making drinks at home, and not only am I finally enjoying them, my girlfriend is also applauding the results. Join us in this epiphany!

✦ *An Example:* Next time you make a sour at home, try this: Using ice straight out of the freezer, prepare two versions of the same drink, one with ice and the other with the same amount of ice plus 1½ ounces of water added. Shake them both for the same amount of time. You'll quickly get a sense of what I'm talking about—the drink with the proper dilution (i.e., the extra water) will be cold enough and Balanced, while the one without the added water will be cold but might taste burny and thick, completely out of Balance.

Now, all that gossip is specific to the ice you're using to shake or stir. The ice you *serve* a drink on is an entirely different story. When we freeze large sheets of ice to make shapes like the chunk† and shard, we let them temper briefly for the carving process (so they are easier to cut), but then hurry them back into a freezer to get cold again. If we were to temper these and then stick them in a bin, they'd stick together, making it impossible to grab an individual cube for a cocktail in the middle of an order. But more important, the vast majority of liquid that is poured over them is already very

---

* When you take your cubes out of the super cold freezer and let them sit for a few minutes until they have a nice wet glistening sheen of water on the surface.

† The term "chunk" has also turned into a verb at the bar. When barbacks talk about making these cubes, they say they're going to go "chunk ice," because the sound of hewing is kind of like that— *chunk chunk chunk*!

One of my favorite things to do at the bar was carving the ice chunks for our Old-Fashioneds. I had to have made thousands. The most meditative moment in all of service, a great opportunity to get to know my fellow barbacks; I fell in love with a friend that way.

—LISA CLAIRE GREENE,
2015–2020

cold—we've already shaken or stirred the cocktail down to a delightful 20°F or so, so when it hits the chunk or shard, the ice is not going to shatter. It'll simply slide down the cube in all its glistening glory, inviting the drinker in for their first sip. Proper Temperature achieved!

MELTING RATE

The final thing you need to know about ice is that the rate at which dilution happens isn't the same with every kind of ice you use because the *surface area* of the cube dictates how much water content and how much chill will enter the drink once you start to shake or stir. This intel is handy when trying to decide what sort of ice to serve your drink over (which will in turn inform how long you shake or stir as we learned in Balance). Generally speaking, crushed ice, which has a ton of surface area, will melt much faster (and thus chill and dilute faster) than a handful of ice cubes, which will melt faster than a single large cube that has less surface area.

Remember how in the Balance chapter I mentioned how I like to say that ice "cooks" a cocktail in the same way that heat cooks food? Heat transforms raw steak into something hot and edible. Ice transforms a glass of gin, vermouth, and bitters into something cold and delicious. With both, you have to choose the right method for the job to get the right results. Do you grill, roast, microwave, or sauté that steak? Do you stir that martini on crushed ice, cubes, or a single chunk? For how long? With how much energy? Do you serve it on crushed ice, cubes, or chunks? How do you choose which sort of ice to use and when? That's ultimately up to you and should be based on the kind of drink you want to make. Test out the options and choose for yourself.

✦ *An Example:* To work this ice intel into the marrow of your bones, try assembling two margaritas using the same shaking length and vigor. Strain one over cubes and the other over crushed ice. Taste every few minutes to see how quickly the one on crushed melts versus the one on the rocks. This is not to say one is better than the other, just different! If you want to serve your marg on crushed ice, as they do at places like Half Step in Austin, you totally can. Just adjust your recipe and shaking technique (using the lessons spelled out in the Balance chapter) to ensure that it will taste as good as the one on the rocks.

SHAPES AND SIZES

Our ice program ensures that we have the right ice for every situation. These varieties are organized in order from LEAST surface area to MOST surface area (i.e., from those that melt the slowest to those that will melt super fast).

CHUNK: Ice cut into cubes about 3 inches in diameter; used for spirits served on the "rock" and any shaken or stirred cocktail served in a double Old-Fashioned glass that isn't à la Sazerac (aka served down*), like the Old-Fashioned, Vieux Carré, and all their riffs. Like the sous vide of ice, the large chunk keeps the drink colder over a long period of time without adding too much dilution.

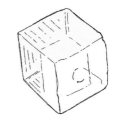

SHARD: Shards are 4½ inches long, 1½ inches wide, and 1½ inches deep so they slide perfectly into a 12-ounce Collins glass. They chill drinks relatively slowly over a very long period of time without adding too much water, and are used for all sorts of drinks that contain bubbles, or for big builds with lengthening juice and/or fortified wine. You could also use cubes for these drinks, but they have more surface area when you're stacking them up, so will dilute much faster than a shard.

CUBES: When TVH opened, we had a great Kold-Draft machine named Lucille. She was as good a KD machine as I ever worked with but was prone to breaking down. We had to add a couple more machines as backup, then it seemed like there was always one, sometimes two machines down, and the repair bills were killer. We switched to Hoshizaki (Hoshi) machines, which have been absolutely fabulous. The cubes are ¼ inch smaller, coming in at 1-inch squares, so they melt slightly faster than KD cubes. It takes a few more cubes to fill up a DOF or Collins glass, but the machine reliably produces them, which is clutch. We use them primarily to shake and stir because they are so sturdy, allowing us to shake long and hard.

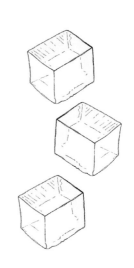

---

* Chilled and served in an Old-Fashioned glass. Not to be confused with a "neat" pour.

~ Coupe ~

~ Sidecar ~

~ Collins ~

~ Nick & Nora ~

~ Delmonico ~

~ Footed Delmonico ~

~ Double Old-Fashioned ~

~ Mug ~

~ Old Man ~

~ Cute shot glass ~

~ Hurricane ~

~ Tall Delmonico ~

* Not to Scale

HAND-CRACKED CUBES: Sometimes drinks call for nonuniform shapes and sizes of ice, in which case we take a Hoshi cube, nestle it in one hand, and whack it with an extra-thick barspoon to break it up into smaller pieces. It's rustic in a charming way, which is great for simple drinks like a Caipiríssima (a rum version of a caipirinha) that need a big hit of cold dilution first thing and then sit on the ice for a bit.

CRUSHED: TVH has an old-style ice crusher from Norlake, with a spinning barrel lined with hungry, jagged teeth. You throw ice in the top hopper and it's ground loudly into nonuniform bits. Similar to the way a deep fryer heats things up fast and aggressively, crushed ice gives drinks a rapid chill and quick dilution because there is so much surface area at play. Usually used for swizzles, juleps, cobblers, and their ilk.

GLASSWARE

As is quite obvious, glassware matters at the bar for many reasons, but the type of glass you use also influences the Temperature of the liquids that reside within. So when considering whether to serve your drink in a Nick & Nora or a coupe, an Old-Fashioned glass or an Irish coffee mug, think about a few of these key points.

MATERIAL

Different glasses hold heat or cold differently. Metal julep cups get cold fast and stay cold when filled with ice. A cobweb-thin white wineglass will be more affected by the heat pulsing out of your fingers than a chunky diner coffee mug will. Thick glass takes a long time to get really cold, but it warms slowly as well. This is why you see Oktoberfest attendees swaying around with those enormous beer steins—the only way those are practical at such ridiculous volume is because that thick glass holds the chill of ice-cold Kölsch for as long as it takes the imbiber to drink 44 ounces.

SURFACE AREA

Glasses with a very large opening allow liquid to come to room temperature faster because of the larger surface area exposed to the air. That's why a Nick & Nora martini stays colder for longer than one served in a coupe. And to that end, a coupe with an enormous surface area will warm a drink faster than one that is more petite. Same goes for Collinses, rocks glasses, and tiki mugs.

---
* SHIFTY *

GLASSWARE IS NEUTRAL

For some reason, people have projected certain sexist and homophobic tropes upon the glasses they drink from. Fuck these guys who see a glass as "girlie" or "gay" and don't want it. That's because they think "girlie" and "gay" is less than. Less than "manly." You may say *I'm* being sexist, but I've been racking my mind for an instance, even one, when a woman asked for a drink served in a less "manly" glass. It's never, ever happened. I've had women request a particular glass because they thought it was more elegant, but that doesn't feel like the same thing.

TEMPERATURE

Pregame chilling will ensure you don't fuck up Temperature, Texture, Balance, or Aroma by putting your cold drink in a hot glass. A freezer is a perfectly fine way to get a glass nice and chilly, especially because during the cooling process, it'll also acquire that great frosted look.* Hold these glasses as low as you can grab them so you don't imprint fingerprints in the seamless exterior frost. It will be slippery, too, so handle with care.

If you are making drinks to order and didn't pop 'em in the freezer ahead of time, you can also chill a glass with just ice cubes or crushed ice, sometimes with ice and water. When you use both, more of the super-cold liquid is touching the glass, resulting in faster and more even chilling than if you use ice alone, so that's good when you need to chill in a jiffy. And if your drink calls for an absinthe rinse, like a Sazerac, or a bold Scotch, like in a Blue Ridge Manhattan (page 156), the slick interior of the glass will pick up those flavors better than a dry one would, so you'll get a better coating and better diluted version of that ingredient.

---

* Except if you have delicate glassware. The freezer can be a treacherous place, where frozen chicken breast can attack and an ice tray can destroy a fragile vessel.

☀TEXTURE☀

I used to think taking my coffee with almost no adulteration made me edgier and more sophisticated. The drier and more bitter the drink, the cooler I was by default. Then one night during setup at Milk & Honey, I had my usual coffee in tow: hot, in the faux-Grecian "We Are Happy to Serve You" paper cup, with just enough milk to turn it gray. Sasha Petraske came in and removed the top, took a sip, grimaced, then immediately reached for Demerara syrup and heavy cream, adding a splash of both. He stirred it thoroughly, took a sip, and walked away.

I was more than a bit annoyed until I took a curious sip and discovered that IT WAS SO MUCH BETTER. I could smell the coffee (because he threw out the top) and the Texture had been completely transformed. Before it was harsh; now it was smooth, and that made all the difference. He had transformed a shitty cup of diner coffee into something drinkable—nay, delightful. The cream and sugar rounded out the harshness, and by adjusting the Balance he had, through bartender alchemy, created something that was a pleasure to drink.

I tell this story all the time because it changed the way I eat and drink more than any other event. More than my time at culinary school, more even than the first daiquiri Sasha made me. It also led to one of the most poignant revelations I've had as a bartender: There is no such thing as an enjoyable cocktail that doesn't have great Texture. It's as simple as that. Nobody makes pajamas out of horsehair or underwear from woven milk thistles. Even if the Balance or flavor of a cocktail is totally out of whack, the garnish ugly and withered, and it's served in a chipped, dingy glass—if it has a nice Texture, it's still drinkable. That is why Texture is the single most important element of a cocktail.

In this section, we'll get real nitty-gritty with the theory by breaking down the elements of a cocktail and explaining how they influence Texture. Then we'll explore the techniques you should master in order to make a Texturally pleasing drink (or troubleshoot one that comes out wonky).

THE BUILDING BLOCKS
OF TEXTURE

Just like every cook knows how sautéing onions, garlic, or mushrooms will produce more delicious results than boiling them, knowledgeable barkeeps must understand the qualities of their spirits, sweeteners, and other adjuncts, and how their Textures will shift depending on what technique is used.

BUBBLES

Whether it's soda water, beer, champers, tonic, cola, or ginger beer, carbonation (in the form of CO_2, aka carbon dioxide) adds a fountain of Texture to cocktails with its ruckus of tiny bubbles. But not all bubbles are equal in their intensity and applications. Here are a few key things to keep in mind when working with bubbles of all sorts—knowing these simple facts will help you choose the right bubbles for your cocktail in the heat of the moment.

✦ Generally speaking, carbonated beverages that were made via forced carbonation (club soda, soda water/seltzer, and tonic) will have larger and more aggressive bubbles than beverages made via natural fermentation (wine, ginger beer, ales, and lagers).

✦ Levels of carbonation vary between brands within a category (tonic, soda, sparkling wine, etc.).

✦ Sugar makes drinks taste fuller and rounder; different brands of sodas and tonics have varying degrees of added sweetness.

✦ More dizzying fizziness of CO_2 is soluble in cold water, so bubbles will come flying out of warm liquid into the ether in a ghostly *poof* but stay packed tight in the liquid if it's chilled.

In regard to technique, when building a cocktail always begin with the carbonated ingredient *at the bottom of the glass* instead of adding it last ("to top") as many bars do, to better integrate the carbonation with the other ingredients. We call this "bottoming."

The first time you add too much soda, you'll know. It's like blowing up a balloon—you want to keep getting it bigger, but then you go too far, it pops, and the middle falls out of your drink.

**—KYLE DAVIDSON,
2007–2010**

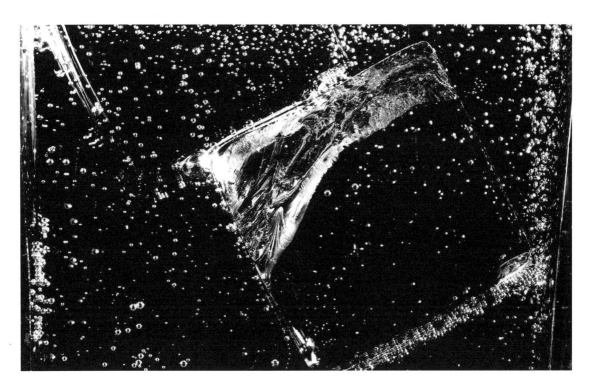

Nobody wants the first sip of their cocktail to be all teetotaler soda and the last to be a shot of booze because the two weren't integrated properly. If you were to gently pour soda on top of a cocktail, it's not going to sink to the bottom of the glass—you'll have to stir it, which is a frankly unnecessary show of force that'll bust all the bubbles you want in the body of the drink itself. A terrible waste of time and energy.

There's no hard-and-fast rule about how much liquid to add when bottoming—it depends on how big your glass is, how voluminous the cocktail is, and what kind of ice you use and how much. Start with about an ounce of liquid and scale up from there. The first cocktail you make will inevitably be fucked up, like the first pancake of the day. You're probably not going to nail your bottoming technique perfectly the first dozen times. It's a thing you have to develop a sense for over time with plenty of practice.

SWEETENERS AND SYRUPS

Many drinkers worry that adding too much syrup to a drink will make it too sweet, but this is not necessarily the case. (And even if you like your espresso black and your white wine bone dry, that doesn't mean your cocktail needs to be the same.) Drinks that are "too sweet" are more often than not just lacking in dilution or acid. It's kind of like adding butter to a pan sauce. Monter au beurre does nothing to change the flavor of the dish, it just adds a more pleasing Texture. You're adding something that reads not "sweet" but rounder in your mouth, more full-bodied and exuberant. That

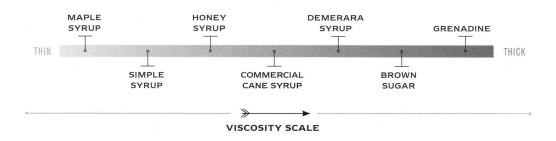

THIN MAPLE SYRUP HONEY SYRUP DEMERARA SYRUP GRENADINE THICK

SIMPLE SYRUP COMMERCIAL CANE SYRUP BROWN SUGAR

≫ ⟶

VISCOSITY SCALE

is why when a cocktail's Texture is too thin or wispy on the second straw taste, we often suggest adding a little more syrup to the mix. Just an eighth or a quarter ounce to buffer up the viscosity.

Different types of sugar have different levels of sweetness, though (and thus different "thickness" or weight in the mouth), so the type of sweetener you choose can have a noticeable impact on the Texture of the syrup, and eventually the drink in which it lands. The difference between the heavy weightiness of Demerara syrup compared to delicate simple syrup, for example, is night and day. Each one can be used to achieve a different sense of weight in the drink. Rank your sweeteners on a scale of thin to thick in your head and use that intel accordingly.

LIQUEURS

I know what you're thinking: Liqueurs are a type of sweetener in cocktails, so naturally they can also ramp up Texture if you add more to a drink, but liqueurs will *adversely* impact Texture if you employ them in the same way as you would honey, simple, or Demerara syrup, because you're adding more flavor *and more alcohol* in addition to sugar. If you've made a cocktail that calls for a liqueur as part of the build, and it feels a bit thin or papery, let a small amount of simple or Demerara syrup do the work. It'll bring a boost to the Texture, and the flavors of that liqueur will shine even brighter alongside their glassmates.

EGGS

Bartenders have been tossing raw eggs into cocktails, using the whites, yolks, or entire globular spheres, since at least the late nineteenth century, when drinks like the flip and the fizz first graced the pages of early American cocktail books. There is one reason only for this: Texture! With proper technique applied, the mysterious and magical egg has the power to change the final feel of a cocktail in a prodigious way. Each component of an egg can be harnessed to achieve a different Textural result in a cocktail.

EGG WHITES: The slippery, transparent liquid that defines an egg white is 90 percent water and 10 percent protein (with traces of minerals, vitamins, and glucose), hosting none of the fat content of the egg as a whole. For this reason, whites add a cloudlike layer of cushy softness to a drink without increasing its heftiness. Think froth without the weight.

EGG YOLKS: The golden yolk is where all the nutrients, calories, and fats of the egg are concentrated, which adds a rich, dense, velvety Texture to a drink. A natural thickening agent.

WHOLE EGG: With both the white and the yolk at play, the great Balance of weighty fats and fluffable proteins adds a combo of both thickness and froth to a cocktail. A doubleheader of Texture!

ALL EGGS: Before you start mixing, remember the eggs in play MUST BE FRESH. A quick way to tell if an egg is fresh without breaking it open is to put the whole egg in water. If it sinks to the bottom and lies flat on its side, it is very fresh. If it's less fresh but still good to eat, it will stand on one end at the bottom. If it floats to the surface, it's no longer usable.

MIME SHAKE: The magic of eggs is how they transform when beaten or bashed (as cooks already know via meringues, mousses, and soufflés). Because of the way an egg's proteins unfold and

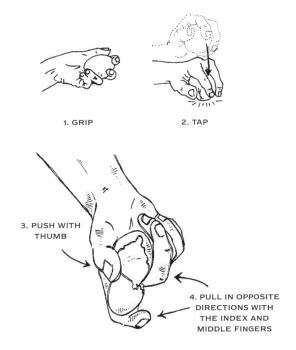

1. GRIP

2. TAP

3. PUSH WITH THUMB

4. PULL IN OPPOSITE DIRECTIONS WITH THE INDEX AND MIDDLE FINGERS

There is nothing more disappointing than an egg white cocktail where you can barely see the spuma on the top. You have to whip the hell out of the drink to create the right meringue. Once you get good at that, you can garnish with bitters to highlight the Texture (and add a nice Aroma). If you've done it right, the bitters just want to stay there, which is really neat. You've created this structure that lends itself to a beautiful presentation.

—ZAC SORENSEN, 2011–2020

unite when subjected to the stress of a whisk or a shake—the forceful introduction of air bubbles into the liquid—a homogeneous foam emerges. That's why whether you're working with the whites, the yolks, or the whole kit and caboodle, you must shake the cocktail. We do this in two stages: first without ice to avoid overdilution, then again with ice to chill. The term "dry shake" is used in bars around the world for this sequence, but that has always driven me a little crazy because you're shaking nothing *but* liquid, so at TVH we call it a mime shake, because the movement is so quiet compared to shaking with Kold-Draft ice. I know, it's a dad joke, and worse than trying to make "fetch" happen, but I'm sticking to it. I think it's fucking funny.

DAIRY

Creamy cocktails have always had a bad rap as being unsophisticated. But there is a reason dairy products are used in so many foods and drinks that we consider decadent and comforting. Products like ice cream and béchamel, whipped cream, milkshakes, and banana pudding have a satisfying Texture that only dairy can offer. At TVH we always go the extra mile to make dairy drinks deeply complex and surprising instead of sophomoric.

The thing to know when working with dairy is how different sources create different Textures based on the fat content of the dairy you choose. Milk doesn't do much in cocktails unless there is another element in the glass to support it, but cream makes for a blissfully luxurious mouthfeel in drinks like the Grasshopper, Irish coffee, the White Russian, and the Ramos Gin Fizz. Usually it just needs a good hard, fast shake to get the right bubbles going. Just be careful not to overshake. In most cases, you want soft, supple peaks, not a solid mass of whipped cream.

COCONUT CREAM

There is a huge difference between coconut water, coconut milk, and coconut cream. We use *only* coconut cream to make cocktails because it's one of the richest things you can impose upon an unsuspecting drink. Like eggs, coconut cream demands a merciless shake, longer and harder and using less ice than your average coupe shake, to get it to emulsify with other ingredients.

---

* SHIFTY *

BE CAREFUL WITH WATER AND FAT

Both dairy products and coconut cream will fall out of suspension quickly, so for best results, consider serving drinks made with these ingredients without ice, or on a giant, very cold cube that will give off precious little water.

FRUITS

If you've ever crunched into a slice of searingly fresh pineapple or a perfectly ripe summer blueberry, you know that fresh fruits and vegetables can bring vibrant flavor to cocktails in a way that spirits and liqueurs simply cannot. Yet whole fruits and their juices are fickle, wildly inconsistent ingredients, not only over different seasons but sometimes within a single container. Who has not been cruelly deceived by a mealy apricot or a sour raspberry? Fruits and vegetables have the best flavor at their peak of ripeness, and not a moment before or after, so always taste your fruit to see how close to ripe it is. If it's underripe, you can add a little more sugar to boost the flavor of the ingredients. If it's overripe, make sure the flavor is still palatable and consider scaling back on the syrup measurement by a skinny bit, since overripe fruit often has more inherent sugar at play.

If you can't get your hands on ripe fruit, or if you're working with something that's out of season, you can work around this by subbing in a fruit distillate or liqueur, which we often do. There are pros and cons to this; using commercial products ensures that we can still make those drinks the exact same way years after they were invented, but I also find there is no substitution for fresh cucumber or strawberry, or other fruits for that matter, so you need to find what works best for you in every situation. Remember to adjust the measurements of booze, acid, and sugar if you are swapping out muddled blackberry for crème de mûre, for example.

I like to give muddled cocktails a quick stir after they've been fully built, because sometimes cucumber bits and orange wheels can get stuck at the bottom of the tin and not integrate with the ice and liquids during shaking, creating a cocktail that has not lived up to its potential. And I always double strain cocktails made with muddled ingredients so no blackberry seed or rogue chunk of strawberry gets stuck in the drinker's teeth. If you have a fine strainer, always double up. If you're working with only a Hawthorne strainer, close the gate as tight as possible to prevent unwanted escapees from entering the glass.

Pineapple

Pineapple juice is a wild card in a cocktail, because it is both sweet and tart and the qualities of the juice will change depending on if you're using fresh versus day-old versus canned juice. Pineapple juice always brings a lovely frothy, rotund Texture to a drink. If you can, use a pulp-extracting juicer to extract the liquid from fresh pineapple, as this preserves the fruit's acidity and sweetness in its purest form.

In lieu of juicing, muddling pineapple is a quick and easy alternative, and almost as good as if you'd employed a juicer, but you must muddle like an angry god and DOUBLE STRAIN under all circumstances to make sure you're not getting gross chunks floating in your cocktail. That's a Textural nightmare. Worst-case scenario, you don't have the right juicer to deal with a pineapple, have no access to presqueezed juice, and don't want to muddle. In a pinch, or on a cold winter's night, you can turn to the canned stuff. Just be aware it has more sweetness and a slick Texture compared to fresh pineapple, with less inherent acidity. Shake it first (separation does occur) and use slightly less syrup than the recipe calls for to achieve the right overall sweetness in the drink.

Citrus

The main reason citrus juice has such a great impact on Texture is that you have to force the juice to bind together with the other liquids in the recipe via a quick shake. Unadulterated citrus will sit dull and lifeless in the glass—a harsh and frankly off-putting Texture for any drink—but shaking whips the liquids all together in a flurry of excitement, introducing a bunch of minuscule bubbles that help connect the two viscosities and creating the most pleasing fluffy Texture in the process. This is why we (almost) always shake cocktails made with citrus—for Textural reasons.

As the great Harry Craddock once said, you should drink your daiquiri while it's still laughing at you. When a properly shaken sour hits the glass, it is all lively bubbles and froth, thanks to the aeration you introduce in the shaking process. As the drink sits, those characteristics fade by the second. Nobody wants to drink a limp sour, so drink shaken cocktails quickly and with gusto and you'll never have to suffer this decidedly un-Hemingway-esque fate.

The intensity of the muddle and how thoroughly you do it should be informed by what you're working with. If it's mint, I'm going to be really gentle, but if it's lime wedges for a caipirinha or another casual cocktail, I'm not going to be too precious about it. You have to be mindful of the ingredients you're working with while channeling the spirit of the drink into each step along the way.

—ROBBY HAYNES, 2007–2013

SHAKING, STIRRING, AND SWIZZLING FOR TEXTURE

Recall how we shake, stir, or swizzle a drink for Balance reasons. How the act of diluting ice into a drink binds together the booze, sugar, acid, and bitters in a way that results in a pleasing cocktail, and how, in the process of that happening, the ice also *chills* the drink to an optimal Temperature for drinking. It is the combination of the two (dilution and chill, or Balance and Temperature) that *creates* a drink's Texture.

SHAKING

Shaking is riling up the drink, getting it excited and ready to go out there and impress with gregariousness. We shake to agitate the liquids, which in turn creates a gossamer web of tiny dancing bubbles. This happens because 1) we're introducing air to the ingredients, a result of the ice knocking about in all directions in the tin when you shake, and 2) when you shake, you also chill, and as the drink gets colder, the Texture of the foam you have manifested tightens up into a wall of frothy goodness. This character is totally desirable for drinks made with citrus because the acid dances when provoked.

If you aren't getting a fucking fluffy fountain of froth when you shake, you probably aren't shaking hard enough. Think jackhammer, not lazy waves. It's a fine line to tread. Shake too much, and your Texture will come out watery and ghostlike, an indication that your dilution went a few steps too far. Shake too little, and the drink will feel flat, boozy, and sweet. Practice, practice, practice, and you'll eventually be able to sense when you've hit the bull's-eye every time.

---

* SHIFTY *

TROUBLESHOOTING TEXTURE

On the second straw taste, if your drink reads:

+ *Too thin, sharp, or watery:* Add a bump of syrup to bring roundness back to the profile. Remember, adding more sugar will not make the drink taste more "sweet," it will just amplify the flavors that have been overwatered and bring the Texture back up to full-bodied.

+ *Too rich, thick, boozy, or viscous:* You likely haven't added enough dilution to calm down the booze and thin out the sugars, so shake or stir a little longer, depending on how your drink will be served.

STIRRING

When done correctly, the Texture and viscosity of a stirred cocktail—that is, one made without citrus, egg, or cream—is lush and velvety and divine. To coax that quality out, you have to work hard not to add any air to the liquids as you stir. And you have to get them really, really, really cold, because as they chill, they transform into something spellbinding.

When you're stirring, be sure to taste often. Keep an eye out for how the Texture of the drink changes at the same time as the chill and dilution. The three are intricately and perilously intertwined, so the moment your martini or Manhattan starts to taste too thin, you'll know the water content has tipped too far—that's when you should stop immediately, add a quarter ounce of booze and strain! Catch it right on the edge of that sigh and your cocktail will remain a ribbon of silk from start to finish.

The point of stirring is to create Texture. You don't want bubbles to show up—you want a silky, rich ribbon of booze because you want to sit and sip and the integrity of the cocktail will maintain over time if you don't shake it. Aim for velvety smoothness.

—ANDREW MACKEY, 2007–2020

SWIZZLING

Swizzling is adding a frightful amount of energy into a cocktail quickly to get a Texture that's delicate and silky. You do this by getting the ingredients down to an arctic Temperature without adding any of the effervescence of shaking. You *could* absolutely stir these drinks in the same way you would an Old-Fashioned; it would just take longer and you wouldn't get the awesome hoarfrost* on the outside of the glass as quickly. The Texture, in that case, would be different. Not as vivacious as when you swizzle.

This is nitpicky, but if I'm thinking the drinker will be constantly fucking with their straw, I will underswizzle the drink before serving. As they are slashing about in the drink while chatting with friends, they're committing a certain level of swizzling themselves, so why not let them bring the Textural qualities of the drink over the finish line while they scratch that fidgety itch?

---

* Crystalline frozen water condensation that forms on the outside of the drinking vessel of a very cold drink.

AROMA

Proust had it wrong. It should have been the *smell* of madeleines coming out of the oven that brought on twelve hundred arduous pages of memory, not the flavor of the first bite dipped daintily into his cup of tea.

Our sense of smell goes beyond the evolutionary need of telling us when we're in danger as well as where to find our next meal. Aromas are also powerful tools for evoking memories and emotions. Real estate brokers use the Aroma of cookies to make a house feel like a home. The fragrance of chicken soup bubbling away as you shake off the chill of a winter's night is more comforting than a crackling fireplace.

The tantalizing smells that come with making and drinking cocktails can be just as evocative. Have you noticed how when you walk into a bar, the space has a signature smell all its own? Milk & Honey always smelled like Brugal Añejo and lime juice, while The Violet Hour smells like citrus, mint, and cucumber because a couple of hours before the thirsty patrons are ushered through the curtains, bartenders are hard at work cutting fruit, picking herbs, and setting the mise for the night.

Introducing a thoughtful and intentional Aroma to a cocktail is doing more than just making it smell pretty. Cocktails are served cold, which dampens their natural fragrance—they *need* an added aromatic element to come alive. A fresh bundle of mint, a generous expression of lush orange oils, or a soft misting of cool absinthe also has the power to make the drink something bigger than the sum of its parts by luring you into the glass, sparking a memory, or toying with your expectations of the sips to follow. It makes the cocktail itself more multidimensional, which in turn elevates the experience of drinking it.

There are many ways in which Aromas can be introduced and manipulated in a cocktail. Let's get to it.

CITRUS

From the perky lemon pigtail coiling on a martini's edge to the orange swath that graces a sultry Negroni,* the garnish is the last touch, the final opportunity to make a cocktail a truly multisensory experience. For that reason, overlooking the garnish is a crime punishable by much shame and ridicule.

The most overt, yet also tastefully dramatic, way to add Aroma to a cocktail is by expressing the oils of a lemon, orange, or grapefruit peel over the top of the drink. It is a ritual that has taken place since the birth of cocktails, a ritual I have performed a million times, yet it still always strikes me as pure magic how the volatile oils spring forth from the peel in a shower of citrusy perfume with just the smallest flex of the fingers. At The Violet Hour, our citrus oil philosophy *starts* there.

A higher-level trick is to think about the way a certain type of citrus aroma will work either in tandem with or as a foil to the way the cocktail tastes. Let's say you have a dark whiskey-laden cocktail in the glass. An orange peel will pull out the warm baking spice notes. It's a comforting journey, with the two coming together merrily and without strife. Add a lemon peel aroma, and the experience changes. The first thing you smell is sunshine and lemon and perky brightness, but when you dip into the drink it turns brooding, with warm vanilla and spice. Your expectations from seeing the drink to smelling it to tasting it have taken you on a roller-coaster ride of unexpected fun. This isn't to say the orange peel was a bad idea—sometimes you want the Aroma and the drink to be matchy-matchy. Sometimes you want a contrast. It's up to you to decide what works for the drink in question and run with it.

Now the next-level shit. The subtle nuances that can emerge between a lemon, a grapefruit, or an orange peel on top of a drink can be quite striking. Depending on what the element is paired with, the citrus aromas can make the drink appear sweeter or drier than it would without that garnish.

✦ *An Example:* Make a drink. Any fucking drink. Split it into several glasses. Peel swaths of all the citrus fruits you have on hand. Go crazy and start with all the greatest hits of the American supermarket: lemon, orange, grapefruit, and lime. First, take a sip of the drink without any added Aromas to get a sense of how it tastes in its pure form. Then squeeze a bit of oil from one of the peels over the top of the drink and take another sip to see how the experience changes. Does the drink taste more or less bitter, sweet, dry? How has it transformed in your mind and in your senses? Do this routine again with every one of the other peels and

---

* I know that an orange wheel is the classic garnish, but it adds no Aroma, and for that reason we use an orange twist of some stripe.

AROMA

73

notice how each one has a totally different impact on the drink. It's like they're completely different cocktails, depending on which citrus peel you choose, right?

Magic.

Let's get more specific. Here's a guide to each type of citrus and what I find its beautiful oils do to a cocktail.

LEMON: Lemon oil is the soaring soprano voice in a booming Wagner opera, the dose of cheer à la summer's first glass of homemade lemonade. It adds a burst of fresh sunshine to a drink and tends to make the cocktail taste drier, adding slightly herbaceous, piney qualities.

LIME: Terpenes (aromatic compounds found in plants, all citrus fruits, cannabis, and hops) give lime peels an Aroma that evokes floral notes with spicy tones. We very rarely use lime peels at TVH because there aren't many drinks that we believe improve with that aromatic quality, but I have had rhum agricole drinks with lime peel that have worked well.

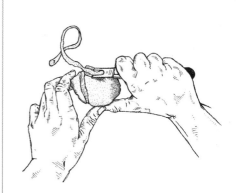

ORANGE: Orange is cozy and brash at the same time. Part fuzzy slippers in front of the fire, part totally gregarious, like having your fifth mimosa by two in the afternoon on a Saturday. Orange peel creates the illusion of warmth and sweetness laced with grandma-spice and floral elements.

GRAPEFRUIT: Neither too sweet nor too savory, Mr. Grapefruit Peel the middleman carries a slightly musky brightness in its aromatics. It has a tropical "rain forest" note that is more subtle than pineapple or passion fruit, more like a sarong knotted just right versus a loud Hawaiian shirt.

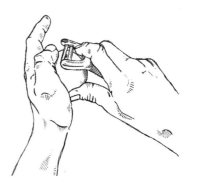

✦ Aromatic garnish is a tricky, fickle thing, losing much of its glimmering freshness shortly after it is cut. At TVH, we cut peels to order, à la minute, instead of preparing them ahead of service. It takes just an extra moment to cut a quick swath, and the freshness you get is worth the effort.

✦ Pay attention to where and how forcefully you garnish a cocktail with citrus oils. Rookies tend to blast with great fervor mere centimeters from the surface of the drink, forcing the oils below the surface, not floating gently upon it. You also don't want a complete and total cluster-bomb of citrus oil, or it will overtake other nuances in the glass, which is not ideal.

✦ Wanna flame an orange peel for aromatic and visual delight? First, wash to remove dirt, wax, and stickers. Dry, then cut a quarter-size disk with hearty pith from where the skin is the thickest, around the poles. There should be no orange "meat" on the back. With the skin side pointing down, gently heat the disk about 3 inches above the flame by moving it in and out of the heat. DO NOT BLACKEN. Hold the flame next to the lip of the glass. Give the peel a deliberate squeeze to let the oils catch flame over the top of the drink. Discard the spent disc—it will no longer serve a visual or aromatic duty.

Expressing citrus oils in a dark bar can be hard, so I always pull a candle close to the glass so I can see that oil float, or whether it flies left or right based on where the AC is blowing in the room. It's 100% nerdy, but it works.

**—KIRK ESTOPINAL,
2007–2008**

✦ In terms of the motion used to express peels, I like to think about it much like the light that "wipes" from one side to the other in a copier. Even. Steady. Not faster or slower on one side or the other. Balanced!

✦ And for the love of all things holy, please do not rub the freshly expressed peel all over the rim of the glass. It's gauche, it's gross. The peel has done its job, so just toss it.

A GUIDE TO
CITRUS GARNISH STYLES

At TVH we take great pride in our assortment of garnish styles. Different styles differentiate what would otherwise be similar-looking cocktails, helping to avoid confusion when dropping off drinks at a table or addressing the "what's that drink" question customers inevitably ask when they see something pretty float by on a candlelit tray.

CITRUS PEEL

ARROW PEEL

NOTCHED PEEL

KNOTTED PIGTAIL WITH BERRY

KNOTTED PIGTAIL

DOUBLE KNOTTED BASKET

TRIMMED CITRUS PEEL

SIDEWINDER

...GTAIL

SKEWERED
CHERRY
WITH PEEL

CITRUS
PEEL ROSE

ROLLER COASTER,
OR MOHAWK,
WHEEL

RADIUS CUT
WHEEL

MINT

Herbs give off aromas to keep insects from eating them, but thankfully, those same aromas signal deliciousness to us humans. Like basil on a caprese salad, or a sprig of rosemary on top of a leg of lamb, fresh herbs bring a beautiful Aroma to cocktails as well. But of all the herbs in the garden, by far and away we use mint the most, almost always for Aroma purposes. Mint comes in many varieties (around six hundred, says *On Food and Cooking* author Harold McGee), but the type most commonly used to garnish cocktails is spearmint. Peppermint has only one menthol-y note to offer, but spearmint has a wild complexity, which is why it has always has a home in drinks like the julep and mojito.

Like citrus peel, mint stores essential oils in glands that grace the surface of the leaves, so to get the most out of the herb, whether it's a big bundle or a single sprig, gently whip the mint on a straw or the back of your hand over the drink to get those oils over the drink. You don't need to overdo this! Just a few light taps will get the job done. We call this giving the mint a good spank. If you're muddling mint inside a glass, just pull it up the sides instead of bruising it (a common term bartenders use for a light muddle of mint, but a grave misnomer, because it suggests too much force). When you do this, also take a second to pull the mint up and around the inside surface of the glass to get the smell to coat the entire area—an ethereal touch most might not consider in their mint practice.

Another super cool thing we do at TVH with mint is spritz absinthe or bitters on top of the leaves for a wild new dimension of olfactory delight. When mint meets absinthe, its cooling effect is second to none, and bitters add the suggestion of dark sweetness that sings in dissonance with the minty herb. Pick and choose what you mist and dribble over mint with the same thoughtful intent you would exert in inventing the cocktail itself, because some combinations will work better than others. For example, in the New Rahm cocktail (page 280), Angostura meets a mint sprig for an explosive contrast—the drink itself is all sun rays and beach breezes so that moment of

Thinking about aroma as part of the whole package is a really cool way of approaching making a cocktail. You don't know what's going to come in that glass, so when you breathe in and notice this invisible garnish that maybe you weren't expecting, that can be awesome.

—STEPHEN COLE, 2007–2011

delicious contrast works wonders. On the flip side, the Tiger Balm cocktail (page 207) is a sort of mojito riff that features a quarter ounce of Branca Menta in the build. For the garnish, a mint leaf gets dusted with a single drop more of the Menta to take the mint from zero to hero. A super cool dynamic that really makes the most out of mint flavor in smart ways that go far beyond a pedestrian muddle.

BITTERS

We all know aromatic bitters like Angostura and Peychaud's play the role of demi-glace or bouillon in a cocktail, but because they are overflowing with herbs, barks, roots, peels, and various other botanicals, they can also be used to influence the aroma of a drink in spectacular ways.

Bitters as an aromatic tool are primarily useful for cocktails made with egg whites, because they sit fixed on the surface, right below the imbiber's inquisitive proboscis, for the majority of the cocktail's life, bringing an extra strata of complexity to the drink. Bitters can also bring a new dimension of Aroma to the surface of eggless drinks in the same respect.

Keep in mind that the bitters you choose to grace the cocktail should be selected because of the conversation they have with the ingredients in the glass. Take the pisco sour, for example. The ray of sunshine that is pisco, egg white, and lemon juice (or another citrus, depending on where you are drinking said pisco sour) takes on striking new meaning when you smatter a few drops of Angostura bitters on top (or even better, the banana-bread-like Amargo Chuncho bitters from Peru). The heavy baking spice notes contrast the drink most beautifully, creating a totally new personality for the drink as a whole. Pick bitters that will Echo (pages 182–84), Complement (pages 186–88), or Juxtapose (pages 189–92) flavors and Aromas inside the cocktail and you're on the road to awe.

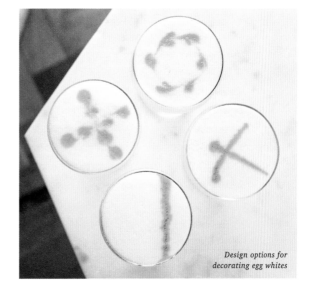

Design options for decorating egg whites

SALT & SPICES

If you've heard the story of how punch got its name (from the Hindi word for "five," referencing the number of components in the drink: spirit, sour, sugar, water, and spice),* you know that spices have played a role in mixed drinks since their very origins. Today that's still the case, especially when it comes to adding Aroma to a drink. Generally speaking, we use cinnamon or nutmeg for the job, depending on the impact we want to gift to the senses.

Remember: Ground, dried prepackaged spices are fine when cooking things for a long time. But to make the Aromas of a cocktail really jump out of the glass you want the volatility of spices grated à la minute.

SALT: One of the world's most ubiquitous seasonings, salt can also help boost the flavors of a cocktail. Salt makes spirits and syrups taste more like what they are, makes one perceive things as savory instead of sweet, and tamps down bitterness. Use sparingly!

CINNAMON: While cinnamon comes in various styles, we typically use two for cocktails: the hot, peppery "Saigon" from Southeast Asia for flavor, and the paperlike Ceylon, for Aroma. Generally speaking, the Aroma of cinnamon on top of a cocktail implies dryness, so if your drink is pretty sweet, this is a great trick to add contrast. It also works swimmingly with spirits like whiskey and rum for the same aforementioned reasons nutmeg does.

NUTMEG: Woodsy and warm, nutmeg creates the illusion that the liquid to follow tastes sweeter than it is. It's also fun to sprinkle a little on top of big, rich, round drinks made with whiskey and rum because when you think about how the spice notes imparted to those spirits from time spent in the barrel can seem similar to the Aroma of the nutmeg, you've got another layer of snowball at play in the drinking experience.

---

* Take this story with a pinch of salt and a shot of tequila.

FLOATS

As seen in the classic Dark and Stormy, the Queen's Park Swizzle, and the New York Sour, amari, bitters, liqueurs, wine, and spirits can also be floated on top of a cocktail. By nature of being the very top component, a float is the first thing the drinker will smell when they get close to the glass, all bluster and showing off. But a float also has a dramatic and short life span, because with each sip, the surface liquid and its aromatic essence sinks further away from the nose (depending on how fast it's being consumed and whether a straw is in play).

When floating a component, you are going for defined strata.* The more compact and intense the float, the more aromatic it will be, which is why the technique of bottoming is especially important in drinks that require a float. If you made a Dark and Stormy by shaking the lime juice, ginger, and rum, pouring that into a glass, and topping it with soda—that soda will float and the blackstrap on top will just diffuse into thin liquid. It won't stay in a nice tight line the way you want it to. Whereas if you put the soda in first, the viscosity of the ginger, lime, and rum is thick and ready to hold the float. This order of things makes it so the blackstrap floats in an intense cloud instead of a brackish malevolence.

On a related note, pay attention to the specific gravity of the liquid you are trying to float, because that will change your plan of attack as well. For example, wine has a thinner body than spirits. Use a jigger or a physical barrier, like the back of a spoon, between the wine and the top of the cocktail to make sure it floats properly instead of sinking into the glass.

To get the most intense Aroma out of floating, which is often utilized with another garnish, like the mint bouquet on the Queen's Park Swizzle, you need to underplay the more potent Aroma. This is predicated on what you do first or last: a smoky Scotch rinse first, then the lemon peel expressed second makes the lemon prevalent initially, and the Scotch brings up the rear with bagpipes blaring. Depending on how volatile or heavy-handed the application of the ingredient, the Aroma will fade at different rates.

* Different layers of experience in a cocktail.

AROMA

81

RINSES

Smell has been linked to religious rituals since god knows when, but really early on. Whether it is burning herbs or incense, roasting an offering, or tossing a supplicant into a volcano, smell is linked to a sense of awe, true awe (not, like, "awesome, bruh!"), because it is *invisible*. For a similar effect in cocktails, we turn to rinsing, a term used for when we wash or rinse the inside of an empty glass with a liquid ingredient like a liqueur, bitters, or spirit before adding the cocktail.

There are a few ways to approach a rinse. The first is by picking out a key flavor or component that is already in the body of the drink to emphasize the element in the smell. You can also rinse with an ingredient that is not found within the rest of the recipe to introduce a totally new strata to the experience—a wicked moment of trickery.

Technique-wise, you could use an atomizer* to do this, but we rinse with the liquid of choice plus crushed ice because the cold water allows the liquor to cling to the glass, resulting in a nice uniform coating. This is especially useful when working with intense ingredients like Scotch or absinthe because water also "opens up" the alcohol, so the aromas and flavors of absinthe or bitters will blossom and materialize in profound ways. Do it quickly and move on! You don't have to be precious about it, and hesitation often results in more liquid on the outside of the glass than the inside. Also, do this over a sink or the trash can—you want to move the liquid around in a way that doesn't allow for drops to escape, but in case that happens, it's best to have something to catch them. Finally, pay attention to your wash lines.† The goal is to make sure the rinse creeps above the level of the cocktail that is going into the glass so the Aroma sticks on top instead of getting lost inside the drink.

Once you've thoroughly seasoned the inside of the glass, toss any remaining droplets and ice, and give it a smell. Think about the cocktail you're working with— do you want this rinse to be loud and bombastic, or more of a subtle whisper? Neither is right nor wrong, it just depends on the drink you're aiming to create. If you need to add a little more liquid and rinse again at this point, that's totally fine; sometimes low-proof liqueurs need a secondary boost to get the smell to the right level of intensity. Then pour your freshly shaken or stirred cocktail into the glass.

---

* I should mention that it is a sad day as I write this, as the inventor of the atomizer has died. He will be mist.

† The level of liquor or cocktail in a glass.

RECIPES

Here are twenty-five original recipes from The Violet Hour that show off the mechanics of mixing. It's *your* job to make these, drink them, and analyze them. When you do, remember to measure with the same care you would apply to fine needlework. Practice your straw tastes, especially the second one—we've included some guidance on what to look for in each recipe, so read the mixing instructions thoroughly *before* you gather your ingredients and begin the process. Use a consistent number of cubes to shake (we recommend five) or stir (fill the mixing glass three-quarters of the way full). What happens to the cocktail when you shake too long or not long enough? Texture too thick or sweet? How would you use Aroma if you were to reinvent one of these drinks yourself? Make the drinks that sound the most delicious to you, and then make them again for your friends and neighbors so you really solidify the technique in your mind. And for fuck's sake, chill your glassware!!!

HUSH & WONDER

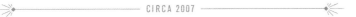

CIRCA 2007

Named after the Bernard DeVoto quote from which we got the name "The Violet Hour,"
this is a warm, vanilla-tinged daiquiri with a sneaky shiv of grapefruit bitters and
a huge floral nose. I would consider this as close to a "signature drink" as we have,
because it touches on most of our core philosophies: it's a barely tweaked, modern take
on a very obvious Mother Drink; it's incredibly complex without being ten touches; and
it relies on solid technique to reach its full, spectacular potential. —TOBY MALONEY

MISE EN PLACE

GLASS . . . . . COUPE

ICE . . . . NONE

GARNISH . . . NONE

METHOD . . . COUPE SHAKE

SPEC

2.0 OZ . . . . . . MATUSALEM RUM CLÁSICO

.75 OZ . . . . . . LIME JUICE

.75 OZ . . . . . . SIMPLE SYRUP

3 DASHES . . GRAPEFRUIT BITTERS

ROTHMAN & WINTER CRÈME DE
VIOLETTE, TO RINSE

PUT YOUR COUPE IN THE freezer. Grab your tin: Dash the bitters and toss in
your simple syrup, lime, and rum. Taste, extrapolating how the crème de violette
is going to round out the drink and make it read sweeter once it merges with the
rest of the liquids. Pull the coupe from the freezer and rinse the glass with the
crème de violette. Violet liqueur is low-proof, so there is no need for ice in this
maneuver, but do it over the sink or trash can so you can angle the glass so there
is no flow back. Add 5 ice cubes and COUPE SHAKE. Taste. Does it need .125
ounce more lime to brighten up? Did you shake long enough that it's frothy and
lively? DOUBLE STRAIN. Fill the glass no more than two-thirds of the way up so
you have plenty of surface area for the rinse to do its part in the cocktail. If there
is more cocktail in your shaker, add it to a sidecar* so it stays chilled but isn't
floating around amid the chewed-up cubes of the shaker tin.

* A small vessel that holds the remaining cocktail that doesn't fit in the coupe or Nick & Nora.

MOTHER DRINKS: PAGE 33 ✳ SIMPLE SYRUP: PAGE 311 ✳ RINSE: PAGE 83

BRIARPATCH

CIRCA 2008

I love a classic Bramble cocktail. It's easygoing and fruity but not frivolous. This is a riff on Dick Bradsell's genius contemporary classic and others of its ilk that followed. Most of them are just a Gin Fix with a fruit component. Like adult pink lemonade. The blackberry syrup has a hefty amount of Angostura, which really ramps up this cocktail.
—TOBY MALONEY

MISE EN PLACE

GLASS . . . . . COLLINS

ICE . . . . CRUSHED

GARNISH . . . BLACKBERRY, KNOTTED
             LEMON PIGTAIL

METHOD . . . WHIP SHAKE, ROLL

SPEC

2.0 OZ. . . . . . BEEFEATER GIN

.75 OZ. . . . . . LEMON JUICE

.50 OZ. . . . . . SIMPLE SYRUP

.25+ OZ. . . . . BLACKBERRY SYRUP,
               TO LACE

IN A SHAKER TIN, COMBINE the simple syrup, lemon, and gin. Put .25 ounce of the blackberry syrup in the jigger and set that next to where you're going to serve the drink. This sets up a nice moment of anticipation to follow. Taste. The drink should be too dry because it will get that final lace of syrup at the end. Prepare your Collins glass by filling it three-quarters of the way with crushed ice. Add 2 ounces of crushed ice to your shaker and **WHIP SHAKE. ROLL** the whole contents of the shaker into the Collins glass. The crushed ice will recede. Top with more crushed ice if you want it to overflow with icy goodness, then lace it with blackberry syrup. Garnish: Use a channel knife to cut your lemon pigtail, holding the fruit so it hovers over the top of the drink and the oils that shower off the peel land on the surface. Don't be shy, get plenty of oil going for a nice and generous coating. Tie the pigtail in a knot, add your blackberry to its soft embrace, and place it in the drink to garnish.

BLACKBERRY SYRUP: PAGE 312 ✳ WHIP SHAKE: PAGE 46 ✳ LACING: PAGE 81

NEW YORK MINUTE

CIRCA 2015

This is a riff on an old Charles H. Baker classic called the Pan American Clipper. Most of the ingredients are the same as in the original recipe, with slightly different ratios and the addition of vodka. The grenadine and apple brandy work really well, and the single dash of absinthe has the unique effect of tying everything together, like adding fresh herbs to a salad. A vodka drink for non-vodka drinkers, it has just enough complexity to be enjoyed by cocktail enthusiasts and is just accessible enough to be enjoyed by casual drinkers. —ALYSSA HEIDT

MISE EN PLACE

GLASS . . . . . NICK & NORA

ICE . . . . NONE

GARNISH . . . NONE

METHOD . . . COUPE SHAKE

SPEC

1.5 OZ . . . . . . VODKA

.50 OZ . . . . . . LAIRD'S BOTTLED-IN-BOND APPLEJACK

.75 OZ . . . . . . LEMON JUICE

.75– OZ . . . . . GRENADINE

1 DASH . . . . ST. GEORGE ABSINTHE VERTE

CHILL YOUR COUPE. IN A shaker tin, combine the absinthe, grenadine, and lemon, then stack the applejack and vodka. Taste. Be extra careful with the absinthe measure. The dash of absinthe should be just that—a very small amount—because once you add dilution through the shaking process, it'll soften and almost disappear into the drink. It's there for just a whisper of complexity and nothing more—this is not an "absinthe drink!" Add 5 ice cubes and **COUPE SHAKE**. Taste. Is it sweet enough, or would it benefit from more grenadine? Applejack is pretty dry, so it might need a little boost of sweetness at this juncture. **STRAIN**. No garnish.

GRENADINE: PAGE 311 ✳ STACKING: PAGE 36 ✳ BULLIES: PAGE 37

THE LIBERTINE

This recipe was inspired by Hemingway-style drinks where absinthe and sparkling wine famously come together, like the Death in the Afternoon. I wanted to do something simple that required the fewest moves possible, so I brought the two together with a sloe gin float, which adds a striking visual component as it trickles down into the cocktail like a creeping spiderweb. —ROBBY HAYNES

MISE EN PLACE

GLASS . . . . . HURRICANE

ICE . . . . HAND-CRACKED CUBES

GARNISH . . . BLACKBERRY; LEMON
              PIGTAIL

METHOD . . . COLLINS SHAKE, ROLL

SPEC

.50 OZ . . . . . PERNOD ABSINTHE

.75 OZ . . . . . LEMON JUICE

.50 OZ . . . . . SIMPLE SYRUP

2.0 OZ . . . . . SPARKLING WINE,
              TO BOTTOM

.25 OZ . . . . . PLYMOUTH SLOE GIN,
              TO FLOAT

PLACE ABOUT 5 HAND-CRACKED ICE cubes in the bottom of the hurricane glass and add a few ounces of sparkling wine so it starts to chill. In a shaker tin, **COLLINS SHAKE** the absinthe, lemon juice, and syrup together with 3 uniform ice cubes. Taste the drink—if it's too sweet, an extra .5 ounce of dry sparkling wine will help achieve Balance. If you're not getting enough of an absinthe punch, you can add a touch more at this time. **ROLL** into the prepared glass. Put the sloe gin in a jigger or in a smaller bottle to make pouring the liquid into the glass gently easier than straight out of a big, 750ml bottle. Use just enough to look cool. Express the oils from the lemon pigtail over the top of the drink as you cut the long and thin ribbon—a crucial move to keep the Aromas bright and refreshing—then twist up the peel so it looks like a pigtail and insert into the drink. Add the blackberry next to the lemon pigtail.

SIMPLE SYRUP: PAGE 311 ✳ COLLINS SHAKE: PAGE 46 ✳
BOTTOM: PAGE 62 ✳ FLOAT: PAGE 81

ORCHARD

CIRCA 2008

Intended as a simple Sidecar riff, this is a straightforward, well-Balanced sour that reminded me of how sweet and tart apples taste when plucked right from the tree. I like how many different layers of nostalgia happen in the drink—it makes you think of fresh apple, caramel apple, and the spice of apple pie or crumble, and all the flavors are very harmonious. Pure autumn. —KYLE DAVIDSON

MISE EN PLACE

GLASS . . . . . COUPE

ICE . . . . NONE

GARNISH . . . 11 DROPS ALLSPICE DRAM

METHOD . . . COUPE SHAKE

SPEC

2.0 OZ . . . . . . LAIRD'S BOTTLED-IN-BOND
APPLEJACK

.75 OZ . . . . . . LEMON JUICE

.50 OZ . . . . . . BLIS BOURBON BARREL-
AGED MAPLE SYRUP

.25– OZ . . . . . ST. ELIZABETH ALLSPICE
DRAM

CHILL THE COUPE. MEASURE YOUR lemon and add to a shaker, then add the maple. Measure your spirit and the allspice dram. Pick out 5 good-looking ice cubes and put them into the shaker. Pop the top on and **COUPE SHAKE**, slowly at first, trying to build a rhythm and a circular movement to the ice in the shaker. Taste to see if the grippiness of the allspice dram has made the Texture of the cocktail unpleasant. If it's too dry, add .25+ oz. more maple syrup, or .25– oz. Demerara. **STRAIN** into the coupe and garnish.

COMFORT: PAGE 133 ✳ MAPLE SYRUP: PAGE 26 ✳
FAT/SKINNY: PAGE 36 ✳ COUPE SHAKE: PAGE 45

BIRD ON A WIRE

CIRCA 2011

This is a whiskey daisy that has a little more interest thanks to the addition of pear liqueur. Like a good piece of pie, it pairs cinnamon's aggressive spice with the softer fruit qualities of delicate pear. Bourbon brings in all the toasty vanilla and baking spice flavors, which Fee's reinforces in exactly the right way. If you were to use Angostura, it would evoke a little more complexity and mystery, but Fee's brings a soda-fountain-like simplicity to the drink. Great for people with a secret sweet tooth. —ROBBY HAYNES

MISE EN PLACE

GLASS.....COUPE

ICE.......NONE

GARNISH...LEMON PIGTAIL

METHOD...COUPE SHAKE

SPEC

2.0 OZ......BUFFALO TRACE BOURBON

.75 OZ......LEMON JUICE

.75 OZ......ROTHMAN & WINTER ORCHARD PEAR LIQUEUR

.50 OZ......CINNAMON SYRUP

9 DROPS...FEE BROTHERS OLD FASHION AROMATIC BITTERS

CHILL YOUR COUPE. PULL OUT your shaker tin and measure the bitters into the tin. Add the cinnamon syrup and pear liqueur, using precision in both measures so the drink doesn't end up "too sweet." Add the lemon juice and bourbon to the shaker, plus 5 ice cubes. **COUPE SHAKE.** Taste. If you need to add more sweetness, try Demerara syrup instead of more cinnamon syrup, since the latter will change the flavor of the cocktail in addition to boosting the sweetness. **DOUBLE STRAIN** with the gate down so you keep as much ice contained in the shaker as possible. Garnish with a nice, tightly wound pigtail. (Using a channel knife, cut a long thin ribbon of peel over the top of the drink, so the oils that spray off the fruit land on the surface of the cocktail. Twist it up tight so it looks like it belongs on Wilbur's backside, and insert the pigtail into the drink in a way that looks visually appealing.)

CINNAMON SYRUP: PAGE 312 ✱ COUPE SHAKE: PAGE 45 ✱ PIGTAIL TWIST: PAGE 77

THE HEARTBREAKER

CIRCA 2018

Call it French 75–esque or a Cosmo-wannabe, but either way, this is a fun and flirty summer vodka drink. Apologue's Aronia liqueur is a berry-forward ingredient that reminds me of pomegranate, so those two ingredients match up right away and are lifted by the inclusion of lemon juice. Vodka helps add ABV, but the Aronia is definitely the star of the show here. It's an effervescent, slightly citrusy cocktail that tastes easy-breezy but has a big mouthfeel for a shaken vodka drink made with sparkling wine.

—ABE VUCEKOVICH

MISE EN PLACE

GLASS . . . . . **COLLINS**

ICE . . . . **ICE CUBES**

GARNISH . . . **GRAPEFRUIT ROSE**

METHOD . . . **COLLINS SHAKE**

SPEC

1.5 OZ . . . . . . **VODKA**

.75 OZ . . . . . **LEMON JUICE**

.75 OZ . . . . . **APOLOGUE ARONIA BERRY LIQUEUR**

.75 OZ . . . . . **GRENADINE**

DRY SPARKLING WINE, TO BOTTOM

GRAB YOUR COLLINS GLASS, ADD ice, and bottom with 2 to 3 ounces of sparkling wine, the former if you want a sweeter drink, the latter if you prefer it on the dry side. It's going to froth up, so it might take a couple of rounds to get enough in there. Set aside. In your shaker tin, combine the grenadine, lemon juice, Aronia, and vodka, plus 3 ice cubes. **COLLINS SHAKE**. Taste. It should be so sweet your teeth ache, because once you add the cocktail to the dry sparkling wine, it'll fall into Balance. **STRAIN**. For the garnish, make sure you squeeze some of the oils over the top of the drink before rolling the peel into a rose shape.

GRENADINE: PAGE 311 ✳ COLLINS SHAKE: PAGE 46 ✳ GRAPEFRUIT ROSE: PAGE 77

IRISH CREAM

CIRCA 2008

For this drink, I was assigned to come up with a recipe for the "cordial" category on the winter menu. It wasn't a type of cocktail I drank very often, so Toby worked with me to compose this pretty simple Irish Cream variation. This is not your grandma's glass of Baileys on the rocks! It's a fresh, spirit-forward digestif that's comforting, warming, bracing, and balanced. Good Irish whiskey and rum come together with a remarkable honeyed savory quality, while the liqueur draws out vanilla notes and the orange peel adds smoky citrus Aromas. Perfect for anyone looking for an after-dinner drink that's not too heavy. —JANE LOPES

MISE EN PLACE

GLASS . . . . . **DOUBLE OLD-FASHIONED**

ICE . . . . **CUBES**

GARNISH . . . **ORANGE PEEL, FLAMED
AND DISCARDED**

METHOD . . . **ROCKS SHAKE, ROLL**

SPEC

1.0 OZ . . . . . . **SAILOR JERRY SPICED RUM**

1.0 OZ . . . . . . **REDBREAST IRISH WHISKEY**

.50 OZ . . . . . **LICOR 43**

.50 OZ . . . . . **DEMERARA SYRUP**

1.0 OZ . . . . . . **HEAVY CREAM**

3 DROPS . . . **ANGOSTURA BITTERS**

IN A SHAKER TIN, ADD the heavy cream, then stack the Demerara syrup and Licor 43. Then stack the whiskey and the rum and add to the tin. Add 5 high-quality ice cubes and **ROCKS SHAKE**. Taste the cocktail: It should have a good Balance between the richness of the cream and the sweetness of the Demerara and Licor 43. Now look at the ice—if it is still mostly intact, you can **ROLL** the drink, ice and all, into a DOF glass. If the ice has shattered into a million shards, you can **STRAIN** the cocktail into the glass over ice instead. Choose your own path. Flame the orange peel over the top of the drink, then discard (it isn't pretty enough to stick around as a garnish).

DEMERARA SYRUP: PAGE 311 ✳ ROCKS SHAKE: PAGE 46 ✳ FLAMED ORANGE: PAGE 75

TRICK PONY

A vodka sour riff with seasonal spring flavors of apricot and grapefruit. I love Cocchi Americano, and like the way the vodka amplifies its intricacies and provides backbone for the cocktail. Everyone likes vodka and everyone likes ponies, but while a vodka soda would be a "one-trick pony," this pony actually knows some tricks. —SUSIE HOYT

MISE EN PLACE		SPEC	
GLASS	COUPE	1.0 OZ.	VODKA
ICE	NONE	1.0 OZ.	COCCHI AMERICANO
GARNISH . . .	RADIUS-CUT LEMON WHEEL	.75 OZ.	LEMON JUICE
METHOD . . .	COUPE SHAKE	.75 OZ.	GRAPEFRUIT JUICE
		.125 OZ.	MARIE BRIZARD APRY APRICOT LIQUEUR
		.50 OZ.	SIMPLE SYRUP

CHILL YOUR COUPE. POUR THE grapefruit and lemon juices into a shaker tin. Stack the Apry with syrup up to a fat .5 ounce. Add the Cocchi, vodka, and 5 ice cubes. Give it a **COUPE SHAKE**. Taste—if it's a little too perky and thin, you'll need to add more syrup. Resist the urge to add more liqueur. If you add more liqueur, you're contributing flavor, booze, *and* sugar, and that will further complicate the drink instead of fixing it. If you can taste the apricot and it feels well-rounded instead of thin, you're good to go. **DOUBLE STRAIN** into your chilled coupe. Garnish with a lemon wheel, floating merrily on top of the cocktail.

SIMPLE SYRUP: PAGE 311 ✳ RADIUS CUT: PAGE 77 ✳ STACKING: PAGE 36

EL TOPO

Spicy drinks are quite popular, and having a solid go-to recipe in your arsenal can be clutch—this has become one of the more popular drinks at the bar for that very reason. The recipe came about after I tried a drink called Gordon's Polynesian Breakfast (gin, lime, cucumber, hot sauce, and salt) at PKNY, may the bar rest in peace. I switched the gin to tequila, added strawberry, and replaced the salt with a splash of mezcal on the top of the drink. It's sweet, sour, spicy, fruit-forward, savory, and smoky—what more can you ask for? —PATRICK SMITH

MISE EN PLACE		SPEC	
GLASS	DOUBLE OLD-FASHIONED	2.0 OZ	REPOSADO TEQUILA
ICE	CHUNK	.75 OZ	LIME JUICE
GARNISH	STRAWBERRY AND CUCUMBER SLICE	.50+ OZ	SIMPLE SYRUP
METHOD	ROCKS SHAKE	.125 OZ	JUGO DEL DIABLO
		1	CUCUMBER SLICE, HALVED, TO MUDDLE
		1	STRAWBERRY, HALVED, TO MUDDLE
		.25 OZ	MEZCAL, TO FLOAT

PUT YOUR CHUNK OF ICE into the DOF glass. Start with the Jugo del Diablo—taste to see how spicy it is, then add a very small amount to the tin. If you add too much hot sauce, it will blow out your palate. This drink toes the line between spice and sweetness, so try to make it balanced AF so you can have another one afterward. Then place the cucumber and strawberry in with the hot sauce mix and **MUDDLE**. Add the syrup, lime, and tequila, plus 5 ice cubes. **ROCKS SHAKE** vigorously. Taste. You want the balance between sweetness and spice to be to your liking. Add more syrup if it lands on the side of too much spice. **DOUBLE STRAIN** into the DOF glass over the ice chunk. Float the mezcal on top of the drink and garnish.

SIMPLE SYRUP: PAGE 311 ✳ JUGO DEL DIABLO: PAGE 315 ✳
JUXTAPOSITION: PAGE 189 ✳ FLOAT: PAGE 81

POOR LIZA

CIRCA 2007

Did you know it takes 20 pounds of pears to get one bottle of pear eau-de-vie? To me, it's obvious from the spirit's succulent grainy texture. This drink tastes like a perfect pear, one that slices like butter, slurped down on a plaid blanket in an alpine meadow with your main squeeze. The Chartreuse plays the same part in complexity as it does in a Champs-Élysées. It doesn't sell for shit on a menu, but it's a killer dealer's choice.
—TOBY MALONEY

MISE EN PLACE

GLASS.....COUPE

ICE.......NONE

GARNISH...ORANGE DISK, FLAMED
         AND DISCARDED

METHOD...COUPE SHAKE

SPEC

2.0 OZ......CLEAR CREEK PEAR BRANDY

.75 OZ......LEMON JUICE

.25 OZ......GREEN CHARTREUSE

.50 OZ......SIMPLE SYRUP

3 DASHES..PEYCHAUD'S BITTERS

CH-CH-CH-CHILL **YOUR COUPE. DASH YOUR** bitters into the shaker tin. Stack the simple syrup and Chartreuse in the small side of your jigger, then toss it in. The lemon juice and eau-de-vie follow suit. Do a quick taste. The Chartreuse is going to necessitate a long **COUPE SHAKE** to soften the blow of the 110-proof liqueur. Shake with 5 ice cubes. Taste for how the pear flavor melds with the botanicals. If it isn't clicking, a few drops of Chartreuse or bitters (depending on which flavor you prefer) can make it pop. **DOUBLE STRAIN** into your coupe and garnish. Practice your flamed garnish away from the glass if you're new to the art; otherwise, let those oils rip over the surface. That Aroma is your garnish, so discard the disk once it has done its job.

SIMPLE SYRUP: PAGE 311 ✳ STACKING: PAGE 36 ✳ FLAMED ORANGE DISK: PAGE 75

THE STROONZ

An after-dinner drink that dials down the base spirit and dials up the amaro. Grapefruit and Cynar taste great together, but grapefruit juice can vary in acidity— even within the same week the flavor can change quite a bit, which is why this drink also has lemon juice as a Band-Aid. If it feels like the grapefruit isn't bright enough, you can up the lemon for more body. The name is Italian American dialect for "little asshole." —EDEN LAURIN

MISE EN PLACE

GLASS.....COLLINS

ICE ....SHARD

GARNISH...NOTCHED ORANGE PEEL,
           EXPRESSED AND INSERTED

METHOD ...COLLINS SHAKE

SPEC

1.5 OZ......CYNAR

1 OZ.......OLD FORESTER BOURBON

.50 OZ......CARPANO ANTICA
           VERMOUTH

.25+ OZ.....LEMON JUICE

.50 OZ......GRAPEFRUIT JUICE

.50 OZ......DEMERARA SYRUP

CLUB SODA, TO BOTTOM

GRAB YOUR GLASS, ICE IT, and put two fingers of soda in the bottom; this is a big build, so it needs only a wink of bubbles. Jigger out your Demerara syrup and pour it into the shaker. Stack your lemon and grapefruit. You of course have tasted the grapefruit juice so you know how tart and bitter it is, so you know how to jiggle the lemon juice (heavier if the grapefruit is not as acidic as usual). Now stack your Carpano and your Cynar at a nice even 2 ounces. Follow with the Old Forester. Taste. Make sure that the Balance between the juices and the Dem is right, paying secondary attention to the bitterness of the grapefruit and the bitterness in the Cynar. Add 3 ice cubes and **COLLINS SHAKE**. Taste, extrapolating that the minimal bit of water content you are getting from soda and ice will eat up most of the existing sweetness. It should taste a bit over-the-top at this point. **STRAIN**. Garnish.

DEMERARA SYRUP: PAGE 311 ✳ COLLINS SHAKE: PAGE 46 ✳ BOTTOM: PAGE 62 ✳
STACKING: PAGE 36 ✳ NOTCHED PEEL: PAGE 76

THE ELDER JACK

CIRCA 2008

Everyone was using St-Germain when it first came out on the market. The name of this drink is a play on the mix of elderflower (Elder) liqueur and applejack (Jack). It's a light, simple, and approachable springtime cocktail using a lot of fresh ingredients. The applejack brings a nice Red Delicious apple flavor to the glass, and the floral St-Germain and house grenadine bring high notes to the mix. Finally, the garnish adds zippy oils to Balance those three elements. I love a good invisible garnish.
—STEPHEN COLE

MISE EN PLACE

GLASS . . . . . COUPE

ICE . . . . NONE

GARNISH . . . ORANGE PEEL, EXPRESSED
AND DISCARDED

METHOD . . . COUPE SHAKE

SPEC

2.0 OZ . . . . . . LAIRD'S BOTTLED-IN-BOND
APPLEJACK

.75 OZ . . . . . LIME JUICE

.50 OZ . . . . . GRENADINE

.125 OZ . . . . SIMPLE SYRUP

.50 OZ . . . . . ST-GERMAIN ELDERFLOWER
LIQUEUR

7 DROPS . . . ORANGE BITTERS

CHILL YOUR COUPE! ADD YOUR bitters to a shaker tin. Grenadine is thicker and more sticky than simple syrup, so measure that into the shaker before you add the simple syrup, lime, St-Germain, and applejack. Deposit 5 ice cubes into the shaker and **COUPE SHAKE**. Taste. If it's too sweet, you could try adding a little lime juice (or a dash of Angostura, if you want to go nuts). **STRAIN** and garnish. Make sure you're getting a good expression of oils over the top of the drink, and that the oils coat the surface as evenly as possible, because that aromatic will help Balance out the drink's sweetness. It also plays well with the grenadine and pulls out pleasing notes from the orange bitters.

GRENADINE: PAGE 311 ✳ SIMPLE SYRUP: PAGE 311 ✳ BULLIES: PAGE 37

STONE COLD FOX

CIRCA 2015

Coming out of a long winter in Chicago, I always want to celebrate by jumping straight into patio-slammer cocktails like this one. It's a cross between a pisco punch and a classic mai tai—two instantly crushable warm-weather drinks. I was determined to make red wine floats a thing at the time (like in the New York Sour), so I poured our house red on top of this already huge mai tai build—it looked beautiful, and you didn't have to think very hard while drinking it. This recipe conjures beachy vibes, no matter the season. —ALYSSA HEIDT

MISE EN PLACE

GLASS.....CYCLONE

ICE ....CUBES

GARNISH...MINT SPRIG,
            ORANGE WHEEL

METHOD ...WHIP SHAKE

SPEC

2.0 OZ......PISCO ACHOLADO

.50 OZ......AMARO MONTENEGRO

.75 OZ......LIME JUICE

.50 OZ......PINEAPPLE JUICE

.75 OZ......ORGEAT

1.0 OZ......CLUB SODA, TO BOTTOM

.50 OZ......LIGHT-BODIED RED WINE,
            TO FLOAT

CHILL YOUR GLASS. IN A shaker tin, add the orgeat, pineapple juice, lime, amaro, then pisco. Add 2 ounces of crushed ice and **WHIP SHAKE** quickly just to chill and combine. **STRAIN** the cocktail into the chilled glass and top with ice cubes, but not to the very top; you need to leave room for the wine to float. Add the orange garnish: This is used à la sangria—it's not doing too much of a job— so you can stick it inside the drink and then eat it at the very end after it's been sitting in the cocktail for a while. A healthy dose of vitamin C. Now the mint: Slap the sprig over the top of the glass, using a handle of a spoon or a straw, so you propel the aromatics of the oil over the surface of the cocktail. Nestle the mint sprig into the drink at six o'clock. Add a straw next to the mint. Gently float the wine on top of the cocktail, either using the back of a spoon or a jigger.

ORGEAT: PAGE 315 ✳ WHIP SHAKE: PAGE 46 ✳ FLOAT: PAGE 81

LONDON FROG

 CIRCA 2019

Before I worked at The Violet Hour, I was a barista for three and a half years. As a nod to this, the London Frog was my attempt at making a cocktail that was inspired by a London fog latte, all bergamot and light lemon notes thanks to the inclusion of tannic Earl Grey tea. Everything in this cocktail is meant to Echo those flavors, and the egg white gives it the frothiness of steamed milk. In the end, it's perfectly Balanced between sweet, dry, and bitter—a good drink for someone who likes vodka but wants to branch out, as well as a person who enjoys delicate amaro and citrus flavors.
—LISA CLAIRE GREENE

MISE EN PLACE

GLASS.....FOOTED DELMONICO

ICE ....NONE

GARNISH...LEMON PEEL, EXPRESSED
            AND DISCARDED

METHOD ...MIME SHAKE, COUPE SHAKE

SPEC

1 OZ.......VODKA

.50 OZ......AMARO MONTENEGRO

.75 OZ......LEMON JUICE

.50 OZ......ITALICUS BERGAMOT
            LIQUEUR

.75 OZ......EARL GREY SYRUP

1 ....EGG WHITE

IN THE TALL SIDE OF a shaker, add the Earl Grey syrup, Italicus, lemon, amaro, and vodka, in that order. In the short side of the shaker, liberate your egg white from its shell, leaving the yolk of bondage behind. **MIME SHAKE.** Taste. The syrup and Italicus should be coming together in a big bergamot keynote; the complexity of the Montenegro should have a warm caramelly quality. If you overdid the lemon juice, you might need to bump up the Italicus to Balance it back out. Separate the tins, keeping the cocktail in the tall half, and scoop 3 ice cubes into the short half. **COUPE SHAKE** the absolute shit out of it. **DOUBLE STRAIN** the cocktail into the glass. Cut a lemon peel and express the oil over the top of your frothy cocktail, then discard. Enjoy promptly.

EARL GREY SYRUP: PAGE 313 ✳ EGGS: PAGE 64 ✳ CITRUS AROMA: PAGE 73

JUNE & HENRY

CIRCA 2016

Cold, spicy, fruity, boozy, fresh, and polite—this recipe was inspired by the Juliet &
Romeo (page 306). It's a spicy drink that you don't have to be in a spicy mood for, and
an agricole drink you don't have to be nervous about trying for the first time. You can
taste the flavors of the ancho chiles in the liqueur very well, but it isn't too spicy for
those with sensitive palates. I think it's the cucumber that holds this drink together—it
cools the chiles and plays nice with the vegetal, grassy notes of the agricole so well.
—DAVID GONSALVES

MISE EN PLACE		SPEC	
GLASS	DOUBLE OLD-FASHIONED	1.0 OZ	LA FAVORITE RHUM AGRICOLE BLANC
ICE	CRUSHED	.75 OZ	LIME JUICE
GARNISH	MINT SPRIG, 3 CUCUMBER SLICES, SALT	1.0 OZ	ANCHO REYES LIQUEUR
METHOD	MIME SHAKE AND WHIP SHAKE	.75 OZ	SIMPLE SYRUP
		3	CUCUMBER SLICES, TO MUDDLE
		1	MINT SPRIG

GENTLY DIP THE EDGES OF the cucumbers in salt, then throw them in the shaker
tin and **MUDDLE**. Add the mint sprig (resist the temptation to muddle), lime juice,
simple syrup, Ancho Reyes, and rum. Be accurate with the simple and lime; be
surgical with the rum and Ancho Reyes. To prepare the garnish, fan 3 beautiful
slices of cucumber like they're a winning poker hand, then take a sprig of mint and
stab it through the seed section of the cucumbers and dip the edges in salt. Set
that aside. **MIME SHAKE**. Add 2 ounces crushed ice and **WHIP SHAKE**. Fill your
DOF glass with crushed ice. **DOUBLE STRAIN** into the glass, moving the stream of
cocktail around the top of the ice so you get good dilution. With a julep strainer,
scoop and press as much ice as you can into the glass and smooth out the top into
a nice mound of ice. In one motion, insert a straw and garnish.

JULIET & ROMEO: PAGE 306 * SIMPLE SYRUP: PAGE 311 * MIME SHAKE: PAGE 65

BITTER GIUSEPPE

CIRCA 2009

Sometimes a cocktail tells you what to do, rather than you telling it what to do. One night an Italian chef I knew came into the bar for a drink. I thought he'd like a Cynar Manhattan. I have no fucking clue why—it doesn't make sense now, because you're just adding a sweet amaro to other sweet flavors, but regardless—I knew it needed something to balance out, and at the time I was playing around with Ti' Punch a lot, with the small medallions of lime. I remember cutting a lemon in that style but with more girth, because it kept needing a touch more acidity. I just kept tasting and trying to correct my fuck-ups to the point where it would take a full quarter ounce of lemon and an aggressive six dashes of orange bitters for it all to come together. I wish I had a better story for this one, but I was blindly moving around trying to make it work, and ended up just knocking it out of the park. —STEPHEN COLE

MISE EN PLACE

GLASS.....DOUBLE OLD-FASHIONED

ICE ....CHUNK

GARNISH...LEMON PEEL, EXPRESSED
            AND INSERTED

METHOD ...ROCKS STIR

SPEC

2.0 OZ......CYNAR

1.0 OZ......CARPANO ANTICA
            VERMOUTH

.25 OZ......LEMON JUICE

6 DASHES ..ORANGE BITTERS

ADD A LARGE CHUNK OF ice to your DOF glass. Add the bitters to a mixing glass—6 dashes is a lot, but the large amount of bitters will add both proof and complexity, which is much needed in this situation. Add the lemon, then the vermouth, and finally the Cynar. Taste, concentrating on how the whisper of lemon is working with the bitterness of the amaro while drying out the vermouth. Add ice, enough to fill the mixing glass three-quarters of the way full, and **ROCKS STIR**. Taste again before it gets too diluted—you want it to go into the glass on the hot side because it will thin out as it sits on ice. **STRAIN** into your DOF glass over the ice chunk. Express the lemon peel to grace the surface of the drink with sunny oils. Then insert the peel, skin side facing inward, placed at eleven o'clock, as garnish.

AROMA: PAGE 72 ✳ TRIPTYCH: PAGE 32 ✳ ROCKS STIR: PAGE 47

IT'S A JUNGLE
OUT THERE

CIRCA 2019

To reinvent one of my favorite drinks—the Jungle Bird—I turned to the specific earthy smokiness of Sfumato and made a strawberry-pineapple shrub with a balsamic vinegar base to add to the bright tropicality of the drink. I adore the combination of the amaro and the strawberry-pineapple shrub, which helps highlight and Balance the stone fruit notes from the amaro in a beautiful way. This drink is good for anybody who's in the mood for something fresh, tropical, and experimental. —EVANGELINE AVILA

MISE EN PLACE

GLASS.....DOUBLE OLD-FASHIONED

ICE ....CUBES

GARNISH...PINEAPPLE LEAF,
          STRAWBERRY

METHOD ...ROCKS SHAKE

SPEC

1.5 OZ......AGED RUM

.50 OZ......CAPPELLETTI AMARO
          SFUMATO RABARBARO

.50 OZ......LIME JUICE

.75 OZ......PINEAPPLE JUICE

.50 OZ......STRAWBERRY-PINEAPPLE
          SHRUB

STACK YOUR STRAWBERRY-PINEAPPLE SHRUB AND the Sfumato and send it to the bottom of the shaker tin. Measure out the lime juice and then the pineapple and pour into the shaker. Add the rum and give it a quick taste. Concentrate on how the vinegar in the shrub and the lime juice are balancing out the sweet pineapple and strawberry. Add 5 ice cubes and **ROCKS SHAKE**. Taste, looking for how the smoky bitterness of the Sfumato doesn't take over the drink; it should sit in Balance with the tropical notes of pineapple and strawberry. **STRAIN**. Garnish (make sure the strawberry is ripe and freshly cut so it has a killer attack).

STRAWBERRY-PINEAPPLE SHRUB: PAGE 315 ✱ STACKING: PAGE 36 ✱
ROCKS SHAKE: PAGE 46 ✱ GARNISH PLACEMENT: PAGE 301

ROOT OF ALL EVIL

CIRCA 2012

It's easy to add one too many ingredients to a cocktail, so learning to use as few ingredients as possible can be quite challenging. This drink is my best representation of that ethos. Good for fans of the Bijou cocktail, the combination of Chartreuse and root beer might seem off, but they're actually a match made in heaven. —PATRICK SMITH

MISE EN PLACE

GLASS.....DOUBLE OLD-FASHIONED

ICE ....CHUNK

GARNISH...5 DROPS BITTERCUBE ROOT BEER BITTERS

METHOD ...CHUNK STIR

SPEC

2.0 OZ......RANSOM OLD TOM GIN

1.0 OZ......CARDAMARO

.25+ OZ.....GREEN CHARTREUSE

CHILL YOUR DOF GLASS UNTIL a lovely frost shrouds the exterior. Grab a mixing glass and contribute your measures of Chartreuse, Cardamaro, and gin, making sure not to over- or underpour, because all three are very special ingredients and it would be a terrific waste to lose any of them if you happened to fuck up with your precision. Fill the mixing glass about three-quarters of the way full of ice and **CHUNK STIR**. Taste periodically until properly diluted and chilled—you'll know it's ready when the heat of the Chartreuse and gin have calmed (but only slightly, because this is going over ice) and the Cardamaro's sweetness stands up to the duo. **STRAIN** into your chilled glass over an ice chunk and garnish by gently dropping the bitters on the top of the drink.

BULLIES: PAGE 37 ✳ CHUNK STIR: PAGE 47 ✳ BITTERS GARNISH: PAGE 79

THE WORLD CUP

CIRCA 2008

A drink that could either be sipped and analyzed or just chugged, this is a caipirinha riff utilizing oily and fragrant tangerine rind. Toby always treated the base spirit as the "protein" of a drink, the item to build around and showcase, so in this circumstance, that's the cachaça. The Amaro Nonino and the tangerine are a lovely supporting cast, pleasantly accentuating the floral, grassy, and funky sugarcane character of the Mãe de Ouro without taking over. I love its harmony and progression. —KYLE DAVIDSON

MISE EN PLACE

GLASS . . . . . DOUBLE OLD-FASHIONED

ICE . . . . CHUNK

GARNISH . . . NONE

METHOD . . . ROCKS SHAKE

SPEC

2.0 OZ . . . . . . FAZENDA MÃE DE OURO
CACHAÇA

.50 OZ . . . . . . AMARO NONINO

.25 OZ . . . . . . DEMERARA SYRUP

1 . . . . LIME QUARTER, CUT IN
HALF, TO MUDDLE

1 . . . . SMALL TANGERINE, CUT
INTO 6 PIECES, TO MUDDLE

1 DASH . . . . REGANS' ORANGE BITTERS

MUDDLE THE LIME IN THE shaker tin first, then add the tangerine and MUDDLE again. Add the Demerara syrup, orange bitters, Amaro Nonino, and cachaça, in that order. Add 5 ice cubes to the mix and give it a ROCKS SHAKE, making sure the ice manages to dilute the mix properly despite its battle with all the muddled citrus in the tin. STRAIN well into a DOF glass over a big chunk of ice; the strain might take a little more elbow grease than usual because of all the muddled citrus, but it's worth the effort to shake out every last delicious drop.

DEMERARA SYRUP: PAGE 311 ✳ MUDDLING: PAGE 68 ✳ STRAINER GATES: PAGE 50

ART OF CHOKE

CIRCA 2008

On a particularly busy night at the bar, Stephen Cole passed me a dealer's choice ticket for a bitter drink with rum. I thought of doing a rum Manhattan with Cynar and a rinse of green Chartreuse. I liked that combination, especially how the Cynar and Chartreuse fought for attention, each wanting to have the last word. From there, I just played with it—the mint brought out all the herbs in the Chartreuse, and I honestly have no idea where the lime came from. But it linked up with the mint, and it was a domino effect from there. We were all so driven to get a drink on the menu back then that we'd often refine these random dealer's choice ideas and drive them home. The drink template has since proved really good for riffing. If Stephen hadn't passed that ticket off, maybe it never would have happened. —KYLE DAVIDSON

MISE EN PLACE

GLASS . . . . . DOUBLE OLD-FASHIONED

ICE . . . . CHUNK

GARNISH . . . MINT SPRIG

METHOD . . . CHUNK STIR

SPEC

1.0 OZ . . . . . . APPLETON WHITE RUM

1.0 OZ . . . . . . CYNAR

.25 OZ . . . . . SIMPLE SYRUP

.25 OZ . . . . . GREEN CHARTREUSE

.25 OZ . . . . . LIME JUICE

1 . . . . MINT SPRIG

CHILL YOUR DOF WITH a nice pretty chunk of ice. Pick a full, lush mint sprig, tear it in half to wake up the essential oils, and drop in your mixing glass. Rub the mint oil all over the base of the mixing glass, then add ice to fill it three-quarters of the way. Stack the simple syrup and Chartreuse, then add the lime juice. Flip the jigger and stack the rum and Cynar. Due to the low proof of the Cynar, this isn't going to need much stirring. Fill the mixing glass three-quarters of the way full with ice and **CHUNK STIR**. Taste, concentrating on the suspicion of lime juice drying out the three sweeteners. If it's still too sweet, you can squeeze a tiny bit more lime juice. Stir some more. Taste again. It should taste like the rum and Chartreuse have relaxed. **STRAIN**. Spank that mint and garnish.

SIMPLE SYRUP: PAGE 311 ✳ STACKING: PAGE 36 ✳ CHUNK STIR: PAGE 47 ✳
SPANK THE MINT: PAGE 78

THE GOLDEN AGE

CIRCA 2007

Our first menu featured mostly classics and a few cocktails that pushed the envelope, like this harebrained creation. It happened at about eleven p.m. the night before we opened to the public. I was so exhausted I don't remember it; I am told that I had an idea, ran around gathering things with purpose, and made it happen in a sleep-deprived fugue state. The combination of egg yolk and crushed ice was weird as fuck in 2007 (well, it's still kinda bizarre), yet the drink is a real banger that's stood the test of time. Remember to ask if the guest has any allergies or is a vegan before mixing, then let them know there is an egg yolk in it after their first few sips.
—TOBY MALONEY

MISE EN PLACE

GLASS.....COLLINS

ICE ....CRUSHED

GARNISH...RADIUS-CUT LEMON
          WHEEL, CHERRY

METHOD ...WHIP SHAKE, ROLL

SPEC

2.0 OZ.....MATUSALEM RUM CLÁSICO

.75 OZ.....LEMON JUICE

.25 OZ.....SIMPLE SYRUP

.50+ OZ....LEOPOLD BROS. MICHIGAN
           TART CHERRY LIQUEUR

1 DASH ....LEMON BITTERS

1 ....EGG YOLK

PLOP THE YOLK INTO YOUR shaker tin—don't be timid, you're *trying* to break it! Add the bitters. Stack the simple syrup and the cherry liqueur so they do not measure more than a single ounce. Add the lemon juice and rum. Stir briefly (or mime shake) to make sure the yolk is incorporated, especially if it didn't split on impact with the tin. Taste! Depending on your cherry liqueur, you may need to add a skinny splash of simple syrup; try to imagine what it's going to be like after you've poured it over crushed ice, which dries out cocktails immensely. Fill a Collins glass three-quarters of the way with crushed ice. **WHIP SHAKE** and **ROLL** the contents of the tin gently into the glass so the crushed ice has time to accept the liquid. Top with crushed ice to just slightly below the rim. The lemon wheel should make it look like this drink is sporting a mohawk with a cherry on top.

EGGS: PAGE 64 ✳ STACKING: PAGE 36 ✳ FAT/SKINNY: PAGE 36 ✳ RADIUS CUT: PAGE 77

METAL FLOWERS

CIRCA 2014

I love the classic Ti' Punch, but rhum agricole can be bombastic, so this drink was intended to be like a Ti' Punch lite. Leopold's tart cherry liqueur tones down the grassy notes of the rum without drowning them out entirely, and the lime cleans it all up. Sometimes you mess with a very minimal classic and you can get something interesting but "flash in the pan," if you will—this cocktail is no Ti' Punch. The cool part is, it doesn't have to be! —ANDREW MACKEY

MISE EN PLACE

GLASS . . . . . DOUBLE OLD-FASHIONED

ICE . . . . CRUSHED

GARNISH . . . LIME WHEEL, ORANGE
WHEEL HALF

METHOD . . . SWIZZLE

SPEC

2.0 OZ . . . . . . NEISSON RHUM AGRICOLE
BLANC

.125– OZ . . . . LIME JUICE

.50 OZ . . . . . . LEOPOLD BROS. MICHIGAN
TART CHERRY LIQUEUR

.25 OZ . . . . . . DEMERARA SYRUP
(OR TVH+)

3 DASHES . . CHERRY BITTERS

THIS IS A SWIZZLE, SO we're going to build it in the glass. Take a DOF glass and dash in the bitters. Stack the Demerara syrup and cherry liqueur, then add the lime juice and rhum, in that order. Taste. The lime juice isn't there to taste like lime, but just to brighten the drink and take the cherry flavor from cherry pie to "fresh off the tree." Fill the glass three-quarters full with crushed ice. With a swizzle stick or barspoon held between your palms as if you are in prayer, **SWIZZLE**. Taste. Depending on the size of the glass and the ice therein, you may need to add a bit more Demerara. Top with crushed ice and garnish with the lime wheel and orange wheel set on the rim.

TVH+: PAGE 311 ✳ CRUSHED ICE: PAGE 59 ✳ SWIZZLE: PAGE 47

THE ART OF SMOKE

CIRCA 2008

This was a riff on Kyle Davidson's Art of Choke (page 115). The framework he created for that drink is a brilliant one, and I think the evolution I introduced is fun. At the time I was really excited about bold flavors—lots of painting with primary colors, as it were. Mezcal and Cynar lead the way, giving the drink a smoky and bitter backbone. The Chartreuse and chocolate bitters are accents that help give the flavor drivers nuance and breadth. —**MIKE RYAN**

MISE EN PLACE

GLASS.....DOUBLE OLD-FASHIONED

ICE ....CHUNK OR SPHERE

GARNISH...MINT SPRIG, 7 DROPS
          OF CHOCOLATE BITTERS

METHOD ...CHUNK STIR

SPEC

1.0 OZ......DEL MAGUEY VIDA MEZCAL

1.0 OZ......CYNAR

.25– OZ.....LIME JUICE

.25 OZ......GREEN CHARTREUSE

.25 OZ......DEMERARA SYRUP

15 DROPS ..PEYCHAUD'S BITTERS

1 ....GRAPEFRUIT PEEL,
           TO RINSE

GRAB A DOF GLASS AND express the oils from your grapefruit peel into the glass with gusto. Add one big, imperfect ice chunk or sphere because a smaller cube will look awkward in such a voluminous vessel. Add the bitters and Demerara syrup, then the lime. Add the Chartreuse, making sure you are precise (or err on the skinny side to be safe, because the liqueur is such a bully), then add the Cynar and mezcal. Add ice to the DOF, three-quarters of the way full, and **CHUNK STIR** to mix. Stop stirring when it tastes just shy of acceptable in terms of dilution. You'll know because the heat of the mezcal will have eased up and the sweetness of the Cynar will shine through. Garnish, being delicate with the chocolate bitters (or not, if you fancy a ton of cocoa aroma).

DEMERARA SYRUP: PAGE 311 ✳ CHUNK STIR: PAGE 47 ✳
MINT/BITTERS GARNISH: PAGE 78 ✳ BULLIES: PAGE 37 ✳ FAT/SKINNY: PAGE 36

LOVE-LIES-BLEEDING

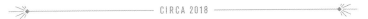

CIRCA 2018

This drink is a take on the Art of Choke (page 115), pushing the flavor boundaries even more by using a super-bitter base and mezcal as the spirit modifier. The dominant flavors come from the Punt e Mes and the mezcal—all baking chocolate, smoke, and even mole notes. Grapefruit from the Aperol and grapefruit bitters play with the lime, which brightens up the profile and Balances out the drink. A summertime digestif with a twist, it's a great option for anyone who enjoys a boozy mezcal cocktail, an absolute must for anyone who likes bitter flavors, and a phenomenal experience for imbibers who love both. —LEVI TYMA

MISE EN PLACE		SPEC	
GLASS	DOUBLE OLD-FASHIONED	1.5 OZ	PUNT E MES
ICE	CHUNK	.50 OZ	MEZCAL
GARNISH	GRAPEFRUIT PEEL, EXPRESSED AND INSERTED	.50 OZ	CARDAMARO
		.50 OZ	APEROL
METHOD	CHUNK STIR	.125 OZ	LIME JUICE
		2 DASHES	BITTERCUBE JAMAICAN NO.2 BITTERS

CHILL A DOF GLASS BY adding your chunk ice. In a mixing glass, combine the lime juice, bitters, Aperol, Cardamaro, mezcal, and Punt e Mes. Add enough ice to fill the glass three-quarters of the way high. CHUNK STIR. Taste. That little hint of lime should be keeping the sweetness in check. If you need a few more drops of lime to tame the sugar, that is good—remember to just be very judicious. The cocktail has a velvety viscosity that we want to maintain, so STRAIN the cocktail *slowly* into the DOF glass over the ice. Garnish with a grapefruit peel, expressing the oils first, then inserting it in the drink between eleven o'clock and one o'clock. Look at it, think about how weird it is that there's lime juice in your stirred cocktail, smell, sip, repeat.

STACKING: PAGE 36 ✳ CHUNK STIR: PAGE 47 ✳ BULLIES: PAGE 37

DRINK PHILOSOPHIES

CONCEPTUALIZING COCKTAILS
WITH COMPELLING BACKSTORIES

Hunter S. Thompson typed out *A Farewell to Arms* and *The Great Gatsby* WORD FOR WORD so he could feel what it was like to write a masterpiece. If that isn't dedication to the craft, I don't know what is. What I like most about Thompson's work is how he manages to tap into the very core of what it means to be human while avoiding any compulsion to make it sound prettier than it really is. With every story, he gave us humanity in all its messy, fucked-up drama. And through that raw and visceral examination of the human spirit, we readers end up feeling connected to something bigger than ourselves and learning something about our own idiosyncrasies, strengths, and character flaws as we enjoy his prose. In short, the vivacious and dramatic storytelling he mastered is not something every writer does well, but it's a crucial element in my favorite books. Without the effort taken to evoke the human spirit and all its perils, stories are just dull penny dreadfuls.

While it's not something everyone waxes poetic about in the same way, cocktails also become something larger and more visceral than a glass of ingredients if you can find a way to imbue them with universal truths and deeper meaning. Like a drink made with the spices that seasoned your childhood family meals, or a cocktail whose flavors reference the time you lost your driver's license in the sand because you drank too much tequila on that spring break trip to Rosarito. Whether it's drawing out soothing nostalgia or playing to a more obvious reference point, a cocktail that comes from a place of storytelling will (more often than not) turn a workhorse cocktail recipe into a Lippizaner* stallion–level glass of wonder. Something that will spark an idea or feeling and knock about in your brain long after the last sip.

In order to learn how to make cocktails like this, you have to start with the basics. You make as many recipes as you can get your hands on, make them over and over again, paying attention to every detail that we've illustrated in this book thus far. You learn the classics, your favorite drinks from Smuggler's Cove, from Death & Co, from Employees Only, from The Violet Hour. As Thompson did, you analyze and digest every word, every comma, every phrase, so you understand the craft inside and out. Once you have that foundation, you learn how to dig deeper. That's where this part of the book comes in.

Recipes also need an identity. Without one, the ingredients fight for attention, like a TV set to static: an ugly mess of muddy, overcomplicated fuzz. Throwing five or six ingredients together in a tin and hoping for the best is rarely going to create anything worth drinking twice. A cocktail that expresses an idea becomes something bigger than itself.

Here we'll walk you through the philosophies and theories of constructing a cocktail with a compelling backstory. Beginning from the flash of an idea, we'll show you how to apply parameters and give context to create a drink that will not only check the boxes of Balance, Temperature, Texture, and Aroma but also resonate on an emotional and intellectual level. The lessons in this section aren't tangible elements you can measure with a laser thermometer or a refractometer. They are theories that tap into the art of invention. The spirit of storytelling. They draw a little from philosophy, a bit from music, a schosh from literature, and a splash of psychology. This is where we earn our barspoon-tattoo-having, blacksmith-apron-wearing pretentious mixologist stripes, striving for cocktail badassery. Through the lessons of Inspiration, Intention, Comfort, and Curiosity, we're going to dig deep into the nerdy subtext of cocktails. We'll wax poetic about the reasons certain combinations evoke strong memories and how to tell better tall tales through drinks.

---

* Wicked cool, world-famous horses known for their acrobatics.

⚞•INSPIRATION•⚟

Chicago has a million places where Al Capone allegedly swilled illegal hootch and nuzzled moles who sported killer getaway sticks. It's kind of like the number of quaint bed-and-breakfasts in New Orleans' French Quarter claiming to be the famous "House of the Rising Sun." There are a fuck ton.

One of the most famous Capone haunts is a jazz club called the Green Mill. A true Chicago institution, where greatness has seeped into its wall murals and red banquettes since it opened as a roadhouse in 1907. Going there in the '90s made me feel sophisticated and worldly. I used to go see Patricia Barber play stripped-down jazz on a baby grand situated behind the bar, and whenever she played "Summertime," my heart would stop. She crawled into that song as if it was a tauntaun and made it her own.

It wasn't until years later that I understood that the saying "Good artists borrow, great artists steal," meant that a great artist will take something and make it their own to the point that you can't imagine that they're not the originator. There are fun covers of songs, like a bluegrass band doing AC/DC, and then there are covers of songs that seem like they were always done that way (thank you, Cyndi Lauper, for doing "Girls Just Want to Have Fun"). I think this is what we tried to do at The Violet Hour with classic cocktails. Like how Patricia took Inspiration from Gershwin and made something new and beautiful all her own, we didn't want to reproduce classic cocktails exactly like they were done pre-Prohibition; we wanted to take those originals and cover them in our style.

Without that specific Inspiration, our program would be, in the parlance of our industry, "a fucking shitshow." A cocktail forged without Inspiration, a core idea, or a backstory might as well be a beer with a lime. When a cocktail communicates a backstory, a journey, a soul, it becomes an *experience* that's worth relishing in the moment and then revisiting.

That's why every recipe has to have its roots hooked into *something*, and it's great when that something is more than "fuck, this is delicious." That is to say, the *way* we develop ideas and *how* we guide them from concept to fruition can make the difference between a decent cocktail and an insanely good one. That's why we start with Inspiration.

FINDING INSPIRATION

At the bar we rotate through new menus every three months to coincide with each season's solstice or equinox. At the halfway mark between each launch, bartenders begin to workshop recipes for the upcoming list. In the early days, we didn't set any parameters on invention, so everyone would come to the table with similar drinks and we'd be left with a dozen gaps in style, spirit, and personality to fill. Now we write down a certain number of prompts on strips of paper and throw them into a hat to kick-start the process. Stemming from the original prompts, Inspiration can come in a bazillion forms: a memory, a favorite song, a season, a mood—everything is fair game.

Try it! Start with an idea. Any idea. The fucking weirder and more stargazing, the better. Write it down. Then push that inkling *beyond* the first easy option to find an Inspiration with more weight to it. This process doesn't demand a full dissertation, but rather a quick flurry of brainstorming. For example, let's say you want to make a cocktail Inspired by fall. That's a large and abstract source, so drill it down to something more concrete. What fall moment is your absolute favorite? Let's say it's the first bite of a fresh cinnamon doughnut dipped into hot cider at your neighbor's apple orchard—that dialed-in version of the bigger idea offers a direct path to combining ingredients in a way that'll speak more clearly to the memory.

Let's do another round: If the broader idea is to make a cocktail that tastes like a walk in the woods, ask yourself a few questions to whittle that concept down to something more specific. Where in the world is this lovely wood? The flora and fauna of an alpine forest in Italy is going to look,

* SHIFTY *

SOURCES TO TAP

Inspiration can come from any source, from today's lunch of leftovers to the floral cologne your best friend wears, but it's not always easy to come up with an idea out of nowhere. Here are a few prompts to consider as sources of Inspiration.

+ Mood + Color + Season
+ Place + Food + Memory
+ Song + Painting + Novel

smell, and taste very different from one in New England, so a cocktail inspired by the former might employ grappa and fernet, while the latter might include wild blueberries and rye whiskey. Take the original idea even further— maybe it's a walk in the woods, but the woods are in the Pacific Northwest and the rain just snuffed out your campfire. What flavors speak to that, and how can you assemble them in a way that tells that story? Homing in on a single aspect of a broad original thought will set a more interesting foundation for flavors to develop.

Travel beyond *literal interpretations* of ideas, because they rarely work well. If I see one more drink called Purple Rain that's made with an obscene amount of crème de violette, I will punch a higher floor. I know *exactly* what that's going to taste like, and it's as lacking in subtlety as the lyrics of "Darling Nikki." Or remember when black cocktails were all the rage? You can make a black cocktail only with something like squid ink, black sambuca, or activated charcoal*—all of which are more novelty than solid flavor choice. Elevate the color swatch idea into something more evocative by thinking about *why* you want to create a black cocktail in the first place.

TVH makes the best cocktails because of their relative simplicity—a riff on a classic, elevated by each bartender's personal inspiration, like adding rose water to the Southside (Juliet & Romeo) or bringing root beer to the Manhattan (Woolworth Manhattan). I think through specific Inspiration, each bartender's weird personality quirks come through in their cocktails and that makes all the difference.

—HENRY PRENDERGAST,
2007–2013

If your goal is to "create a cocktail as dark as the bass riffs from my favorite goth rock track," one way to take that Inspiration to the next level is by thinking like a synesthete: Choose an amaro-and-vermouth combo that round out in the same way each pulse drives the beat forward, grab a bottle of dry-as-hell rye whiskey to match the gravelly vocals, pepper it with the reverb of blackstrap bitters, and hit the top with a spritz of lemon oil as the cymbal clash of garnish. Now you have a Manhattan riff that speaks volumes about your penchant for darkness, rather than a boring vodka soda dyed with black food coloring.

---

* An ingredient that interacts negatively with certain medications. Not a great offering to unsuspecting or uneducated guests.

⟡ INTENTIONS ⟡

Landscape architect Frederick Law Olmsted was fucking cool. His jam was designing the intersections where parks and cities interacted with humans, and vice versa. He worked to create outdoor spaces that could be easily and intuitively enjoyed by people from all walks of life.

To do this, he harnessed the power of Intention in his designs. By tapping deeply into the context of each plan—taking in the weather and how it changes, the flora available that time of year, the fauna, the guests (whether local squirrels or migrating business travelers), the who, what, when, where, and why of each place and what might be right for it at that moment, he used common sense and empathy to create parks, parkways, and housing developments—literally over one hundred parks and recreation spaces, including Brooklyn's Prospect Park—that to this day are still considered some of the best ever created.

Intention comes into play after Inspiration happens. It is the moment when you ask yourself *how* you will take that Inspiration and make something inspired out of it. The parameters and goals. The moment when the bartender puts on their architect hat and takes into consideration how the ingredients, the weather, and the specific human will interact. Many choices are made when considering all three. When and where is the drink going to be consumed? Why? How? All good questions to ask to get you started, because they will put guardrails up for the research and development process to follow. Maybe it's the glass you will serve the drink in, the dryness or nap of the ice, the balance of bitterness to booziness, a light effervescent Texture or a contemplative velvety one. Up or on crushed ice? Mint or sage? Tiki-esque or Algonquin Round Table? Cinnamon or nutmeg? All of these choices are determined by an *Intention* for how you hope the cocktail will be enjoyed by a guest. When you work with a combination of empathy and common sense, like Olmsted did, amazing things can happen.

Let's look at several ways you can use the idea of Intention to help guide your Inspiration from the tadpole of an idea to a fully fledged, er . . . cocktail.

SETTING INTENTIONS

One of the first places to start this journey is by considering your audience—that is, the drinkers on the receiving end of your cocktails. From day one at The Violet Hour, we aimed to get people to think beyond the ubiquitous Red Bull and vodka and dip a toe into new flavor experiences. We made all our whiskey cocktails with rye instead of bourbon to ease folks into the embrace of the rugged grain spirit. Then we added six gin drinks to the list for those willing to explore its juniper-fueled wonder. That spoke to our ethos as a bar, but also made it easier to create cocktails because we knew what the bigger picture should look like.

Our Intention has shifted over the years. Now we offer a mix of super accessible cocktails—i.e., simple, easy patio pounders and other "roast chickens" that will sell well—and more adventurous drinks with weird, expensive ingredients like big, bold amari, and hyper-peaty Scotch. The middle third of the menu casts a wide net of styles and flavors. With the Intention of making many different types of drinkers happy while still slightly nudging them to break out of their Comfort zone, it is easy to create menus that check all the right boxes.

Intentions should apply to a more individual level, too. One of the biggest rookie mistakes bartenders make is inventing drinks only *they* will enjoy. That's fine if it's just you mixing up a drink at home for Sunday brunch, but if you're inventing cocktails for other people, you should consider *who that person is* and *what kind of drink* will bring a smile to their face. Are you making a cocktail for a whiskey novice? Or are you making it for a whiskey geek who wants something bitter and rich? That could be the difference between whether you make a Manhattan or a Black Manhattan.

The *when* and *where* of drinking—the setting and occasion—should be taken into consideration at this stage of development to make sure the idea you had will translate to the moment the drink is being consumed. Are you

---

* SHIFTY *

INTENTION PROMPTS

Intention has a lot to do with how an Inspiration comes to fruition. Try one of these tried-and-true submission prompts from our menu meetings and see what evolves from there.

+ Shaken/Vodka/It's Gonna Be Hot Out

+ Shaken/Accessible/Gin

+ Stirred/Savory/Gin

+ Aquavit/Any Way

+ Shaken/Tequila/No Mezcal

+ Shaken/Rum/Adventurous

+ French 75 Riff/With Beer

+ Potable Bitters/Shaken/Refreshing

+ Stirred/Whiskey/Friendly and Familiar

+ Agricole/Stirred

+ Shaken/Adventurous/Whiskey/Safari

making drinks for a house party in the Gold Coast neighborhood or a Riot Fest afterparty in your friend's basement? Are you envisioning an aperitif to stimulate the senses before a gut-bomb of a meal, or throwing together a round of shots for a bachelorette party? Jim Troutman designed a "spicy margarita" by the name of Tex-Anne (page 169) for searingly hot summer days in the Lone Star State, while the Intention behind Lisa Claire Greene's Tall Order (page 199) was a margarita for a drinker who would appreciate the brooding notes of Sfumato. Both started as a tequila-based sours and evolved in distinct and unique directions based on the situation and sort of drinker Jim and Lisa envisioned.

Intentions are the starting line for development, because oftentimes, regardless of your Intent, the *impact* of a cocktail will differ based on who is drinking it. For a hot minute back in the early '90s, I lived in Thailand, where I worked at a beach resort serving the best food in Koh Lanta. We had these big aluminum serving bowls for rice that stood 10 inches off the table, and I realized quickly that they were light and stackable versions of a punch bowl. Using that vessel, I came up with a drink called the Devil's Cup, intended for people who needed something to occupy their hungry minds while they waited for their food. It was so time-saving to pour a pint of whiskey, a bottle of Sprite, some pineapple juice, and a little coconut water into a vessel and eschew cups for straws. One night, I was slammed, so I brought the Devil's Cup accouterments to a table, built it, and then instead of placing the straws nicely in front of everyone, I held them over the middle of the bowl, released them to fall where they may, and said, "GO!" To my surprise, everyone jumped into the fray, claiming a straw with their mouth and sucking greedily. It had become a competition with just one small syllable. The drink was gone in less than 15 seconds. I cheered and they laughed. The Intention I started with—of creating a big drink that would occupy a group for a long time—instantly became the opposite, and something infinitely more fun.

> *We had forty-three bourbons and seventeen pisco bottles on the back bar. If someone used Buffalo Trace in their whiskey sour variation, they would be asked why during our menu-tasting sessions. Not because it was wrong or bad, but really: "Why did you choose that one? Why not x, y, or z?" And it wasn't a rhetorical question. It was asked with an expected response. If you used an ingredient, it had to be well thought out and work with everything else in the drink.*

—OWEN GIBLER, 2011–2012

❊ COMFORT ❊

One cold winter night a few years ago, my girlfriend and I went to Milk Room at the Chicago Athletic Association to visit the bar the extra-ordinary Paul McGee set up with more vintage spirits than you could shake a swizzle stick at. In the small and moody former speakeasy—named after a time when enterprising gentlemen* could visit and receive their "milk" (illegal spirits) during Prohibition—I ordered a Vieux Carré made with terrifically preserved expressions of whiskey, Cognac, vermouth, and Bénédictine.

Even before I tasted the drink, I was transported. It smelled just like the tack room at the stable where I used to ride horses. Reminiscent of burnished leather, saddle soap, clean dry straw, rich earth, and seasoned hardwood, it evoked such a powerful sense memory that it shook my body like a hiccup. I could almost see the dust motes floating in sunbeams and hear Cassidy nickering.

This is experiencing a cocktail through emotion. Specifically, evoking feelings of well-being, nostalgia, or peace. This theory is ultimately about what is in the glass and how it might resonate with the drinker. What happens when you take that first sniff or sip of a drink? Does it transport you to a time or place, or raise questions or concerns? Does it stimulate the *mind* as well as the body? That's when a cocktail turns into something bigger than itself. When even the simple thought of it sticks to your rib cage for days to come.

There is a school of thought that says when you have positive emotions, it makes whatever you are eating or drinking better. More enjoyable. This is why we sometimes approach the Inspiration process by looking at ways to evoke Comfort in a cocktail. Think about the crunch of your mom's signature chocolate chip cookies. The smell of fresh-cut grass in the summertime. The warm humidity that hangs in the air in the wake of a rainstorm. Something familiar and friendly. Finding ways to translate those sentiments into a cocktail isn't always terribly difficult—most of the time you simply think about the sights, sounds, and smells from a certain time and place and work to translate that into ingredients. When it works, the results are a runaway success.

---

* At the time, it was a men-only club.

EVOKING COMFORT

One approach to Comfort is to draw out a distinct and specific memory associated with a certain ingredient. Let's revisit Proust's famous madeleine. The first bite took him right back to the old gray house where his aunt first made him dip the cookie into tea—an instant, vivid sense memory that earned a legendary place in literary history. To flush out an Inspiration around this moment, think about the time of year, the place, the smells or mood, then home in on what flavors or aromas are connected to that memory. Work backward from that point to invent a drink. If we were to be Proustian about it, perhaps it's a brandy cocktail made with a tea syrup, vanilla bitters, and a spray of sunny lemon oil as the garnish.

Another example: If you were a particularly entrepreneurial child, maybe you ran a lemonade stand, and now the Tom Collins—an "adult" lemonade, with its simple mix of gin, lemon, and soda—takes you back to days spent sitting on your lawn behind a rickety card table, fortified with a sweating pitcher of liquid shade and waxy Dixie cups, hoping to make a few extra quarters from thirsty passersby. That flavor memory can be harnessed to invent a cocktail that makes you sink into the warmth of nostalgia. Maybe you grew up in Georgia and sold lemonade only at the height of peach season. How can you work a subtle thread of the stone fruit into the story of that drink so that when you taste it, or when someone else from Georgia reaches for a glass, you both find yourselves wiping a bead of sweat from your brow, with a slow grin spreading across your face?

Sense memories like that can also be linked to an Aroma or flavor with a deeper cultural connection. In the early days of The Violet Hour, we made a lot of recipes using orange marmalade. The US isn't as big a market for that kind of flavor as the UK is, but we like to think it's so specific and unique to British cuisine that the ingredient would get even the most stubborn expats to emote.

Playing to familiar reference points works in a similar way. Even if you've never been to a Kentucky Derby party, seen the horses shake flies from their manes and smelled the sweat of the jockeys, chances are, a mint julep is going to stir up images of fancy hats and galloping hooves. Simply understanding the reference can evoke a sense of

> *A classic example of The Violet Hour method: Make classic drinks classically, let variations and inspirations abound, but the drink should remain, at the end of the day, recognizable as a classic in form and build.*
>
> **—TYLER FRY, 2011–2016**

Comfort. And if you're lucky enough to have clasped an ice-cold cup at Churchill Downs in the month of May, that emotional connection will ring even stronger. How can you, the cocktail inventor, find a time or place or celebration that's universally enjoyed and make a drink that taps into that spirit?

Sometimes it is as simple as finding a classic cocktail that is already a favorite and finding tiny ways to change the drink to make it even more personal. For me, the Manhattan is the quintessential Comforting drink. Where a martini is a bit snooty and persnickety, a Manhattan is a cool friend who is easy to hang out with. When whiskey is drunk straight and neat, it can be a bit brash—like a New Yorker with the grit to wade through a trash-strewn sidewalk or argue about which dollar slice is the best—but with a little, or a lot, of vermouth, it becomes a sophisticated cocktail that's complex and enjoyable without the attitude. A Manhattan, placed on an end table and forgotten when you go out to get more firewood, is still delicious when you get back, even at room temperature. Think about every element in the drink and how you might be able to make your version even more unique to *you* and what you like.

In a similar sense, Comfort also connects directly with ritual or habit. When teaching bartenders about Sazeracs or martinis, I always say, "Every good drug has a distinct, intricate ritual, from heroin to Catholicism," because humans find solace and comfort in doing something by rote. The sounds and the smells of cocktails woven together in repetition creates Comfort for the bartender. Making your own cocktail or ordering "the usual" from your local purveyor of fine spirits can create Comfort for the non-bartender. It doesn't even have to be fancy or overblown; if you crack open a cold Miller High Life and pour a shot of Very Old Barton when you get home from work every day, that combination becomes Comfort. Mixing up a quick Negroni before dinner or pouring a dram of a fernet after a gut-busting meal—these kinds of drinking rituals and habits also create Comfort and can be played with when inventing new cocktails.

Comfort is one of those theories that can be highly personal. What might be Comforting to you won't necessarily resonate with everyone else. That's not a bad thing, though. You can't always make every single person who walks through the door happy, let alone send them off into the night awash in warm-fuzzy sentimentality. Instead, accept the ambiguity. There are a million "right" and "wrong" answers. That flexibility will set you free to be as creative as you please, and that's what drives the beautiful, labyrinthian world of cocktails we all love. Whether your Intentions resonate thoroughly with other people or not, it's the journey to creating something with depth (and deliciousness) that matters.

☀ CURIOSITY ☀

Chicago, the City of Broad Shoulders, home of the stockyards and slaughterhouses that form the backdrop of the pro-union socialist novel *The Jungle*, is also the home of the hot dog. You might already know that we take our hot dogs as seriously as a heart attack. The derision and shame that will be heaped upon you for putting ketchup on a dog at The Wieners Circle at four thirty a.m. would make a statue blush and slink away into the good night.

And yet amid all this frankfurter snobbery, a man by the name of Doug Sohn upturned the entire establishment when he opened a place called Hot Doug's, a "Sausage Superstore and Encased Meat Emporium," in a working-class neighborhood on the northwest side. It was here that Doug sparked endless waves of Curiosity in his guests by taking the beloved genre and turning it into something unexpected. He made his sausages wild and whimsical and culinarily inspired. Doug made dogs of rabbit and foie gras and wild boar. White wine and fancy cheese went into his dogs.

Before going, I admit I was a bit skeptical; it seemed gimmicky and show-off-y. It wasn't—it was great technique and high-quality ingredients coming together to make deliciousness that fit in a poppy seed bun. Even when they were extravagant as fuck, they were still, objectively, hot dogs. It was a sausage you would never worry about seeing being made. A dog that had gone to finishing school. Doug set out to surprise people and create repeat customers out of the adventure, and it worked. We lined up around the block to smash them in our faces.

Curiosity is one of the most entertaining and enjoyable theories to tap into when inventing drinks. Like Comfort, Curiosity can spark nostalgia and memory. But with Curiosity, we're going for a slightly different end goal. Not necessarily one of soft longing or reminiscence, but one where the first sip opens your eyes wide in surprise or raises your eyebrows in alarm. Drinks that have that "what the fuck?!" magic. Where there's something floating around in that glass that takes you somewhere you can instinctively remember but have a hard time putting your finger on. Like a sneeze that's about to arrive. Or even simpler: an "I have no idea what's going on in this drink" kind of moment. That's Curiosity.

SPARKING CURIOSITY

Do you remember the first time you saw an egg cracked with one hand? That slimy plop into the shaker tin always jolts the senses and provokes a question. When we light orange peels on fire, it always stops drinkers mid-conversation. In these moments, the drink stimulates *intellectually* as opposed to emotionally. It makes you pause and inspires wonder. A cocktail that employs Curiosity asks questions you might not be able to answer. A lot of the time this can arise from the sheer number of ingredients in a drink and the individual character of each, but there are more nuanced approaches, like setting up and slaying expectations and preconceived notions, just as Hot Doug did at his sausage temple. Let's talk about a few ways to conjure up Curiosity.

In its simplest form, Curiosity derives from sheer complexity, like in the 20th Century cocktail, which plays host to gin, lemon, Cocchi Americano, and crème de cacao. I remember my first sip made me do a Scooby Doo–style double take, take another sip, then put the cocktail down as if it had wronged me. I was stymied. I knew something wholly familiar was going on in that kaleidoscope of flavors, but I could not for the life of me place it. Once I was told that the confounding element was the chocolate notes of crème de cacao, it all made sense—but it took a wild and winding ride on the Curiosity train to get me to that destination.

Other times, Curiosity comes about from an unexpected *combination* of ingredients. Robby Haynes's 2013-era Rye Tai cocktail (page 209) combines a small portion of Jamaican rum with rye whiskey as the base, together with the square-shooting combo of lime and orgeat. Things get really crazy as Aperol weasels its way into the recipe; the nuttiness of the orgeat sits in shocking contrast with the bittersweet orange notes of the Italian liqueur. Somehow, inexplicably, they walk together side by side, without argument, despite how different their profiles are from one another.

Sometimes Curiosity happens with an expectation or assumption that gets challenged, leading to a great reveal or moment of surprise. For most of the cocktail dark ages (from approximately 1920 to 2000, or the beginning of Prohibition to the opening of Milk & Honey), if you were to breathe the word "daiquiri," the first thing most people would think of was the sticky-sweet neon slush cranked out of frozen drink machines in New Orleans. This was my initial expectation when I first ordered a dealer's choice at Milk & Honey. When Sasha Petraske said he'd make me a daiquiri, I couldn't shake the image of the swirling slosh from Bourbon Street. I put on a straight face at the time, but my teeth hurt just thinking about it. When he delivered a perfect classic daiq made with rum, lime, and simple syrup, shaken together in sublime simplicity, my world changed.

I love this idea of playing expectations. I like to always underpromise and overdeliver. It's something we do pretty regularly. We had loads of pink drinks on our early menus, and back in 2007 that came with all sorts of assumptions—namely, that a pink drink would be sweet and fruity. What the unsuspecting drinker rarely knew was that the pretty hue was almost always because of Campari, Aperol, or some other bitter red Italian liqueur. With the Riviera (page 162), for example, we set out to make a poolside cocktail that incorporated Campari because the Italian bitter was a weird conundrum for most drinkers. Made with pineapple-infused gin, Campari, Luxardo maraschino liqueur, and orange bitters, the drink starts familiar, reminiscent of a classic piña colada, but ends somewhat mind-bogglingly with hints of bitterness from the Campari and the maraschino liqueur. Heads turned and questions were asked, and the drink ended up being one of our greatest hits for its element of surprise, confusion, and delight.

Someone once said that poetry is making new things familiar and familiar things new, and in the same way, there can be Curiosity in the Comfort and Comfort in the Curiosity. The two are not always binary. In fact, they have more in common than they have differences. Making drinks that stir Curiosity helps you engage with cocktails in a way that's driven by surprise and intellect. Comfort stirs the same but roots itself in the heart. Applying this thrilling Möbius strip of concepts to the cocktails you make and drink means you will never be bored again. If you are, you just aren't fucking paying attention.

Comfort and Curiosity is a delicate balance that can be applied to everything from a delicious cocktail to an enthralling story over the bar. First you want to create a Comfortable vessel or environment, or narrative, to draw people in and make them relax. The Curiosity element can't come bursting out like Trojans from the horse. It needs to be subtle enough to fit within the narrative but bring people slightly out of their Comfort zone. The surprise differs for every individual, but when you dial in the levels just right, the result is magical.

**—AUBREY HOWARD,
2010–2016**

RECITES

RECIPES

Ⓐll right, y'all, set up your mise en place and get mixing! This is one of the more fun collections of recipes because it is all about storytelling and finding creative ways to express an idea through a recipe. In most cases, the bartender has explicitly shared the backstory, Intentions, or emotional touch points behind the drink. Read those introductions, then look at the specs to hypothesize how the recipe manifested from that vision. Notice how some backstories are simple, while others serve a more utilitarian purpose. When you make each recipe, consider what type of person might enjoy the drink the most (or the least). How would you describe the cocktail and its personality to someone in a way that will get them excited to order it? Close your eyes and picture the mood or season or context. Is it obvious? Or not so much? Does it matter, if the drink tastes fucking great? You decide.

NOT A CARE

CIRCA 2015

I had the idea for this drink based on the lack of enthusiasm people at The Violet Hour had for vodka. I wanted to take a section of the menu where nobody was investing a lot of time and make it mine. Granted, I did put gin in it. Either way, the Inspiration came from my time bartending in Japan, where cassis is a super popular ingredient. The Kir Royale is one of the least saccharine cassis drinks, so this recipe was about mashing that up with a stirred vodka drink like the Vesper, which is a go-to for so many people. —PAT RAY

MISE EN PLACE

GLASS.....COUPE

ICE ....NONE

GARNISH...CHERRY; GRAPEFRUIT
          PEEL, EXPRESSED AND
          DISCARDED

METHOD ...COUPE STIR

SPEC

1.5 OZ......VODKA

.50 OZ.....LONDON DRY GIN

1.0 OZ......DEL PROFESSORE BIANCO
            VERMOUTH

.25 OZ......BRIOTTET CRÈME DE CASSIS
            DE DIJON

SPLASH OF SPARKLING WINE

COUPES WERE MADE FOR SPARKLING wine cocktails, but if you don't chill the glass beforehand, you're doing a disservice to the drink. In a mixing glass filled three-quarters of the way with ice, combine the crème de cassis, vermouth, gin, and vodka and **COUPE STIR**. Taste it: Is there a good balance between tart, sweet, and booze? The wine will help dry things out, so it's okay to be a touch sweet at this stage. Splash a whisper of sparkling wine into the mixing glass. **STRAIN** into the chilled coupe. Garnish with a quick spray of grapefruit peel over the top of the drink and throw the peel aside. Add a cherry—the drinker's reward for finishing the drink—and you're good to go.

SIMPLE SYRUP: PAGE 311 ✷ GARNISH: PAGE 73 ✷ COUPE STIR: PAGE 46

VODKA COBBLER

CIRCA 2007

This is not a classic cobbler (fortified wine, syrup, and fruit garnish), but I was so exhausted at the time that I called it one because I liked the sound of the name and it shared a few aspects with the original. It's really just a fortified sour with berries. The Cocchi Americano lengthens and adds complexity and a back-end bitterness that's easy-delicious like Sunday morning. I'd make this one by the carafe, as they go down just as easy; just change the ounces to cups in the recipe to scale up accordingly.
—TOBY MALONEY

MISE EN PLACE		SPEC	
GLASS.....	COUPE	1.5 OZ......	VODKA
ICE	NONE	.75 OZ.....	COCCHI AMERICANO
GARNISH...	3 BERRIES OF CONTRASTING COLORS, SKEWERED	.75 OZ.....	LEMON JUICE
		.75 OZ.....	SIMPLE SYRUP
METHOD ...	COUPE SHAKE	ABOUT 5 ...	FRESH BERRIES

CHILL YOUR COUPE. GRAB ABOUT 5 berries. If they are nice and ripe and sweet, you should stick to a firm .75 ounce of simple syrup; if it's the middle of winter and the berries read pretty perky, you should increase that measure of syrup to a fat pour. Throw the berries into your shaker tin and **MUDDLE**. Add the simple syrup, lemon juice, Cocchi, and vodka. Give it a quick stir to make sure the berries aren't all stuck at the bottom of the tin. Add 5 lovely cubes of ice and **COUPE SHAKE**. Taste. If it's heavy on the sweetness, give it a little more lemon juice. **DOUBLE STRAIN** into a coupe glass and garnish with three pretty berries, ideally in colors that will contrast with the color of the drink for a little visual oomph!

SIMPLE SYRUP: PAGE 311 ✳ MUDDLING: PAGE 68 ✳ DOUBLE STRAIN: PAGE 50

ASTA COLLINS

CIRCA 2007

The first and only vodka drink on our opening menu was intended to be the opposite of what vodka drinkers expected, so it's pretty and pink and long and bubbly, but also has a decent bitter kick. Surprise! Pink doesn't always mean sweet as candy and less sophisticated. So many eyebrows raised in alarm upon first sip, then eased into the deliciousness with a satisfied smile (okay, some were quickly sent back, too—it was 2007, after all). For those who want an even more adventurous ride on this train, try the drink made with a big juniper-y gin or a blanco tequila instead of neutral vodka.

—TOBY MALONEY

MISE EN PLACE		SPEC	
GLASS	COLLINS	2.0 OZ	VODKA
ICE	SHARD	.75 OZ	LIME JUICE
GARNISH	RADIUS-CUT LIME WHEEL	1.0 OZ	GRAPEFRUIT JUICE
METHOD	COLLINS SHAKE	.25 OZ	CAMPARI
		.75 OZ	SIMPLE SYRUP
		SODA WATER, TO BOTTOM	

INTO YOUR SHAKER TIN, STACK the Campari and simple syrup. Both have sugar, so make sure you don't overpour either. Donate the grapefruit and lime juices to the shaker and finish with the vodka. Grab your Collins, add the shard of ice plus about 1 ounce of soda (depending on the size of the glass), and set aside. Pop 3 ice cubes into your shaker—a couple fewer than usual because between the ice and the soda, most of your water content is already in the glass—and **COLLINS SHAKE**, like a quick staccato. **STRAIN** into the Collins over the ice shard. Be conscious to aim the stream coming through your Hawthorne directly into the soda at the bottom of the glass, not slowly dribbling down the sides of the ice, so you get complete integration of the two liquids. Garnish with a fresh lime wheel poised on the rim of the glass.

SIMPLE SYRUP: PAGE 311 ✳ STACKING: PAGE 36 ✳ BOTTOM: PAGE 62 ✳
COLLINS SHAKE: PAGE 46 ✳ RADIUS CUT: PAGE 77

SINGER'S FLIP

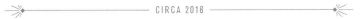

CIRCA 2018

Invented for a friend who likes rich, sweet dessert drinks, this is a flip that tastes like salted butterscotch. It was one of those magic moments where the ingredients I put together worked on the first try—with the dryness of cinnamon, nuttiness from orgeat, and the softness of a blended Scotch (versus an Islay or similarly grandiose style), it is a pretty comforting cocktail. The egg makes it taste a little like cake batter, and with a little sea salt sprinkled on top, you get these big pops of saltiness when you sip it, like biting into a candy bar. —ANEKA SAXON

MISE EN PLACE

GLASS . . . . . COUPE

ICE . . . . NONE

GARNISH . . . FLAKY SALT (SEA SALT,
IF POSSIBLE)

METHOD . . . MIME SHAKE, COUPE SHAKE

SPEC

2.0 OZ . . . . . . PIG'S NOSE BLENDED
SCOTCH WHISKY

.50 OZ . . . . . . ORGEAT

.25 OZ . . . . . . CINNAMON SYRUP

1 . . . . WHOLE EGG

A FEW GRANULES OF SALT

CHILL THE COUPE FIRST. DROP your whole egg in the small side of your shaker tin. Combine the pinch of salt (a super tiny amount—you can always add more later if you need to), cinnamon syrup, orgeat, and Scotch in the big side of the shaker. Combine the two and **MIME SHAKE**, a bit longer than usual because it has an entire egg and not just the white or yolk. Add 5 cubes of ice and **COUPE SHAKE** until the tin feels cold. Taste. If the sweetness of the orgeat and cinnamon syrup combined gets too intense, you could add a tiny splash more Scotch to snuff that out. **DOUBLE STRAIN** into a coupe and garnish with a sprinkle of sea salt, something like Maldon that's nice and flaky so it sticks to the top.

ORGEAT: PAGE 315 ✻ CINNAMON SYRUP: PAGE 312 ✻ MIME SHAKE: PAGE 65

WOOLWORTH MANHATTAN

CIRCA 2008

I grew up in a small town in Michigan, and when I was little, we still had a Woolworth's with a lunch counter. Merciless fluorescent lighting, cherry-red vinyl stools, a letterboard menu of five items—for me, it was heaven on earth. Strolling down aisle after aisle and studiously comparing equally pointless objects—or so a shopping trip with my mother seemed to me—always ended with an expertly griddled double cheeseburger with endlessly caramelized edges, topped with cheddar cheese of dubious origin and served on a toasted sesame bun, with super-skinny and perfectly crispy fries and a fragrant fountain root beer alongside. Such were the visceral Proustian recollections that sparked the inspiration for this drink. I knew the Manhattan would be the best vehicle. Our root beer bitters had that perfect wintergreen note that really made the aromas sing. I still like the drink, and I still make root beer bitters to this day. —MICHAEL RUBEL

MISE EN PLACE

GLASS.....COUPE

ICE.......NONE

GARNISH...CHERRY, 12 DROPS
          BITTERCUBE ROOT BEER
          BITTERS

METHOD ...COUPE STIR

SPEC

2.0 OZ......BUFFALO TRACE BOURBON

.75 OZ......CARPANO ANTICA
            VERMOUTH

.25 OZ......CYNAR

9 DROPS ...ANGOSTURA BITTERS

PUT YOUR COUPE IN A cold place (in Chicago, sometimes that means the back porch in the middle of winter) to let it get nice and frosty. In a mixing glass, combine the bitters, Cynar, vermouth, and bourbon with enough ice to fill the glass three-quarters of the way full, and **COUPE STIR**. Taste the drink—if you're using a vermouth that doesn't have as much body (and soul) as Carpano, you might need to add a little Demerara syrup to boost the Textural qualities. Nobody likes a thin Manhattan. **STRAIN** into that frosty coupe, garnish, and relish how the root beer bitters bring a totally new aroma to the contents of the glass when you drop them on the surface of the drink as garnish. A marvel of a Manhattan.

COUPE STIR: PAGE 46 ✱ BITTERS GARNISH: PAGE 79 ✱ AROMA: PAGE 72

LAUGHING STALK

CIRCA 2013

Around the time I made this cocktail, everyone was trying to make savory drinks because we'd tried everything else at that point. Celery has such a subtle and refreshing green flavor, with the ability to add just the right amount of vegetal personality to a cocktail without being overpowering, so I knew it would pair well with the light botanicals of gin. And back then the challenge was always to make an approachable cocktail with one subtle curve ball, so that's where the rinse of cassis comes in; it has an earthy, stone fruit quality going on, kind of like when you include fruit in a vegetable salad. I knew together with the offset of something citrusy, it'd make the perfect warm-weather combo. —HENRY PRENDERGAST

MISE EN PLACE

GLASS.....COLLINS

ICE ....CRUSHED

GARNISH...LIME WHEEL

METHOD ...WHIP SHAKE

SPEC

2.0 OZ......PLYMOUTH GIN

.75 OZ......LIME JUICE

.75 OZ......CELERY "OLEO-
SACCHARUM"

.25 OZ......CRÈME DE CASSIS, TO
RINSE

TO RINSE THE COLLINS GLASS, add the crème de cassis and roll it softly around the inside so it sticks to the sides in a thin layer. Fill the glass about three-quarters of the way with crushed ice and set aside. In a shaker tin, combine the lime juice, celery "oleo-saccharum," and gin. Add 2 ounces of crushed ice. **WHIP SHAKE.** Give it a regular old **STRAIN** into the Collins glass over the crushed ice. Don't make the lime wheel garnish too thick or too thin—about ¼ inch thick is best, because you don't want this massive dumb thing flopping all over your cocktail and getting in the way. A big ugly garnish looks shitty, so make sure you're using a pretty lime with no blemishes or brown spots.

CELERY "OLEO-SACCHARUM": PAGE 314 ✳ WHIP SHAKE: PAGE 46 ✳ CRUSHED ICE: PAGE 59

SPANISH MARGARITA

CIRCA 2007

Why are spicy margaritas so popular? One of my theories is that it has to do with the chef's axiom "What grows together goes together." Mexico is the home of tequila, limes, and a wild variety of spicy peppers. But spicy margs are so delicious because you have fiery chile and cooling lime in the same glass. There is almost no way they would not all taste great together. —**TOBY MALONEY**

MISE EN PLACE

GLASS.....DOUBLE OLD-FASHIONED

ICE ....CHUNK

GARNISH...LIME WHEEL, 5 DROPS
            BITTERMENS HELLFIRE
            HABANERO SHRUB

METHOD ...ROCKS SHAKE

SPEC

2.0 OZ......LUNAZUL BLANCO TEQUILA

.75 OZ......DRY CURAÇAO

.75 OZ......LIME JUICE

.25 OZ......LICOR 43

.25 OZ......SIMPLE SYRUP

7 DROPS ...BITTERMENS HELLFIRE
            HABANERO SHRUB

ADD THE BITTERS TO A shaker tin (if you aren't sure how big a kick you want, add 3 drops and adjust on the second taste). Stack the curaçao, Licor 43, and simple syrup so you have 1.25 oz. ounce and no more. Follow that with the lime and tequila. Taste. Not spicy enough? Throw in a touch more bitters. Too hot already? Pump in a little more Licor 43, but not too much since there is liquor in that liqueur and adding too much proof at this juncture could tipple the scales of Balance. Five cubes go into the tin before you **ROCKS SHAKE**. Taste, looking at the "heat" factor. It's going to get a bit more Hellfire as a garnish, but do you want to ramp up the bitters in the body of the drink? **STRAIN** into your DOF glass over an ice chunk. Garnish with the bitters toward the center of the cocktail so it's about the Aroma and doesn't just sting the drinker's lips. That lime wheel better be fresh.

STACKING: PAGE 36 ✳ ROCKS SHAKE: PAGE 46 ✳ BITTERS GARNISH: PAGE 79

MIRAFLORES

CIRCA 2008

The Iron Cross was a huge seller on our first menu, and I wanted to craft a sequel using pisco. At the time, I had never been to Peru, but while doing some basic research I came upon the name of a popular tourist neighborhood in Lima and thought it was a perfect name—evoking that extraordinary city but also referencing the floral qualities the Italia grape brought to the drink. Use the tremendously expressive Tabernero piscos from Chincha Alta, whose Italia often possesses the Aroma of fresh-cut spring flowers.
—MICHAEL RUBEL

MISE EN PLACE

GLASS.....COUPE

ICE ....NONE

GARNISH...3 DROPS PEYCHAUD'S
BITTERS

METHOD ...MIME SHAKE, COUPE SHAKE

SPEC

1.0 OZ......TABERNERO PISCO ITALIA

1.0 OZ......TABERNERO PISCO PURO
QUEBRANTA

.25 OZ......LIME JUICE

1.0 OZ......GRAPEFRUIT JUICE

.50 OZ......HONEY SYRUP

9 DROPS ...GRAPEFRUIT BITTERS

1 ....EGG WHITE

CHILL YOUR COUPE. JIGGLE YOUR egg white into the small side of a shaker tin. In the large side, combine the bitters, lime juice, honey syrup, grapefruit syrup, and piscos. If you managed to measure each ingredient correctly, combine the tins and **MIME SHAKE** to bring them all together in perfect unison. Add 5 ice cubes and **COUPE SHAKE**. Taste. If it's a little thin, you can add a bump of simple or honey syrup (the former if you just want to boost the Texture, the latter if you think the drink would benefit from both more roundness and honey flavor). If the grapefruit element is too aggressive, add a little more lime juice to make it friendlier. **DOUBLE STRAIN** into the chilled coupe and garnish with the electric pink Peychaud's.

HONEY SYRUP: PAGE 311 ✳ EGGS: PAGE 64 ✳
MIME SHAKE: PAGE 65 ✳ BITTERS GARNISH: PAGE 79

BEVERLY MAE

CIRCA 2019

My grandmother's favorite cocktail was a Wisconsin-style dry brandy Manhattan. She'd drink them with whatever the cheapest brandy in her cabinet was, with dry vermouth, Angostura, and 7UP. I wanted to reinterpret the drink within the framework of what we do at The Violet Hour, so to cut down on the sandpaper dryness of a straight dry vermouth build, I split the dry with Dolin Blanc (which is a touch sweeter) and brought in a little Italicus (which I jokingly say tastes like a 7UP syrup). This combination brings sweetness to the drink without having to introduce any sugar. You still get that dry Manhattan feel. —ZAC SORENSEN

MISE EN PLACE

GLASS . . . . . COUPE

ICE . . . . NONE

GARNISH . . . LEMON PIGTAIL

METHOD . . . COUPE STIR

SPEC

2.0 OZ . . . . . . PIERRE FERRAND 1840 COGNAC

1.0 OZ . . . . . DOLIN BLANC VERMOUTH

.50 OZ . . . . . DOLIN DRY VERMOUTH

.50 OZ . . . . . ITALICUS BERGAMOT LIQUEUR

CHILL YOUR COUPE. IN A mixing glass, stack the two vermouths, then add the Italicus and Cognac. Add ice cubes, enough to fill the glass three-quarters of the way, and **COUPE STIR**. Taste. Dolin Blanc is more viscous than dry vermouth, and the Italicus adds to that viscosity, so this could get too sweet too quickly if you don't twirl it around long enough (this is also the reason you stack the vermouths during measuring). Stir more if it needs to calm down further, then taste again to make sure it's ice-*ice*-cold. The pressure is on here, because you've got to get it right and ready to hit the coupe and be consumed immediately. **DOUBLE STRAIN** into the chilled coupe and garnish.

CHILLED COUPE: PAGE 60 ✳ STACKING: PAGE 36 ✳ DOUBLE STRAIN: PAGE 50

MERIT BADGE

CIRCA 2018

Fernet Branca has a eucalyptus quality that reminds me of Thin Mint Girl Scout cookies—hence the name of the drink. It's got that mad good flavor but for some, it can come across as really aggressive, so I added chocolate and mint as familiar companions for anyone who might not be comfortable with the bitter bite of the amaro. All in all, this is a cool Old-Fashioned-style cocktail that's spirit-forward and super aromatic thanks to the big bundle of mint used as the garnish. —ANEKA SAXON

MISE EN PLACE

GLASS . . . . . OLD-FASHIONED

ICE . . . . CHUNK

GARNISH . . . MINT SPRIG

METHOD . . . CHUNK STIR

SPEC

1.5 OZ . . . . . . FERNET BRANCA

.50 OZ . . . . . REPOSADO TEQUILA

1.0 OZ . . . . . . COCCHI VERMOUTH
DI TORINO

.50 OZ . . . . . . TEMPUS FUGIT
CRÈME DE CACAO

1 DASH . . . . CHOCOLATE BITTERS

1 DASH . . . . PEYCHAUD'S BITTERS

DASH YOUR BITTERS INTO the tin. Stack your cacao and tequila before pouring it into the tin. Then jigger your vermouth and the fernet to donate in quick succession. Taste. There is going to be a riot of chocolate and mint and menthol, along with fennel and vanilla. How do you feel about the Balance of these elements? Ice your mixing glass three-quarters of the way full. **CHUNK STIR**. Taste. Do more than a few turns with the spoon and then taste again. It should go from jagged and boozy to mellow and cookie-like. **STRAIN** into an Old-Fashioned glass over an ice chunk. Garnish with a mint sprig to echo the eucalyptus, spanking the leaves first to release their wonderful oils and Aromas.

VIEUX CARRÉ: PAGE 35 ✳ STACKING: PAGE 36 ✳
CHUNK STIR: PAGE 47 ✳ JUXTAPOSITION: PAGE 189

BLUE RIDGE MANHATTAN

CIRCA 2007

I love a good pulled pork sandwich. To make a Manhattan riff inspired by those flavors, I knew I couldn't take the literal route of fat-washing whiskey, infusing peaches into a simple syrup and garnishing with an onion, because that would be too ham-fisted. Instead, I chose rye whiskey as the grain element for its bright and savory notes (versus the dessert-like flavors of bourbon), then used the heavy cherry notes of Carpano Antica sweet vermouth to serve as the BBQ sauce. To make it dynamic, Dolin dry came into play with its summer herb qualities, and the Laphroaig mimics hours spent in the smoke pit. For the vinegar aspect, I used just a smattering of lemon oil to imitate that note present in so many "mop" sauces. The final drink has all the whispers of the original pulled pork sandwich but manifested in a way that tastes like a cocktail and not a literal pile of meat. —TOBY MALONEY

MISE EN PLACE

GLASS . . . . . **COUPE**

ICE . . . . **NONE**

GARNISH . . . **LEMON PIGTAIL**

METHOD . . . **COUPE STIR**

SPEC

2.0 OZ . . . . . . **RITTENHOUSE RYE WHISKEY**

.75 OZ . . . . . . **CARPANO ANTICA VERMOUTH**

.50 OZ . . . . . . **DOLIN DRY VERMOUTH**

2 DASHES . . **PEYCHAUD'S BITTERS**

1 DASH . . . . **BITTERCUBE BOLIVAR BITTERS**

LAPHROAIG SINGLE MALT SCOTCH WHISKY, TO RINSE

GET YOUR COUPE AND ADD a couple of ice cubes and a whisper of Laphroaig to rinse the glass. This will chill the coupe and add water content to the Scotch, without taming the whisky. You will just get a blast of alcohol and none of its umami-like seaweed notes and saltiness. Let the ice and liquid rest in the coupe while you mix the drink. Add the bitters, the vermouths, and the rye to your mixing glass, plus enough ice to climb three-quarters of the way up the glass, and **COUPE STIR**. Taste for booziness as well as how well the bitters are coming through. You can add a bit more Peychaud's if they aren't forward enough for your liking. Keep stirring as the ice falls. Add a couple more cubes for a final arctic blast of water. Dump the ice out

of the coupe and **STRAIN** the contents of the mixing glass into the vessel. This drink should go only about two-thirds up the glass so you leave a lot of room for the rinse to affect the nose of the drink. You don't need much lemon oil for garnish—it's an accent, not a main player in the Aroma of this drink—so cut the pigtail from your lemon from up high, then hang it over the edge of the glass at eleven o'clock.

RINSE: PAGE 83 ✳ COUPE STIR: PAGE 46 ✳ PIGTAIL GARNISH: PAGE 77

DRINK PHILOSOPHIES: RECIPES

PARADISE PERDIDO

CIRCA 2013

At its core, this drink wants to be an Amaretto Sour. It appears one-dimensional, but I like to think the first sip invokes a subtle turn of the head. Suitable as an after-dinner drink, more closely related to comfort food like a cinnamon and strawberry crumble. The palo cortado sherry is the rug that ties the room together. —JOHN SMILLIE

MISE EN PLACE		SPEC	
GLASS	TULIP	2.0 OZ	REPOSADO TEQUILA
ICE	ICE CUBES	.25+ OZ	PALO CORTADO SHERRY
GARNISH	5 DROPS PEYCHAUD'S BITTERS	.75 OZ	LEMON JUICE
		.25+ OZ	STRAWBERRY SYRUP
METHOD	MIME SHAKE, ROCKS SHAKE	.25+ OZ	CINNAMON SYRUP
		1 DASH	ANGOSTURA BITTERS
		1	EGG WHITE

IN THE LARGE SIDE OF your shaker tin, add the bitters, stack the syrups, then add the lemon, sherry, and tequila, in that order. Crack the egg white into the small tin and discard the yolk (or add it to your protein shake tomorrow morning). **MIME SHAKE**. Add 5 ice cubes to the tin and 2 cubes to a tulip glass so it starts to chill while you shake. **ROCKS SHAKE** until frost develops on the exterior of the tins. Donate a few more ice cubes to the tulip glass to ready it for the cocktail. **DOUBLE STRAIN** into your prepared glass. Garnish with the Peychaud's, replicating the look of the five-dot side of a die.

STRAWBERRY SYRUP: PAGE 312 ✳ CINNAMON SYRUP: PAGE 312 ✳
BITTERS GARNISH: PAGE 79

2-2

CIRCA 2008

Right around the time the absinthe ban was lifted in America, I got really into the French spirit because we had this crazy string of customers coming in wanting to try it, asking questions about why it had been banned, etc. This particular cocktail was me trying to reverse the flavors of a tiki drink, so instead of using absinthe as a bridge between bigger tropical flavors, it comes to the forefront as the base. The bitter orange of the Aperol goes with the anise of the absinthe really well—they're both nice fresh flavors—and the bitters help blend those two aspects together perfectly with a darker candied note. —STEPHEN COLE

MISE EN PLACE

GLASS . . . . . COUPE

ICE . . . . NONE

GARNISH . . . ORANGE DISK, FLAMED
AND DISCARDED

METHOD . . . COUPE SHAKE

SPEC

1.5 OZ . . . . . . APEROL

1.0 OZ . . . . . . LUCID ABSINTHE

1.0 OZ . . . . . . LEMON JUICE

.25 OZ . . . . . . SIMPLE SYRUP

6 DROPS . . . REGANS' ORANGE BITTERS

CHILL THAT COUPE! WITH A meticulous eye, measure out the bitters into your shaker tin, then the simple syrup, lemon juice, Aperol, and absinthe. Bring 5 ice cubes to the tin and **COUPE SHAKE**. Taste—if the absinthe is pushing its way to the front of the stage too forcefully, you need more dilution to temper that blow. Shake more. Pull your coupe from the icebox and **DOUBLE STRAIN** the contents of your tin into the glass. If you've never flamed a peel before, give it a few practice runs before ruining your hard-earned cocktail with a spray of charred oil so you don't garnish with singed aromas. Once you feel comfortable, flame that baby lightly over the surface of the drink to garnish, then discard.

SIMPLE SYRUP: PAGE 311 ✳ CHILLED COUPE: PAGE 60 ✳ FLAMED ORANGE: PAGE 75

THANK YOU, LORRAINE

 CIRCA 2018

Nobody knows exactly who invented the chocolate-covered strawberry, but a woman by the name of Lorraine Lorusso has a strong claim to the title. As the story goes, she came up with the idea at the Stop & Shop on Washington Street in Chicago. That local connection led me to create a Pimm's Cup that would have the same flavors as the sweet treat. In true TVH fashion, the best way to get fresh strawberry flavor into a cocktail is by putting fresh strawberries in the drink, so I made a classic Pimm's Cup and muddled some fruit. From there, the Tempus Fugit crème de cacao has a great chocolate flavor without being too syrupy, and the Cognac helps pump up those chocolate notes. It took a few versions to get it down, but once I took the first sip of this one, I knew it was perfect. —PAT RAY

MISE EN PLACE

GLASS . . . . . COLLINS

ICE . . . . SHARD

GARNISH . . . HALF STRAWBERRY
ON THE RIM

METHOD . . . COLLINS SHAKE

SPEC

1.5 OZ . . . . . . PIMM'S NO. 1

.50 OZ . . . . . . COGNAC

.50 OZ . . . . . . LEMON JUICE

.75 OZ . . . . . . TEMPUS FUGIT
CRÈME DE CACAO

1 . . . . STRAWBERRY, HALVED,
TO MUDDLE

SODA WATER, TO BOTTOM

PREP YOUR COLLINS GLASS BY adding a shard of ice and bottoming with soda water, then set aside. Toss your strawberry halves into the shaker tin and **MUDDLE** 'em. Add the lemon and crème de cacao, then stack the Cognac and Pimm's and add that to the party. Give the drink a quick stir to make sure the berries don't get stuck to the bottom. Add 3 ice cubes and **COLLINS SHAKE**. Taste. Make sure the crème de cacao isn't overwhelming—if it is, add more Cognac. **DOUBLE STRAIN** into the Collins over the ice shard. Garnish with the fresh-cut strawberry.

BOTTOM: PAGE 62 ✳ COLLINS SHAKE: PAGE 46 ✳ INSPIRATION: PAGE 126

THE RIVIERA

CIRCA 2007

A lot of the drinks we created in the first years of The Violet Hour were attempts to introduce people to bitter ingredients like Campari in a way that would feel Comfortable and familiar. How do we get someone to love this weird, sharp, bittersweet flavor? In this case, we paired it with pineapple. The Riviera is a big glass of sunshine, with a gin infused with pineapple, Campari, Luxardo maraschino, and orange bitters. —TOBY MALONEY

MISE EN PLACE

GLASS.....NICK & NORA

ICE ....NONE

GARNISH...SPANKED MINT LEAF,
           3 DROPS ORANGE BITTERS

METHOD ...MIME SHAKE,
          COUPE SHAKE

SPEC

2.0 OZ......RIVIERA MIX

.75 OZ......LEMON JUICE

.75 OZ......SIMPLE SYRUP

1 ....EGG WHITE

CHILL YOUR GLASS. PUT THE egg white in the small side of your shaker tin. In the large side, combine the simple syrup, lemon juice, and Riviera Mix. **MIME SHAKE**. Add 5 ice cubes. Cap and wipe down your tin, because inevitably, there is an errant bit of wicked slippery liquid somewhere. **COUPE SHAKE**, trying to whip as much air as possible into the drink. Taste it! You should have added enough dilution to the mix during your shake that the drink tastes like one long seamless delicious drink and not a glass of disparate flavors. Shake more if you need to, until it becomes palatable and you can estimate that it will stay as such for the entire time it takes you to drink it. **DOUBLE STRAIN** into the Nick & Nora and garnish, floating the mint leaf softly and spacing the bitters out around the little boat-like herb evenly.

RIVIERA MIX: PAGE 315 ✳ SIMPLE SYRUP: PAGE 311 ✳
EGGS: PAGE 64 ✳ SPANKED MINT: PAGE 78

IRON CROSS

CIRCA 2007

I wanted an egg white drink on The Violet Hour's first menu, which meant either a whiskey sour or a pisco sour. It was summer, so pisco made more sense, and I thought it would be an easier sell at the time. Pisco is like a summer meadow in spirit form. In the drink, the pisco's whimsical floral notes dance together with the orange flower water, while contrasting with a bright floral note of grapefruit from the bitters. Yes, it is a pisco sour, but one snazzed up with a great brooch and handbag. —TOBY MALONEY

MISE EN PLACE

GLASS.....COUPE

ICE ....NONE

GARNISH...5 DROPS ANGOSTURA
            BITTERS, SWIRLED

METHOD ...MIME SHAKE,
            COUPE SHAKE

SPEC

2.0 OZ......SANTIAGO QUEIROLO PISCO
            ACHOLADO

.75 OZ......LEMON JUICE

1.0 OZ......SIMPLE SYRUP

3 DROPS ...ORANGE FLOWER WATER

9 DROPS ...GRAPEFRUIT BITTERS

1 ....EGG WHITE

CHILL THE COUPE. SEPARATE THE egg white into the small side of your shaker and add the bitters to the large side. When you add the orange flower water, measure it out into a jigger if you're new at mixing cocktails—you want to be as precise as possible because it is an Aroma bomb and will ruin your drink if you add too much. Add the simple syrup, lemon, pisco, and bitters. **MIME SHAKE.** Taste. Does it have enough sweetness for your liking? Egg white can dry out a drink, so this is the time to check that element and adjust. Five ice cubes meet the ingredients and then launch into your **COUPE SHAKE.** Taste again, adjusting the sugar as you see fit. **DOUBLE STRAIN** into your chilled coupe. Let your bitters garnish rest peacefully on top of the egg white for a second to let it stabilize, then swirl it around into a pretty flourish of art.

SIMPLE SYRUP: PAGE 311 ✳ EGGS: PAGE 64 ✳
MIME SHAKE: PAGE 65 ✳ BITTERS SWIRL: PAGE 79

SO MANY KISSES

CIRCA 2012

I love a good pisco sour, and for this recipe wanted to see what pisco could do outside of that Comfortable presentation. The spirit has a minerality to it, like clay, plus a ripe fruit note like banana and green vegetal flavors, so the other ingredients in this drink are there to support those features. With the vermouth and vermouth-like ingredients (Lillet has great depth because it has a wine base), the drink reads almost like a pisco martini, if you will. —ANDREW MACKEY

MISE EN PLACE

GLASS . . . . . COUPE

ICE . . . . NONE

GARNISH . . . ORANGE PEEL, EXPRESSED
            AND DISCARDED

METHOD . . . COUPE STIR

SPEC

2.0 OZ . . . . . . CAMPO DE ENCANTO
                PISCO ACHOLADO

1.0 OZ . . . . . . COCCHI VERMOUTH
                DI TORINO

.50 OZ . . . . . . LILLET ROUGE

.25 OZ . . . . . . APEROL

1 DASH . . . . REGANS' ORANGE BITTERS

7 DROPS . . . BITTERMENS XOCOLATL
                MOLE BITTERS, TO RINSE

PREPARE A COUPE GLASS BY filling it with the mole bitters and crushed ice. Rinse, then throw the ice out. The glass should be coated in a thin icy layer of bitters, which will create a wonderful Aroma. In a mixing glass, combine the bitters, Aperol, Lillet, vermouth, pisco, and fill about three-quarters of the way full with ice. Taste, looking at how the pisco and the vermouth play tag with one another. It's a big vermouth and pisco can be delicate, so be sure you still taste the summer of the pisco among the jammy fruit of the sweet vermouth. **COUPE STIR**, slowly, so you don't add any bubbles. **STRAIN** into your chilled coupe. Express the oils from the orange peel high over the top of the drink and discard—you only want a touch of orange so as to complement the mole, not overpower it.

RINSE: PAGE 83 ✳ COUPE STIR: PAGE 46

ATTITUDE ADJUSTMENT

 CIRCA 2013

I probably had the name "Attitude Adjustment" written in my notebook long before I moved to Chicago. It goes back to the early days of scouring the eGullet and LTH forums, studying Toby's builds, methods, and witticisms. His favorite "Attitude Adjustment" was crappy beer and a shot of Matusalem rum or Chartreuse, so the ingredients for this cocktail were all chosen as a "few of my favorite things" for Mr. Maloney. The drink itself is just a daisy like a margarita or a Daisy de Santiago—it isn't a "beer cocktail," it's a daisy with beer in it, like adding Corona to your marg. Definitely a deeper, more brooding, autumnal kind of fizz, like the old-world dark ale punches of antiquity. —TYLER FRY

MISE EN PLACE

GLASS.....**COLLINS**

ICE ....**CUBES**

GARNISH...**LIME WHEEL**

METHOD ...**COLLINS SHAKE**

SPEC

1.5 OZ......**MATUSALEM RUM CLÁSICO**

.75 OZ......**LIME JUICE**

.25 OZ......**GREEN CHARTREUSE**

.50 OZ......**SIMPLE SYRUP**

MILLER HIGH LIFE, TO BOTTOM
 (AND AS A SIDE-SIPPER)

BUILD IN THE SHAKER TIN—FIRST stack the simple syrup and Chartreuse, then add the lime juice and rum. Taste. Miller High Life is deceptively sweet, so before the cocktail gets strained into your glass, it needs to be on the dry side. Grab your Collins glass and add 4 ice cubes, then bottom with some of the beer; set aside. Add 3 ice cubes to the tin and **COLLINS SHAKE**. Taste again. Does it feel a little too hot and boozy right now? That's okay! It's going to mingle with the beer, which will stretch out the dilution. **STRAIN** into the prepared Collins glass. We serve the beer remaining in the pony bottle alongside the cocktail. Garnish.

SIMPLE SYRUP: PAGE 311 ✳ COLLINS SHAKE: PAGE 46 ✳
BULLIES: PAGE 37 ✳ BOTTOM: PAGE 62

DRINK PHILOSOPHIES: RECIPES

HUNTER GATHERER

CIRCA 2012

As a staff we made lots of hot drinks, flips, and cream-based cocktails on winter menus, but I veered more toward stirred drinks with deep flavors. It sounds corny, but this Boulevardier-like number was inspired by apple pie. It has vanilla, spice, and baked apple notes without being a stupid straightforward apple cocktail. For the Scotch, use something subtle with a nice malt character (not something peaty because it could be overpowering) and pair it with a bitter red liqueur like Luxardo, Cappelletti, or Aperol—something tamer than Campari—to fit the overall tone of the drink. —HENRY PRENDERGAST

MISE EN PLACE

GLASS.....DOUBLE OLD-FASHIONED

ICE ....CHUNK

GARNISH...LEMON PEEL, EXPRESSED
          AND INSERTED

METHOD ...CHUNK STIR

SPEC

2.0 OZ......PIG'S NOSE BLENDED
           SCOTCH WHISKY

.75 OZ......COCCHI VERMOUTH
           DI TORINO

.25 OZ......LUXARDO BITTER ROSSO

.125 OZ.....ST. ELIZABETH ALLSPICE
           DRAM

11 DROPS ..BITTERCUBE BOLIVAR
          BITTERS

ADD THE ALLSPICE DRAM TO a mixing glass; go easy—even a tiny, tiny eighth of an ounce can be a bully, and you can always add a touch more later if it needs the spice. Add the Luxardo, vermouth, and Scotch. Fill the mixing glass three-quarters of the way full with ice and **CHUNK STIR**. Slightly understir this one so it will taste just barely hot on the first sip. That way it'll still taste good as it sits on a large chunk of ice in the glass. Taste. Do you have enough allspice? If not, add a little more now. **STRAIN** into a DOF glass over an ice chunk. I like to add the bitters at the end so you can smell those when you take the first sip. I also like a very light expression of lemon oil over the top for brightness. Insert the lemon peel at the drink's eleven o'clock, and you're set.

BULLIES: PAGE 37 ✳ CHUNK STIR: PAGE 47 ✳ GARNISH PLACEMENT: PAGE 301

TEX-ANNE

CIRCA 2013

Inspired by a friend of mine from Texas (who narrowly escaped being given the name Tex-Anne), this savory but refreshing cocktail is a real crowd-pleaser—something you might pine for if you're parched from a long afternoon spent whiling away the hours in the hot Texas sun. Basically, a mezcal margarita with more spice from the Chartreuse and Tabasco and nuttiness from the orgeat. Make one or two for you and a friend or a whole pitcher to bring to a BBQ. —JIM TROUTMAN

MISE EN PLACE

GLASS . . . . . OLD-FASHIONED

ICE . . . . CHUNK

GARNISH . . . GRAPEFRUIT PEEL,
EXPRESSED AND INSERTED

METHOD . . . ROCKS SHAKE

SPEC

1.0 OZ . . . . . . DEL MAGUEY CREMA DE
MEZCAL

1.0 OZ . . . . . . SIETE LEGUAS BLANCO
TEQUILA

.75 OZ . . . . . . LIME JUICE

.25 OZ . . . . . . YELLOW CHARTREUSE

.50 OZ . . . . . . ORGEAT

1 DASH . . . . GRAPEFRUIT BITTERS

5 DROPS . . . GREEN TABASCO

MEASURE OUT ALL YOUR INGREDIENTS into your shaker tin—Tabasco first, because if you accidentally dash out too much you can dump it and start over, then the bitters, orgeat, lime, Chartreuse, tequila, and mezcal—and have a taste. If it's too spicy, you can add a little simple syrup and that should smooth out the capsicum qualities. **ROCKS SHAKE** with 5 ice cubes. Taste. If the spirits have stepped off their "hot hot heat" cliff and settled into harmony with the orgeat and lime, **STRAIN** into the Old-Fashioned glass over an ice chunk. If not, shake a touch longer before straining. Thoroughly express the oils from the grapefruit peel over the cocktail, then insert the peel in the glass upright, so it almost looks like a tongue sticking out of the glass. Now you're flyin' high over the great state of Texas.

ORGEAT: PAGE 315 ✳ STACKING: PAGE 36 ✳ GARNISH PLACEMENT: PAGE 301

FRESH METAL

CIRCA 2017

Fresh Metal is intended to be a deceptively boozy tiki-esque cocktail. The tropical presentation may lead you to think you're about to enjoy something cooling and bright, but there's more to it than meets the eye. As an over-the-top, evocative mai tai variation, it has layers of nuance up front followed by a dry, absinthe-spiked ending. When I finish with this cocktail, I like to pour a few ounces of water over the remaining ice and enjoy the remnants of what's still in the glass. It's that good.
—JIM TROUTMAN

MISE EN PLACE

GLASS.....TULIP

ICE ....CRUSHED

GARNISH...MINT SPRIG

METHOD ...WHIP SHAKE, ROLL

SPEC

1 OZ.......PLANTATION 3 STARS
WHITE RUM

.50 OZ.....ABSINTHE

.75 OZ.....LEMON JUICE

.25 OZ.....ORGEAT

.50 OZ.....LICOR 43

1 ....MINT SPRIG

.25 OZ.....GREEN CHARTREUSE,
TO FLOAT

DROP YOUR MINT SPRIG IN a shaker tin, followed by the stacked Licor 43 and orgeat, then lemon. Because this cocktail calls for liqueurs as the sweetening agents, it can be finicky in terms of finding the right Balance, so don't go too heavy on the Licor 43. Add the absinthe and rum. Taste! If it needs more sweetener, use simple syrup or a bit more orgeat (that'll also add more body to the drink, so decide if that's desired or not). Next, take a Collins glass and fill it three-quarters of the way with crushed ice. **WHIP SHAKE** the contents of the tin with 2 ounces of crushed ice and immediately **ROLL** into your glass. Top off with more crushed ice. Garnish with a mint sprig and a float of Chartreuse—if you're a beginner, you should measure the Chartreuse in a jigger and then float it.

ORGEAT: PAGE 315 ✳ WHIP SHAKE: PAGE 46 ✳ FLOAT: PAGE 81

ALL BARK,
ALL BITE

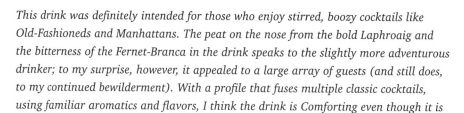

CIRCA 2018

This drink was definitely intended for those who enjoy stirred, boozy cocktails like Old-Fashioneds and Manhattans. The peat on the nose from the bold Laphroaig and the bitterness of the Fernet-Branca in the drink speaks to the slightly more adventurous drinker; to my surprise, however, it appealed to a large array of guests (and still does, to my continued bewilderment). With a profile that fuses multiple classic cocktails, using familiar aromatics and flavors, I think the drink is Comforting even though it is very strong. —LEVI TYMA

MISE EN PLACE

GLASS . . . . . DOUBLE OLD-FASHIONED

ICE . . . . CUBES

GARNISH . . . 2 SPRAYS OF LAPHROAIG
SINGLE MALT SCOTCH
WHISKY

METHOD . . . ROCKS STIR

SPEC

1.0 OZ . . . . . . COPPER DOG SPEYSIDE
BLENDED MALT SCOTCH
WHISKY

1.0 OZ . . . . . . WILD TURKEY 101 RYE
WHISKEY

.25 OZ . . . . . . FERNET-BRANCA

.25 OZ . . . . . . DEMERARA SYRUP

CHILL THE DOF GLASS. IN a mixing glass, combine the syrup, Fernet-Branca, rye, and Scotch. Add ice, enough to fill the mixing glass three-quarters of the way full. **ROCKS STIR**. Taste. We are tasting for the Balance of flavors but also to make sure the drink has not been *over*stirred. The tipping point is razor-thin with this drink because the blended Scotch is delicate, but the rest of the ingredients are quite aggressive, so you might have to taste a few times and pay close attention to finding the perfect point to stop. Remember, the drink will be served over ice, so it should still be a little aggressive but not bite-your-head-off hot. **STRAIN** into the DOF glass over ice. Garnish with 2 sprays of Laphroaig, ideally using a little atomizer that you found easily online or at a drugstore.

DEMERARA SYRUP: PAGE 311 ✳ BULLIES: PAGE 37 ✳ ATOMIZER: PAGE 83, SEE FOOTNOTE

GOODBYE NOW, TA TA THEN

CIRCA 2017

This drink was an attempt at making a simple pie-esque sherry cobbler with a silly name to catch people's attention. More lush than your typical dry and fruity sherry cobblers, this is a "cozy up with a big thick blanket" sort of cocktail. The palo cortado has baked goods notes like vanilla and almonds, the Pineau des Charentes adds citrusy acidity, and the falernum swoops in with spice. —ABE VUCEKOVICH

MISE EN PLACE

GLASS.....JULEP

ICE ....CRUSHED

GARNISH...NONE

METHOD ...SWIZZLE

SPEC

2.0 OZ......**PALO CORTADO SHERRY**

.75 OZ......**PINEAU DES CHARENTES**

.75 OZ......**FALERNUM**

.25– OZ......**DEMERARA SYRUP**

1 DASH ....**BITTERCUBE BOLIVAR BITTERS**

CHILL YOUR JULEP GLASS UNTIL frosty, then combine the bitters, Demerara syrup, falernum, Pineau des Charentes, and sherry in the glass. Taste. Did you get everything in the drink? Does it seem Balanced, or do you need more sugar or bitters? Adjust. Add crushed ice. **SWIZZLE** with energetic fervor to get it as cold as possible as quickly as possible. Taste. If you've overswizzled into a sad trombone of flavor, add a little more booze, then give it a quick stir (not another swizzle because that would be too aggressive). You don't need a huge cone of extra ice on top of this drink because there is no garnish, so just let the ice rest in its happy pool so you can smell the Aroma of the drink as you dive in.

FALERNUM: PAGE 314 ✳ DEMERARA SYRUP: PAGE 311 ✳ SWIZZLE: PAGE 47

PB&J

This is one of those drinks where the ingredients chose themselves. Aquavit steps in as a substitute for rye bread (I know, nobody makes their PB&J on pumpernickel, but simply evoking "bread" is enough to justify the flex), the orgeat is your nut butter, and the jelly comes from rich, jammy Carpano Antica brightened up with a little Peychaud's. We could have easily gone more literal with our interpretation of the ingredients, but this was merely meant to be "evocative" or reminiscent of a PB&J sandwich. More than the flavors of bread, peanut butter, and jam, we're tricking the mind into screaming "PB&J" with the Texture of egg yolk. —TYLER FRY

MISE EN PLACE

GLASS . . . . . **COLLINS**

ICE . . . . **CRUSHED**

GARNISH . . . **ORANGE KNOT AND BASKET
                WITH CHERRY**

METHOD . . . **MIME SHAKE, WHIP SHAKE**

SPEC

2.0 OZ . . . . . . **AALBORG TAFFEL AKVAVIT**

.75 OZ . . . . . . **CARPANO ANTICA
                     VERMOUTH**

.75 OZ . . . . . . **LEMON JUICE**

.50 OZ . . . . . . **ORGEAT**

.25 OZ . . . . . . **DEMERARA SYRUP**

2 DASHES . . **PEYCHAUD'S BITTERS**

1 . . . . **EGG YOLK**

DEPOSIT THE EGG YOLK IN the small side of the shaker tin. Build the cocktail in the large side, adding the ingredients in this order: bitters, Demerara syrup, orgeat, lemon, vermouth, and aquavit. Taste. Depending on the size of your glass and how much ice you have, you might need to add a little extra Dem so the Texture holds up over time; it'll taste a touch sweet and hot and that's how you know it's right. Bring the two tins together and **MIME SHAKE**. Prep your Collins: Fill halfway full with crushed ice, because this is a big build (over 4 ounces!). Let the Collins sit there happily chilling while you **WHIP SHAKE** just to cool off the contents of the tin. Then **DOUBLE STRAIN** into the Collins over the ice. Garnish.

ORGEAT: PAGE 315 ✳ DEMERARA SYRUP: PAGE 311 ✳
EGGS: PAGE 64 ✳ GARNISH: PAGE 76

DRINK PHILOSOPHIES: RECIPES

AMAROS & SORROWS

CIRCA 2016

Geared toward the seasoned cocktail drinker, this Sfumato-based cocktail is reminiscent of a crisp fall morning. The combination of the dryness of the Sfumato and the juice from the pineapple is divine. When your drink is finished, the ice cubes should look like a snowcapped mountain inside your glass. Tell me that doesn't make you want to hit the slopes! —JIM TROUTMAN

MISE EN PLACE		SPEC	
GLASS	DOUBLE OLD-FASHIONED	1.5 OZ	CAPPELLETTI AMARO SFUMATO RABARBARO
ICE	CUBES	.50 OZ	LUXARDO BITTER ROSSO
GARNISH	LEMON PEEL, EXPRESSED AND INSERTED	.50 OZ	LEMON JUICE
METHOD	MIME SHAKE, ROCKS SHAKE	1.0 OZ	PINEAPPLE JUICE
		.75– OZ	SIMPLE SYRUP
		1	EGG WHITE

CHILL THE DOF GLASS BY adding a few ice cubes. Measure out the liquid ingredients into the large side of a shaker tin in this order: simple syrup, pineapple, lemon, Luxardo, and Sfumato. Next, drop the egg white into the smaller shaker. Merge the two tins together and **MIME SHAKE**. Open the tins, pop in 5 cubes of ice, and **ROCKS SHAKE**. Once the shaker is frosty and ice-cold, you're good to dive in for a quick taste. It should be like a well-Balanced, fluffy Jungle Bird, without the heat of high-proof booze. **DOUBLE STRAIN** into the DOF glass over the ice. Lastly, take a lemon peel and express as much oil as possible on top of the drink, then place it into the glass, sticking straight up.

SIMPLE SYRUP: PAGE 311　✳　EGGS: PAGE 64　✳　MIME SHAKE: PAGE 65

RECIPE FLOURISHES

BRINGING DEPTH AND SOPHISTICATION TO A SPEC

Cocktails are art. You've heard this a million times, I'm sure. We bartenders love thinking of ourselves as artists. But I mean *literally* like art, in the sense that there is always more to creating a great drink than meets the eye, and the best recipes manage to express a flavor or idea in a way that walks the razor's edge between beautifully minimal subtlety and organized chaos.

Imagine you're studying the original *Don Quixote* by Picasso, a brilliant example of restraint. With simple black silhouettes sketched out on a white canvas, there is nothing frivolous going on in the painting, which makes the negative space striking. On the flip side, fix your eyeballs on Jackson Pollock's *Blue Poles (Number 11)*. While complex and chaotic, there is still unified and recognizable Texture and Balance in the work. Both artists applied a strategic underlying technique to an intentional structure, which can be seen if you study them long enough. If you don't, they're just cool to look at.

Cocktails are the same! A gin gimlet, with just three ingredients, is all about the gin. It's delicious if you just want to sip one and not think too hard about it. But split base the gin, or add an amaro, liqueur, or flavored syrup to the mix, and you've taken that simple canvas and exploded it into a riot of color and flavor—you've taken *Don Quixote* and fluffed it up into a Pollock. In this section, we are looking at ways of building complexity and structuring flavors that will result in a cocktail that has depth and sophistication. Some of you will look at it and think "any kid could do that," but I've found that every kid fucks up the gin/vermouth ratio in my martini, time and time again, so what I am saying is there is a lot more legwork and brainpower required to do this than meets the eye.

In this lesson, we'll introduce several ways you can layer flavors in a way that will transform a *good* drink into an *extraordinary* one. We do this through a series we like to call Echoing, Complementing, Juxtaposition (E/C/J), and Narrative Arc. Each offers a way to manipulate flavor, whether that's through repetition of certain aspects of a single flavor, combining affinities to stack complexity, introducing elements that are a counterpoint of existing ones to create new meaning, or using technique to ensure the drink changes over time in the way you prefer. All of these skills will make your cocktails fascinating and thoughtful.

These are tools for intellectual analysis: four ways to look at how ingredients play with one another to create the right mix of reasonable pandemonium or radical harmony. Sometimes when you are really lucky, you get all the theories living in the same drink concurrently in an explosion of nuance.

These concepts also build on the lessons we've laid out in the program so far. If you Juxtapose or contrast ingredients that read sharp or stabby with ones that bring roundness to the drink, you achieve a better overall Texture. When you Echo the muddled mint of a mojito with the fresh sprig of herbs that garnishes the drink, an intense Aroma emerges. Juxtaposition can create Balance, too, because if you layer ginger syrup with blackstrap rum, the bitter and sweet components click together in contrasting harmony. Bundle them together and a banger of a cocktail starts to unfold. Keep your basic mechanics in mind as we dig into this section, and you should stay gold.

✦ ECHOING ✦

The echo is a marvel. It is a sound that seems exactly the same as the original but fades without changing in any respect but volume. It's said that humans can't tell the difference between the original sound and the echo that comes from it, but each echo is slightly different due to the resulting distance and the time lag.

This always reminds me of a call-and-response context. Like when Freddie Mercury played Live Aid at Wembley Stadium in 1985—he would sing to the audience and then stand in rapture as 72,000 people sang the same lines back to him. The notes, the words, the sentiment was all the same, but the character and delivery of each phrase was wildly different.

In cocktails, we look at Echoing through a similar lens, but with a focus on the ingredients, both inside the glass and hovering above it. For example, lemon bitters, lemon peel, limoncello, and lemon juice are all lemon at heart, but each one represents a different shade, and when you combine two or three or all of them, you are compiling a fan of lemon flavor that is complex and layered. Like that stadium chorus shouting out the refrain from "Radio Ga Ga," Echoing is layering various shades of the same flavor within a drink to create ripples of personality.

The goal is amplification, not simple repetition, of a certain aspect of a drink. Like how many tiki drinks call for three types of rum to create the booming statement "This is a RUM drink!" Every one of the four rums used to make a Zombie is rum, but with one rum from Puerto Rico plus one from Jamaica, one overproof white rum, and a sugar-rich Demerara rum meet in the glass, you have four different personalities coming together to create a blend that showcases a rounded version of what it means to be a rum more than any one of those spirits served solo could ever achieve. More examples await—hey, ho, let's go!

ECHOING FLAVORS

Each new Echo must add something new to the conversation or flush out the personality of that original flavor in novel or interesting ways. Think about orange: Some "orange" ingredients taste like Jolly Ranchers, while others taste like orange marmalade or orange bread pudding or Orange Julius. The dark stewed orange flavor you get from curaçao is very different from the fresh orange oil found in an aromatic garnish, a contrast we harnessed in our version of the classic Sidecar cocktail. To create an amplified version of the drink, we chose to Echo the orange curaçao with orange bitters and an orange peel garnish. Between the warm sweet notes of curaçao, the candied flavor of the bitters, and the smack of fresh citrus in the garnish, we compiled many layers to create a very complicated orange profile that tastes harmonious in the glass.

Look at the classic Ward 8 cocktail for another instance, a simple cousin of the whiskey sour made with rye whiskey, lemon juice, orange juice, and grenadine. We aren't fans of OJ here, so we make a riff on this drink called the Daisy 17 (page 201), with rye whiskey, lemon juice, grenadine, orange bitters, and a flamed orange garnish. See the Echoing between the orange bitters and the flamed orange garnish? There is also orange oil cooked into the grenadine, so now you have orange three ways—like how a schmancy restaurant gives you lamb braised, confit, and pulled on the same plate. The exaggerated orange notes take this classic from a jalopy to a rip-roaring muscle car.

A lot of this is devising how you can bring a different *shade* of a flavor into a drink. St. George's spiced pear liqueur, with its bounty of warm baking spice and molasses-like sweetness, has a different "pear" personality than the searingly crisp and fresh nature of an unaged pear brandy, right? What happens when you bring both together in the same recipe (while adjusting for booze and sweetness per good Balance practices, of course)? Or give "cherry" a whirl: cherry Heering tastes wildly different from Rothman & Winter's cherry liqueur. If you have a recipe that calls for "cherry liqueur," you could even split base with one of each to mix up a microcosm of cherry flavor. Add cherry blossom bitters to the mix, and you've got a bouquet of wild fruit and floral qualities sharing space in the glass.

Or have a gander at the Merit Badge cocktail (page 155), where a cave full of Echoes comes into play, shattering the sound waves from every direction. In the drink, a bracing base of Fernet-Branca sets a foundation of minty bitterness, which is Echoed by a fresh mint sprig garnish. Lucious, chocolaty crème de cacao finds an Echo in the rich cocoa notes of chocolate bitters. When the aged tequila (vanilla from the barrel and vanilla in the bitters) and sweet vermouth (sweet vermouth and Fernet have dozens of ingredients in common!) join the party, everything explodes with complexity.

ECHOING THEMES

Echoes can be less straightforward than picking out a single flavor element, too. It could be a theme or a *category*, like bitterness or citrus. Look at the Paloma—the simple highball made with tequila, grapefruit soda, and a wedge of lime can take on new depths if you layer the grapefruit soda with real grapefruit juice, then overlay a sheet of lime juice to Echo the acidity of the fresh citrus while adding a little more snappiness to the sweetness of the grapefruit. One could even throw in a dash of grapefruit bitters to make it a citrus trifecta. With these citrus qualities layered, the cocktail becomes cold, bright waves of joy. Like drinking the laugh of a baby.

Echoing can also happen with colors, moods, or ideas, like "summer" or "winter." How do ingredients evoke certain seasons, and how can you play up those qualities to make the entire cocktail speak to a time of year? Summer tiki drinks can be a riot of Echoing, for example. In the Painkiller cocktail, rum hearkens back to warm sandy island beaches, which Echoes the cooling tropical breezes of sweet pineapple and the rays of sunshine that shoot out of fresh orange juice. All of a sudden, you are basking in a beach chair, a wad of soggy dollars in your pocket and a stack of cups as high as your sunburned shoulder piled next to you, the mood buoyant and "Kokomo" leaking from the speakers behind you.

ECHOING AROMAS

Finally, Echoing can also happen between the body of the cocktail and its Aroma. Take the mojito. Many bartenders use a lime wedge as the garnish, but I will argue, to just shy of fisticuffs, that the lazy wedge is not the right choice, because the lime is not the star of the cocktail and it doesn't add any Aroma. The star of the mojito is the mint, so the best way to take a mojito from good to *good god, that's great* is to Echo the mint in the recipe with mint as the garnish. Now you get a smack of cool herbaceousness on the nose in addition to the pool of herbaceousness that swims through the body of the cocktail itself. Several layers of mint make the mojito a far more exciting drinking experience.

⊱ COMPLEMENTING ⊰

In 1922, the *Chicago Tribune* put out a call to the paper's stringers to collect rocks from architecturally significant buildings all over the world to add to the base of the Tribune Tower, the eponymous skyscraper that would house the newspaper's offices.

An engineering and artistic marvel, the tower still stands near the river today, bearing almost 150 stones and architectural features from amazing structures and spaces around the world. Stones from Angkor Wat and the Berlin Wall, from the Great Wall of China and Notre-Dame (the Paris one, not the South Bend one), from the Parthenon, the Alamo, and the Great Pyramid of Giza, and petrified wood from California and Corregidor Island were all incorporated into its structure. These things were the same—almost all of them stone or rock—but different, in that they represented other amazing structures from around the globe. And yet, despite their differences, they made sense hanging out together. A study in Complementing.

Complementing is all about things that go together. Tried-and-true combinations of flavors that everyone knows and loves, like PB&J, or tequila, salt, and lime. In *The Flavor Bible,* one of my favorite books, authors Karen Page and Andrew Dornenburg call these "flavor affinities": tried and true, tested, and verified ingredient combinations that simply work well together. It's throwing stuff together that makes sense in your head to create a cocktail that's going to taste like flavor fireworks.

On the first read, the concept is almost too simple to put on paper, but potential approaches vary wildly, so we've laid out a few for you here. Whether you're thinking about traditional flavor pairings, ones that speak to larger cultural values, or more intellectual paradigms, harnessing the friendly interplay that can result from Complementing is a fabulous way to make your cocktails more vibrant and interesting.

FLAVOR AFFINITIES

The easy place to start with Complementing is by looking at ingredients that simply go together: cinnamon pairs well with strawberries, vanilla with peaches, coffee with brandy, and so on. Literally pick up a copy of *The Flavor Bible,* flip to an ingredient, and let their suggestions guide you. The book is a great place to go when you're stymied by a flavor or trying to overcome writer's block, but for drinks.

You can also kick-start Complementing by thinking about broader flavor pairings you love and how you can transform that into a cocktail. Combinations that ring true to your palate specifically. Maybe it's a pistachio chai latte, or a simple peanut butter and jelly sandwich. In 2013, we put a PB&J cocktail (page 175) on the menu, with orgeat and egg yolks to mimic the rich, nutty goodness of peanut butter; Peychaud's to boost the cherry and vanilla qualities of the Carpano Antica to the point of resembling jam; and aquavit to channel the soul of a good rye bread thanks to its inherent caraway spice. I don't know what kind of monster makes PB&J on rye, but it made a damn fine cocktail, with lemon juice coming in to hold everything together and add an element of surprise: a shaken PB&J!

* SHIFTY *

FIVE GREAT COCKTAIL COMPLEMENTS

Pisco and Pear Brandy

Tequila and Hibiscus

Apple Brandy and Orange Oil

Oxidized Sherry and Berries

Vanilla and Root Beer

CONCEPT AFFINITIES

Another way to think about Complementing is to look at larger cultural pairings that have stood the test of time, like mirepoix in French cooking, or garam masala from India. We often play by the old culinary adage "What grows together goes together," so looking at ingredients with similar geographic roots can result in something super cool. Chile peppers and spices like clove, anise, cumin, and cinnamon all grow in Mexico, right? That's why mole is one of the country's most iconic dishes. Or think about traditional Italian ingredients: If you know that lemons from the Amalfi Coast, fresh basil, and melon go well together, what Italian bitter or liqueur might work with those flavors? Find the connections and step through the looking glass.

You could also look at a classic cocktail like the Old-Fashioned or Manhattan and consider ways to bring in slight tweaks that still Complement the traditional base of the drink. In the Rhymes with Orange (page 204), the richness of Scotch brings a new layer of Complementary interest to the Manhattan framework when matched with spicy rye and the sweetness of Carpano Antica. Splitting the base with two whiskeys of different origins just pumped up the volume on the entire cocktail. Then things take an even bigger swerve, because Italian amaro and orange bitters come into play—each component Complements the others, resulting in a beautiful tangled mishegas of a Manhattan riff. You could split base tequila cocktails with mezcal or rum drinks with rhum agricole to achieve similar results. Think outside the box!

Remember, this concept is entirely subjective. Your Complementing could be someone else's Juxtaposition. This subjectivity is part of the reason a bar in Monaco might make cocktails differently than a bar in Vegas does. If we all had the same palate, we'd all like the same drink, bartenders would only ever make that one drink, and that would be boring as fuck.

⊱•JUXTAPOSITION•⊰

Many years ago, I saw a Japanese drumming group called Kodō (which means "heartbeat") at Carnegie Hall. It was breathtaking. There were moments I could literally not breathe because the air was so full of vibrations.

Taiko drums come in all sizes, from very small ones, played with basic drumsticks, that make a sharp, high-pitched sound to Gigantor drums the size of the grill on a Mack truck, played with, for all intents and purposes, Louisville Sluggers. The combination of these two drums—one bass, one treble; one a foghorn, the other a glass-shattering high C—made the air thick with opposing forces. When all the drums built up to a head, the air rattled to the point that my shirt sleeves brushed the gooseflesh on my forearms. And then at the very top of the earthquake of percussion floated the graceful melody of a flute, bringing a much-needed high note to the assembly.

This contrast made the riot of noise so complex and satisfying. Without the low notes, the high notes would have been lacking. One sound without the other equals less than half of what they are together. This speaks to the concept we call Juxtaposition, using contrasting flavor combinations (or ideas) to create new meaning or complexity in a drink. The stark opposite of Complementing, Juxtaposition is all about bringing opposing forces together.

Juxtaposition can happen in myriad ways. It can be as simple as pairing two flavors that have different characteristics. Or it can be more cerebral, like summer versus winter, sharp versus round, dried versus fresh. Spicy margaritas are one of the bar world's most popular calls because of the contrast between hot peppers and cooling boozy limeade. Irish coffees, with their cold layer of cream over piping-hot whiskey and coffee, is a dissonance that's helped the drink stand the test of time. And the list goes on! There are so many ways we can use this concept to make cocktails that are spectacularly interesting. Let's dig in.

CONTRASTING INGREDIENTS

Think about flavors that have qualities that oppose one another, like spicy and sweet or floral and earthy. By putting something sharp and dry like cinnamon against the round softness of vanilla, you get a thought-provoking dynamic. A good example of this concept is the stinger, because Cognac and crème de menthe could not be more different. Cognac is this lovely warm spirit redolent of simmered stone fruit, and crème de menthe is a big sip of ice-cold menthol, but when you put them together and shake the living fuck out of them, you get a delicious drink. That's Juxtaposition!

Or think about the pisco sour, made with pisco, lemon, and egg white and garnished with the darkness of bitters. South American brandy tastes like summer and sunshine and flowers, so pair that with breezy lemon juice, plus pretty frothy egg whites, and all those elements play perfectly in sync with one another. That's all very Complementary, but when the bitters come into play, they challenge the senses with a dark richness. Peruvian bitters taste like a warm slice of banana bread, all walnuts and molasses and baking spices, and the contrast makes you pause and wonder why the two work so well together when, in reality, they are totally unrelated ingredients.

Consider a binary like cooked versus fresh. Our house grenadine plays with this notion because we combine half fresh pomegranate juice, which is bright and acidic, with an equal quantity of pom juice that has been reduced by half, which is thick and sweet and "cooked." The brightness of the fresh juice and its floral nature pit perfectly against the dark sweetness of the molasses. Look for this contrast in the Elder Jack (page 103), a spin on the Jack Rose, where the bright side of grenadine Complements the florality of St-Germain, while the darker notes align with the aged qualities of applejack.

In any cocktail, the components have to have a fair fight of equal intensity between the two; otherwise, one ingredient gets bullied out of the way. You can't Juxtapose a whisper of lavender with Fernet-Branca because the amaro will kick the shit out of the demure herb. But St-Germain and Fernet-Branca punch in the same weight class, so when you put those together in a drink, there is a symmetry to how the floral note in the St-Germain shows off the bitter, earthy notes in the Fernet-Branca. I've spent years trying to make this combo work in a cocktail, and by hook or by crook someday I will make it happen.

TEXTURAL DIFFERENCES

Consider textural differences. In haute cuisine, a great dish plays with Texture in many different contrasting ways. In a drink, finding ways to Juxtapose Texture can be an incredible exercise. In the Golden Age cocktail (page 116), which we put on the first summer menu at The Violet Hour, we tinker with Textural expectations by making this gorgeous thick egg yolk cocktail and throwing it over crushed ice. Elements like warm aged rum, egg yolk, and cherry Heering speak to winter richness and thick, creamy cocktails, while the addition of lemon juice, lemon bitters, and crushed ice transport the drink to the middle of July.

AROMATIC OPPOSITIONS

Garnishes are a simple way to achieve Juxtaposition, too. A drink becomes something mystifying when it smells like one thing and tastes like another. In my humble opinion, a whiskey Old-Fashioned should be garnished with an orange (when using rye) or lemon peel (when using bourbon) because the drink is lacking without that final aromatic contrast. Similarly, Juxtaposition is one of the many reasons a mint julep without a big bountiful bouquet of mint on top is just a glass of whiskey and sugar on crushed ice.

People always ask me why we don't have olives for martinis at the bar, and the answer is simple: because a lemon twist on an ice-cold martini creates this gorgeous contrast between the summery sunshine of lemon and the wintry personality of cold gin and juniper. An olive is just a fucking salty snack and does nothing to illuminate the drink the way a lemon peel does. (A wag much smarter than I called them "the anti–ice cube" because they are often dropped room temperature into the hard-won arctic temps of a martini. Yet another reason to disdain them.)

Juxtaposition is an amorphous concept because it's asking you to consider metaphorical and subjective ideas. What is the opposite of apple? Is it orange? Or is that just because of the saying? To me, vanilla is warm and round and cinnamon is dry and sharp, so yes, those are opposites. But maybe for you, cinnamon and nutmeg occupy the opposite poles! It doesn't really matter how you sort flavors in your head; what is important in relation to Juxtaposition isto simply *have* a theory, because that is what will make the cocktail more interesting at the end of the day.

Juxtaposition has always been an imperative tool in our bartender back pockets. I've loved playing with the layering of flavors to make surprising contrasting complements. Like "rich" mixed with "light" or "oily" complemented with "bright." In a way, it's the dialing down of creating Balance by tipping both sides of a scale.

—EDEN LAURIN, 2008–2020

⟡ NARRATIVE ⟡
ARC

William Shakespeare's *Romeo and Juliet* is one of the most iconic love stories of all time. A tempestuous thrill ride in which six deaths, the sullying of a clergyman's virtue, lying to parents, and unprotected teenage sex unfold in iambic pentameter over the course of three days.

It's very Tarantino, like a lot of the Bard's greatest hits. But it's that three-act structure—the way it starts all cute and innocent with giddy first love and party crashing and stolen kisses, then takes a sinister turn with street fights and banishment, then lucky for us (less so for them) ends in more bloodshed and reciprocal suicide—and that makes it a story for the generations. In short, its Narrative Arc is one wild ride.

Like all great tales, a well-written story takes you on a journey from point A to point B, starting in a specific time and place, evolving through conflicts and tension as the action rises, then peaking at a climax and sliding into a resolution. In literary circles, this progression is formally called Narrative Arc. It's the drama and excitement as characters change and transform. It's what ultimately makes stories satisfying. This theory can be applied to any medium where stories happen: TV, movies, songs, books, and (yes, you know where I'm going with this) also cocktails.

The story, or Narrative Arc, of a cocktail is how the ingredients come together and then play out in the glass, usually with a beginning that hooks ya, a building-up of flavor and complexity in the body, and a gentle and satisfying ending that makes you sad it's over. In the Balance and Temperature chapters, we detailed how the arc of a drink will shift depending on whether it is served on ice, but that is only one small facet of how a cocktail's Narrative Arc shifts. Just as in conventional storytelling, all elements of the drink will influence the way its arc unfolds. The characters, the mise-en-scène, and the audience—or in this case, the ingredients, the prep, the garnish, the delivery, the temperature of the room, and the drinker—always work in tandem with one another to tell a story. Let's look at some of the many (many) ways an arc appears and can be manipulated in a cocktail.

ATTACK,
MID-PALATE, FINISH

Like a sublime amuse-bouche, the Narrative Arc of a drink can happen within the scope of a single sip. We call this progression attack, mid-palate, and finish. Take the Queen's Park Swizzle: The garnish makes the first whiff feel like doing snow angels in a mint garden; then in the first sip (if you drink it with a straw), you get a tiny hint of Angostura bitters, followed by flavors of a mojito, then a full-on Ango assault at the end. Attack, mid-palate, and finish. In a New York Sour, the attack is a quick hit of dry red wine, the mid-palate is the searing brightness of lemon juice, and the finish is all smoldering notes of oak, vanilla, and honey from the whiskey.

If you want to shift this progression, the garnish is an obvious place to start. If you want the attack of an Old-Fashioned to taste more bitter, float or spray the Angostura over the surface in addition to mixing it with the rest of the ingredients to create a surprising entry to a familiar cocktail. To change the mid-palate, play with the sweetening agent. Maple syrup will draw out a lumberjack character, while honey will add understated complexity that'll step in time with the nuances of the booze. And what about the finish? Angostura bitters tend to lend a dry, lightly bittersweet finish that is moreish,* but try hopped grapefruit bitters for a dank twist, or Peychaud's for its bombastic conclusion of round vanilla and anise.

HOW THE COCKTAIL
IS SERVED

Narrative Arc expands beyond each individual sip, applying to the entire cocktail and how it evolves through time, too. A mint julep, a great linchpin in the history of American cocktails, will charge in like a thoroughbred on the homestretch with a flourish of vivacious mint and toothsome flavor of ice-cold whiskey if you swizzle it with enough moxie. As it sits, the booze softens and eases into a bed of crushed ice, sauntering out like a debutante. When a Negroni is served on ice, the introduction tastes bold, boozy, and sweet, while the denouement has a significantly more mellow character thanks to the added dilution.

---

* "Moreish" is a British term for something so delicious, you want more of it before the glass even hits the table after your first sip.

Play with this arc at will! If you serve a mint julep on a single rock instead of on crushed ice, you will have a very different evolution. For the Negroni, strain it into a coupe with no ice, and the first sip will taste punchy and cold while the last will be the boldest because the ingredients have warmed and intensified over time.

OTHER ARCS

Aroma can have its own mini arc, especially in drinks with floats. If there is a straw included, the guest might stir the float into the body of the drink immediately, which presents a very different story than if they were to let the aromatics bob merrily on top of the drink the entire time. Citrus oils have a fleeting arc, as they dissipate rather quickly after the first sip, while big bundles of mint will remain at the attack almost every time when placed on top of a drink in abundance.

Glassware can also impact Narrative Arc. A stirred cocktail sitting in a comically enormous martini glass will come to room temp before most can neck the pint of hard liquor, whereas one served in a Nick & Nora will maintain its cool a little longer. That's why we serve our martinis in a 5½-ounce chilled coupe, then drive the story a step further by presenting the rest of the liquid in a chilled sidecar—the mouth of the sidecar has almost no surface area compared to that of the cocktail glass, meaning the liquid inside will stay chilled for a good amount of time. We train bartenders to strategically place the mini carafe away from the guest's hot little hands so they don't warm up the vessel prematurely. When the barkeep re-ups the drink (or the impatient drinker does so themself), the icy-cold goodness brings an unexpected blast of arctic frost to the cocktail, making the entire experience start anew. That is the story you want to present with your martinis!

The end goal should be to make sure the cocktail maintains quality and integrity as its flavors and personality fluctuate. This always makes me think about one of Audrey Saunders's philosophies on cocktail making at Pegu Club: After creating a new recipe or deciding on a house spec for a classic, she would let that polished drink sit and come to room temperature, then taste it to make sure the last drops stood up to the first. Nobody in the real world (and in their right mind) would wait until all the ice melted to drink a Tom Collins, but Audrey wanted to know that it would still taste "good" if they did. I am still in awe of her commitment to quality and her superhuman palate. That drive for consistency and control over Narrative Arc is one of the things that made Pegu Club cocktails some of the best of their time.

RECIPES

T his is practice, this is gym time, this is study. Dig into the following recipes with the theories of Echoing, Complementing, Juxtaposition, and Narrative Arc at the forefront of your mind. Look at the spec *before* you mix to see if you can pick out these theories. In some cases, the bartender has given you explicit intel in the headnote, but in others, we're leaving the sleuthing up to you. A lot of times, a recipe can hold all four theories at once, so remember to consider those broad concepts and how they intersect and intertwine. Do you find it interesting to look at cocktail recipes through this lens? How does one bartender's imagining of Complementing coincide or clash with yours? Does Narrative Arc make the experience of drinking the cocktail more exciting? Share your discoveries with a friend.

TALL ORDER

CIRCA 2020

Smoky and earthy with a pop of citrus, this is a refreshing but bitter cocktail with roots in the Tom Collins. I love how the reposado tequila plays with the Sfumato, a sometimes polarizing amaro I frequently describe to folks as tasting like "sweet dirt." The cocktail skews somewhat too intense to be a widely acceptable tequila drink, but it's refreshing and can be good for someone who wants a margarita or amaro cocktail that's a little more outside the box. —LISA CLAIRE GREENE

MISE EN PLACE

GLASS.....COLLINS

ICE ....SHARD

GARNISH...LONG ORANGE PEEL

METHOD ...COLLINS SHAKE

SPEC

1.5 OZ......REPOSADO TEQUILA

.50 OZ......CAPPELLETTI AMARO
SFUMATO RABARBARO

.75 OZ......LIME JUICE

.75 OZ......EARL GREY SYRUP

2 DASHES ..BITTERCUBE BOLIVAR
BITTERS

1 TO 2 OZ...CLUB SODA, TO BOTTOM

PREPARE YOUR COLLINS GLASS WITH the ice shard and hit it with a spritz of soda, roughly 1 ounce depending on the glass size. The build is only 3.5 ounces, so it's on the smaller end of the spectrum. In the large side of a shaker tin, combine the bitters, Earl Grey syrup, lime juice, Sfumato, and tequila, then add 3 ice cubes. Give the cocktail a quick **COLLINS SHAKE**. Taste. Let this drink be a little bold and assertive because it will sit on ice and club soda, where it should mellow out a touch over time. **STRAIN** into the Collins glass, aiming it down the side so it incorporates with the soda. Using a Y-peeler, make a long-ass orange peel—use the whole orange if you have to—and either tuck it down one side of the glass or wind it aesthetically around your ice.

EARL GREY SYRUP: PAGE 313 ✳ COLLINS SHAKE: PAGE 46 ✳
BOTTOM: PAGE 62 ✳ GARNISH: PAGE 76

DAISY 17

CIRCA 2007

I'm still happy with this recipe many, many years later. As a spin on the classic whiskey daisy, it has a great richness from our grenadine, which has a fruity umami note, like cherry leather or cranberry compote. This richness of the pomegranate syrup is why I went rye instead of bourbon for the build; it needed that dryness. The orange bitters hook into the orange oils in the garnish in a lovely way—flaming the disk may seem like sheer swank, but it adds just a bit of desired danger to this cocktail.
—TOBY MALONEY

MISE EN PLACE

GLASS . . . . . COUPE

ICE . . . . NONE

GARNISH . . . ORANGE DISK, FLAMED AND DISCARDED

METHOD . . . COUPE SHAKE

SPEC

2.0 OZ . . . . . . WILD TURKEY 101 RYE WHISKEY

.75 OZ . . . . . LEMON JUICE

.50 OZ . . . . . GRENADINE

.25 OZ . . . . . SIMPLE SYRUP

3 DASHES . . BITTERCUBE ORANGE BITTERS

TOSS THE BITTERS INTO A shaker tin, stack the grenadine and simple syrup, then jigger the lemon juice, rinsing out any bit of sticky residual grenadine with it. The rye is last but not least. Taste, concentrating on how your ingredients are playing together. Grenadine can be quite tart, so you might have to add a little more simple, up to a fat eighth of an ounce, if there isn't a decadent mouthfeel. Add 5 ice cubes and **COUPE SHAKE**. Taste. If the whiskey has finally settled deep into the embrace of the pomegranate, you know it's ready. **DOUBLE STRAIN** into a chilled coupe. Flame your orange disk over the top of the drink, and discard the spent disk.

SOUR: PAGE 33 ✳ STACKING: PAGE 36 ✳
COUPE SHAKE: PAGE 45 ✳ FLAMED ORANGE DISK: PAGE 75

TATTOOED SEAMAN

— CIRCA 2009 —

My dad loved root beer, but it wasn't until I became an adult that I began to enjoy it. This cocktail is all about nixing the aspects of root beer I didn't like, and finding ways to Complement the remaining flavors. Spiced rum, with its huge vanilla note and gingersnap vibe, felt like the right fit for the sarsaparilla, birch, and wintergreen elements inherent in the house root beer bitters that Michael Rubel and I came up with. For the garnish, lemon seemed too sharp and jarring for this drink, so I went with orange, which sidles up to the other flavors, not looking for a bit of fisticuffs. It feels and reads as an adult version of a root beer float and has a cheeky name to say.
—TOBY MALONEY

MISE EN PLACE

GLASS . . . . . **DOUBLE OLD-FASHIONED**

ICE . . . . **CHUNK**

GARNISH . . . **ORANGE PEEL, EXPRESSED AND INSERTED**

METHOD . . . **CHUNK STIR**

SPEC

2.0 OZ. . . . . . **SAILOR JERRY SPICED RUM**

.25 OZ . . . . . . **DEMERARA SYRUP**

9 DROPS . . . **BITTERCUBE ROOT BEER BITTERS**

GENTLY ADD YOUR CHUNK ICE to the DOF glass with a barspoon. In your mixing glass, combine the bitters, Demerara syrup, and rum. Taste. Depending on the spiced rum you are using, the Texture might not be as nice and big and round as you want—if that's the case, add a scant dose of additional Demerara to boost the body. Add enough ice to fill the mixing glass three-quarters of the way full and **CHUNK STIR**. Straw Taste. Sailor Jerry is 92-fucking-proof, so chances are, when you taste the drink at this point it will be too hot and you'll need to stir a bit longer to get that fire to settle. Just remember it's going over that ice chunk, so don't take it *too* far. **STRAIN** the cocktail into the DOF over the ice. Express the oils from the orange peel atop the drink for a bittersweet contrast to all the brooding flavors in the glass and garnish with the peel.

DEMERARA SYRUP: PAGE 311 ✳ CHUNK STIR: PAGE 47 ✳
GARNISH PLACEMENT: PAGE 301

RHYMES WITH ORANGE

— CIRCA 2011 —

A smoky Manhattan with depths that stretch fathoms deep. This is a contemplative cocktail, something to sip leisurely at the end of a night, after a meal of delicious meats grilled over a fire and served alongside chewy red wines. It's also a good way to begin to appreciate the brawny, smoky, peaty nature of Islay Scotch. Almost brutal in the repetition of orange notes (in the Carpano Antica, the Ramazzotti, the orange bitters, and of course the orange oils from the garnish), this fireside sipper will keep you warm even on the coldest Islay night. —TOBY MALONEY

MISE EN PLACE

GLASS . . . . . DOUBLE OLD-FASHIONED

ICE . . . . CHUNK

GARNISH . . . ORANGE PEEL, EXPRESSED
                 AND INSERTED

METHOD . . . CHUNK STIR

SPEC

2.0 OZ . . . . . . WILD TURKEY 101
               RYE WHISKEY

.125– OZ . . . . LAPHROAIG SINGLE
               MALT SCOTCH WHISKY

1.0 OZ . . . . . . CARPANO ANTICA
               VERMOUTH

.50 OZ . . . . . . RAMAZZOTTI AMARO

17 DROPS . . BITTERCUBE ORANGE
               BITTERS

ADD YOUR CHUNK OF ICE to the DOF glass to chill. Set aside. Fill your mixing glass three-quarters of the way full with ice and drop the orange bitters in, sliding them down the side so they end up at the bottom, not stuck to ice near the top. Stack the vermouth and amaro in your jigger and add to the mixing glass before adding the rye and whisper of heavily peated Scotch. **CHUNK STIR**, taste, stir, taste—the amaro and the bitters both have orange qualities that will come out as the drink dilutes. Also analyze how bold the Scotch is—if you loooove smoke in your cocktails, you can add another whisper. When you get it to a place that feels a little boozy (because it will dilute further over ice when it goes into the glass), **STRAIN** into the DOF over the ice chunk. Garnish.

MANHATTAN: PAGE 34 ✳ STACKING: PAGE 36 ✳
BULLIES: PAGE 37 ✳ CHUNK STIR: PAGE 47

GENIUS OF LOVE

CIRCA 2019

At its core, this drink is a kind of a minty, vegetal Tom Collins-meets-mojito. The classic gin-based Collins cocktail is a great drink, but it can be a little boring—this adds a few more levels of depth, with the herbaceousness you get from mint green tea syrup and Cocchi Americano, plus the earthiness of the Old Tom gin. It's a very approachable drink, and an easy way to take a tiny step outside the Comfort of a classic Collins. —ZAC SORENSEN

MISE EN PLACE		SPEC	
GLASS	COLLINS	2.0 OZ	HAYMAN'S OLD TOM GIN
ICE	SHARD	.75 OZ	COCCHI AMERICANO
GARNISH	NOTCHED LEMON PEEL	.75 OZ	LEMON JUICE
METHOD	COLLINS SHAKE	.50 OZ	MINT GREEN TEA SYRUP
		4	MINT LEAVES
		SODA WATER, TO BOTTOM	

KICK THIS ONE OFF BY adding the mint and mint syrup to the shaker tin. Swirl the leaves around to wake up the oils. Then add the lemon, Cocchi, and Old Tom. Taste. These are all very lightweight and subtle ingredients, so it takes finesse to bring them together correctly—if you need to nudge up the syrup for sweetness or the lemon for brightness, this is the time to make those adjustments. Prepare your Collins glass by adding the ice shard and soda water— just a little, because it will be easy to overwater the cocktail as a whole. Set that aside while you add 3 cubes and follow up with a **COLLINS SHAKE**. **STRAIN** into the prepped glass and garnish.

MINT GREEN TEA SYRUP: PAGE 313 ✳ COLLINS SHAKE: PAGE 46 ✳
BOTTOM: PAGE 62 ✳ NOTCHED PEEL: PAGE 76

TIGER BALM

I wanted to make a mojito that didn't look like one or require the amount of work a mojito demands, so this is a daiquiri-like version with an adventurous vibe. The Brugal was a big utility rum for us at the time; it has this cool honey vibe to it, which gives the drink a nice viscosity that doesn't get gross. If you use a rum that's too thick, the drink will get pretty gnarly as it warms. Today I'd probably put it on the rocks to make sure it evolved in a delicious way. —KIRK ESTOPINAL

MISE EN PLACE		SPEC	
GLASS	COUPE	2.0 OZ	BRUGAL AÑEJO RUM
ICE	NONE	.75 OZ	LIME JUICE
GARNISH	MINT LEAF, 1 DROP BRANCA MENTA	.75 OZ	SIMPLE SYRUP
		.125 OZ	BRANCA MENTA
METHOD	COUPE SHAKE	6 DROPS	ANGOSTURA BITTERS

ADD A DASH OF ANGOSTURA to your shaker tin, then the simple syrup. Measure out EXACTLY .125 ounce of Branca Menta. If you want to pour skinny to start to be on the safe side, go for it—just remember you might have to add that extra amount later if the bitterness tastes too wimpy. Jigger the lime and rum. Add 5 ice cubes and **COUPE SHAKE**. Taste. Look for the soul of the daiquiri in there. The mint flavor should be present but not overwhelming. If your Texture reads too thin, you could add a touch more syrup to boost that element. **DOUBLE STRAIN**. Take one nice mint leaf and bend it into the shape of a boat. It will break, releasing the smell of mint. Drop it on the surface of the drink and put one drop of Branca Menta on the aft of the boat. Knock that bad boy back fast. Much like the Tiger Balm it's named after, this drink is ugly ferocious when warm.

SIMPLE SYRUP: PAGE 311 ✳ FAT/SKINNY: PAGE 36 ✳
COUPE SHAKE: PAGE 45 ✳ GARNISH: PAGE 78

THE WITCH DOCTOR

CIRCA 2018

This is a warming, earthy drink with just the right amount of honeyed goodness to make drinkers see the full potential of Angostura and how it can work wonders beyond its normal small measures. The way the honey syrup and the orange oils from the garnish Complement and soften the baking spices is great, and I've always liked the way the smoke and earthiness from the agave spirits work to Balance everything out.
—PATRICK SMITH

MISE EN PLACE

GLASS.....DOUBLE OLD-FASHIONED

ICE ....CUBES

GARNISH...ORANGE PEEL, EXPRESSED
　　　　　　AND INSERTED

METHOD ...ROCKS SHAKE

SPEC

.75 OZ......ANGOSTURA BITTERS

.75 OZ......MEZCAL UNIÓN UNO

.75 OZ......LUNAZUL BLANCO TEQUILA

.75 OZ......LEMON JUICE

.50 OZ......HONEY SYRUP

.25 OZ......SIMPLE SYRUP

IN A MIXING GLASS, STACK your simple syrup and honey. Add the lemon juice. Use the same stacking method for your agave spirits, because combining the tequila and mezcal in the same side of your jigger will ensure you're not adding too much proof to the drink, which can tilt your Balance in the wrong direction. Add the Angostura bitters. Ango in this volume can be quite the bully, so use pinpoint precision! No meniscus! Taste to make sure you didn't skip any ingredients. Consider how the Balance feels at this point, remembering that all the brashness will soften when you **ROCKS SHAKE**. Add 5 ice cubes to the tin and have at it. Taste again. Shake longer if you need more water content, but if not, go ahead and **STRAIN** into a DOF glass over ice, then slide the garnish in at eleven o'clock.

HONEY SYRUP: PAGE 311 ✳ ROCKS SHAKE: PAGE 46 ✳ BULLIES: PAGE 37

RYE TAI

CIRCA 2013

I came up with the name of this drink based first on the question of what would happen if you made a mai tai with rye whiskey, and the spec followed. When you split base a cocktail, you can do it a few ways: You can use equal parts to make interesting new fireworks from clashing flavors, or you can feature one spirit prominently and accent with the other. With this one, the rye was the focal point, and the Smith & Cross comes in to give a lot of bang for your buck in terms of big, funky flavor. I love the way the orgeat and Aperol contrast one another—the nuttiness that Juxtaposes the complex bitter orange flavors of the aperitif is pretty awesome and unexpected. —ROBBY HAYNES

MISE EN PLACE

GLASS.....COLLINS

ICE.......CRUSHED

GARNISH...MINT SPRIG, 3 DROPS
          ANGOSTURA BITTERS

METHOD ...COLLINS SHAKE

SPEC

1.5 OZ......RITTENHOUSE RYE WHISKEY

.50 OZ......SMITH & CROSS JAMAICA
            RUM

.75 OZ......LIME JUICE

.25+ OZ.....APEROL

.25- OZ.....SIMPLE SYRUP

.50+ OZ.....ORGEAT

IN A SHAKER TIN, STACK the orgeat, simple syrup, and Aperol. Then add the lime, followed by the rye whiskey. Add 3 ice cubes and use a very short **COLLINS SHAKE** to mix. Taste the drink to make sure the Texture is rich enough; if not, add a little more simple syrup and shake again briefly just to combine. **STRAIN** into a Collins glass over crushed ice. To garnish, find the best-looking mint sprig you have and place it on top of the cocktail. Decorate the sprig with a few drops of Angostura bitters for an added moment of theater—you can really play up that moment to make it memorable.

ORGEAT: PAGE 315 ✳ COLLINS SHAKE: PAGE 46 ✳ GARNISH: PAGE 79

CHAPULINE

── CIRCA 2007 ──

I have had some shitty '70s drinks in my life and made tens of thousands of shitty '80s and '90s drinks I wish I could have made better. That's why I really wanted to have a grasshopper variation on the first menu at The Violet Hour. I set out to prove that I could take a gauche drink and make it at least interesting, at best delicious. With a riot of opposing elements—the richness of cream, the breezy pisco, the rich crème de cacao, and the jangling crème de menthe—this is a study in how to bring disparate flavors together in happy unison. **—TOBY MALONEY**

MISE EN PLACE

GLASS . . . . . COUPE

ICE . . . . NONE

GARNISH . . . . MINT LEAF

METHOD . . . COUPE SHAKE

SPEC

1 OZ . . . . TEMPUS FUGIT CRÈME DE CACAO

1 OZ . . . . MARIE BRIZARD GREEN CRÈME DE MENTHE

.75 OZ . . . . . SANTIAGO QUEIROLO PISCO ACHOLADO

1 OZ . . . . HEAVY CREAM

A GOOD HABIT WITH CREAM-BASED drinks is to smell everything that could go bad before you add it to the drink. If the heavy cream smells nice and fresh, add it to the shaker tin. Stack the crèmes de cacao and menthe (always use the green variety of the latter, the white pales in comparison), then add the pisco to the tin. Add 3 ice cubes and **COUPE SHAKE** (like it owes you money!). Taste, seeing if you have the right Balance of mint and chocolate. You can add a suspicion of either to change the character of the cocktail if that is more to your liking. **DOUBLE STRAIN.** Make sure there is a lovely layer of bubbles on top, but not so thick it's almost butter. Now for the garnish: Make sure you get a heavy dose of mint Aroma on top via an astute slap of the leaf.

HEAVY CREAM: PAGE 67 ✳ STACKING: PAGE 36 ✳ COUPE SHAKE: PAGE 45 ✳ MINT GARNISH: PAGE 78

BLINKER

The original Blinker, a mix of rye whiskey, grapefruit juice, and grenadine, is a 1934 recipe from Patrick Gavin Duffy's The Official Mixer's Manual, *but before I knew about that one I had discovered Ted Haigh's version, which has raspberry syrup instead of grenadine. For my version, I grabbed Rittenhouse, an over-the-top dry and spicy rye for the base, then muddled a bunch of raspberries and added way more bitters than needed, looking for their big vanilla and fennel note to Complement the grapefruit juice, kind of in a Don's Mix way. I added the lemon juice for Balance. This is without a doubt the greatest brunch drink of all time. —*TOBY MALONEY

MISE EN PLACE

GLASS . . . . . **COLLINS**

ICE . . . . **CUBES**

GARNISH . . . **NOTCHED GRAPEFRUIT PEEL, EXPRESSED AND INSERTED**

METHOD . . . **COLLINS SHAKE**

SPEC

2.0 OZ . . . . . . **RITTENHOUSE RYE WHISKEY**

.75 OZ . . . . . . **LEMON JUICE**

1.5 OZ . . . . . . **GRAPEFRUIT JUICE**

.75 OZ . . . . . . **SIMPLE SYRUP**

5 . . . . **RASPBERRIES, TO MUDDLE**

3 DASHES . . **PEYCHAUD'S BITTERS**

GRAB YOUR COLLINS GLASS AND add ice cubes to chill it briefly while you mix. Add the bitters to your shaker tin, then add the raspberries and **MUDDLE** nice and evenly. The simple syrup goes into the tin next, followed by the citrus juice duo and the rye. This is a huge build, and even though it has no soda, you want to **COLLINS SHAKE** with 3 ice cubes anyway. Taste for Balance between the acid and the sugar and the booze. If one peeks out above the others, you might want to shake a little longer—the extra dilution will help smooth out the rough edges. Or add a kiss more of the simple if it still needs a little oomph. Just a peck will push the Balance and Texture toward greatness! **STRAIN** into the Collins. Garnish with a notched grapefruit peel, placed on the edge of the glass so it doesn't sink down to the bottom of the drink.

SIMPLE SYRUP: PAGE 311 * COLLINS SHAKE: PAGE 46 * GARNISH: PAGE 76

MONKEY'S HEART

CIRCA 2011

This cocktail is a variation on the Monkey's Paw from The Varnish in Los Angeles, a drink made with pisco, Jamaican rum, lime, orgeat, and triple sec. In this iteration I bumped up the baking spice by adding allspice dram and using our house orange bitters in lieu of triple sec. Pisco and Angostura are a classic flavor duo (think pisco sour—this drink plays off that by adding more spice character, plus the funk of a hearty Jamaica rum). It's a desert island sort of drink. —PATRICK SMITH

MISE EN PLACE

GLASS . . . . . DOUBLE OLD-FASHIONED

ICE . . . . CHUNK

GARNISH . . . MINT SPRIG, ANGOSTURA
BITTERS

METHOD . . . ROCKS SHAKE

SPEC

1.5 OZ . . . . . . PISCO

.25+ OZ . . . . . SMITH & CROSS
JAMAICA RUM

.75 OZ . . . . . . LIME JUICE

.125 OZ . . . . . ST. ELIZABETH
ALLSPICE DRAM

.50 OZ . . . . . . ORGEAT

1 DASH . . . . ORANGE BITTERS

1 . . . . ORANGE WHEEL HALF,
TO MUDDLE

GUIDE YOUR CHUNK OF ICE into the cradle of the DOF glass so it earns a chill while you mix. Add the orange wheel half to a shaker tin and **MUDDLE** slightly. Add the bitters, lime juice, orgeat, allspice dram, and rum. Be careful with the Smith & Cross—it's there to give depth and funk, but not too much. Add the pisco, followed by 5 ice cubes. Taste. Make sure it's sweet enough to hold up when served over the ice chunk. If it's not, add an eighth or quarter of an ounce of Demerara to get it nice and robust. **ROCKS SHAKE. DOUBLE STRAIN** in the DOF over the ice chunk. Grab a good-looking sprig of mint and give it a coating of about 5 dashes of bitters to get the leaves soaked. Garnish. Then add 5 generous dashes of bitters to the top of the drink so your first sip is all baking spice goodness.

ORGEAT: PAGE 315 ✳ ROCKS SHAKE: PAGE 46 ✳ GARNISH: PAGE 78

LINCOLN COUNTY REVIVAL

CIRCA 2012

I do my best cocktail work when I'm asked to make a drink from a concept that has substance. In this instance, Robby Haynes challenged me to make a cocktail that'd be a reflection of the Deep South. It's one of those drinks that really is more than the sum of its parts: The maple is there, as are the peach and coffee, but it's hard to focus on any particular flavor as the ingredients fall into irreverent harmony. Every ingredient speaks to the region in some way, tying back to the central theme. —DAMIEN VANIER

MISE EN PLACE

GLASS . . . . . COUPE

ICE . . . . NONE

GARNISH . . . NONE

METHOD . . . COUPE SHAKE

SPEC

2.0 OZ . . . . . . GEORGE DICKEL TENNESSEE WHISKY

.75 OZ . . . . . . LEMON JUICE

.50– OZ . . . . . BLIS BOURBON BARREL-AGED MAPLE SYRUP

.50– OZ . . . . . BRIOTTET CRÈME DE PÊCHE

1 DASH . . . . PEYCHAUD'S BITTERS

1 DASH . . . . BITTERCUBE BOLIVAR BITTERS

HERBSAINT, TO RINSE

GRAB YOUR (PRECHILLED) COUPE AND fill it with ice and a couple of dashes of Herbsaint. Set aside. Into your shaker tin, add the bitters followed by stacking your crème de pêche and maple syrup together. Donate the lemon juice and the whiskey. Taste. The whiskey and bitters should be fighting for attention without the handshake of dilution. Add 5 ice cubes and **COUPE SHAKE.** If the whiskey comes in above 80 proof, like Dickel does, that little extra burn is going to be helpful in elevating the maple and peach flavors, but will require an extra shake or two. Taste. It should be a dazzling combo, but if it isn't, try another tiny dash of bitters. Dump the ice and Herbsaint from your coupe. Give it a smell to ensure the Aroma has fully opened up, then **DOUBLE STRAIN** into the coupe.

MAPLE SYRUP: PAGE 26 ✳ RINSE: PAGE 83 ✳ COUPE SHAKE: PAGE 45

FOXHUNT

CIRCA 2008

I loved Toby's recipe for a Pimm's Cup and wanted to make a similar one served up. Kirk Estopinal was instrumental in workshopping this drink with me—we took it down to its bones with just Pimm's, lemon, and sugar and then juiced it back up with gin for some spine, plus Cynar for depth and finish. Peychaud's and Pimm's proved to be so good together, it was like they were separated at birth. With a little bit of a darker, bitter edge to it than the house Pimm's Cup, this was still a fairly delicate and mild drink that worked well in seasons other than just summer. —KYLE DAVIDSON

MISE EN PLACE

GLASS . . . . . COUPE

ICE . . . . NONE

GARNISH . . . 7 DROPS PEYCHAUD'S
BITTERS

METHOD . . . COUPE SHAKE

SPEC

1.5 OZ . . . . . . PIMM'S NO. 1

.50 OZ . . . . . TANQUERAY GIN

.75 OZ . . . . . LEMON JUICE

.50 OZ . . . . . SIMPLE SYRUP

1 DASH . . . . PEYCHAUD'S BITTERS

CYNAR, TO RINSE

CHILL YOUR COUPE IN THE freezer, because if you use the ice-and-water method to chill here, you won't get the right concentration of Cynar in the rinse. Once it's nice and cold, rinse with the Cynar. Build the drink in a shaker tin, starting with a single dash of Peychaud's, then the simple syrup and lemon juice, culminating with the stacking of the base spirit gin and the Pimm's. As you **COUPE SHAKE** this cocktail (with 5 ice cubes as usual), remember that the base spirit is low-proof, so you want to get this cold quickly but not overdilute it. **DOUBLE STRAIN** the cocktail into the coupe so it lands just shy of the wash line from the rinse and garnish with a few more drops of Peychaud's.

SIMPLE SYRUP: PAGE 311 ✳ RINSE: PAGE 83 ✳ COUPE SHAKE: PAGE 45

GILDED CAGE

CIRCA 2008

As a very simple iteration of the Bee's Knees, this drink is really all about the honey. Sure, it's going to be fine with honey-bear honey, but if you can get your hands on some interesting stuff like wildflower or buckwheat honey, it'll knock your socks off. We were using orange blossom honey at the time, which is why we Echoed that flavor in the drink with orange bitters. If you switch up the honey, consider using bitters that will Complement or Juxtapose. **—TOBY MALONEY**

MISE EN PLACE

GLASS . . . . . COUPE

ICE . . . . NONE

GARNISH . . . 5 DROPS PEYCHAUD'S
BITTERS

METHOD . . . MIME SHAKE, COUPE SHAKE

SPEC

2.0 OZ . . . . . . VODKA

.75 OZ . . . . . LEMON JUICE

.75 OZ . . . . . HONEY SYRUP

7 DROPS . . . REGANS' ORANGE BITTERS

1 . . . . EGG WHITE

USING THE LIP OF YOUR shaker tin, crack your egg and separate the white so it lands in the tin (discard the yolk). Add the bitters, honey syrup, lemon juice, and vodka and **MIME SHAKE**. Add 5 ice cubes and **COUPE SHAKE**. Taste. The Texture should be rich and the honey and orange bitters should both come through in tandem with one another. If it's ready, tap the bottom of the large side of the shaker a few times against the bar or a table to get the bubbles to settle before straining (like how you might see a barista tap the freshly frothed milk when they are making your cortado). **DOUBLE STRAIN** into a chilled coupe. Garnish with 5 drops of Peychaud's—swirl them around on top of the foam in a way that's visually pleasing.

HONEY SYRUP: PAGE 311 ✳ EGGS: PAGE 64 ✳
MIME SHAKE: PAGE 65 ✳ BITTER SWIRL GARNISH: PAGE 79

DRAG ME THROUGH THE GARDEN

SPRING 2019

There's nothing more exciting than spring approaching after a harsh Midwest winter. I really wanted to highlight vegetal ingredients in this cocktail, something reminiscent of that crisp spring day when you can start harvesting herbs from your garden. The fresh ingredients help pull and Echo the verdant flavors from the liqueurs. The caraway from the aquavit adds a touch of spice and the fennel, ginger, and cucumber all work gloriously together. This drink is crisp, lush, and leafy with a nice tinge of spice. It'll make you dream of warm, sunny days in your garden. —EVANGELINE AVILA

MISE EN PLACE

GLASS.....COUPE

ICE ......NONE

GARNISH...THIN CUCUMBER WHEEL

METHOD ...COUPE SHAKE

SPEC

1 OZ.......VODKA

1 OZ.......AQUAVIT

.75 OZ.....LEMON JUICE

.50 OZ.....DON CICCIO & FIGLI FINOCCHIETTO LIQUEUR

.50 OZ.....GINGER SYRUP

2 ....CUCUMBER WHEELS (¼ INCH THICK), TO MUDDLE

SALT

CHILL THE COUPE. DUST THE cucumber wheels with a tiny pinch of salt—don't oversalt—and add them to the shaker tin. **MUDDLE** to break up each wheel and get the salt into the crevices. Stack the ginger syrup and liqueur to make sure they do not total more than a sharp ounce. Add the lemon, vodka, and aquavit to the shaker, plus 5 ice cubes, and **COUPE SHAKE**. Taste. There isn't much you can do if you added *too much* salt up front, but if you'd like to brighten up all the flavors in the drink, add some salt now to taste. **DOUBLE STRAIN** into your coupe. Sprinkle a thin cucumber wheel with a very small pinch of salt and garnish.

GINGER SYRUP: PAGE 313 ✱ STACKING: PAGE 36 ✱
ECHOING: PAGE 182 ✱ COUPE SHAKE: PAGE 45

LIT LACE

Lit Lace was intended to be a tiki-inspired drink that was clearly not tiki, so I used tequila as the base instead of rum. With the depth of the blackstrap rum, the brightness of pineapple, and the spices in the syrup—on their own, each ingredient would be bland, but when they come together, it's a great layering of flavor.
—EDEN LAURIN

MISE EN PLACE

GLASS . . . . . COLLINS

ICE . . . . ICE CUBES

GARNISH . . . LIME WHEEL

METHOD . . . COLLINS SHAKE

SPEC

2.0 OZ . . . . . . REPOSADO TEQUILA

.25 OZ . . . . . . CRUZAN BLACKSTRAP RUM

.75 OZ . . . . . . LIME JUICE

1.0 OZ . . . . . . PINEAPPLE JUICE

.50 OZ . . . . . . SPICE TRADER SYRUP
(OR TVH+)

SODA, TO BOTTOM

TASTE YOUR PINEAPPLE JUICE TO get a sense for its Balance. In your shaker tin, combine the syrup, pineapple, lime, rum, and tequila. Prepare your Collins glass by filling it three-quarters of the way with ice and add roughly 1 to 2 ounces of soda; set aside. Taste. If the drink tastes thin or too acidic, add a little more syrup. This will help smooth over the rough edges and will amplify a nice round Texture. Give the cocktail 3 ice cubes and a quick **COLLINS SHAKE**. Taste again. If it's a bit dull, you should add more syrup—it'll help all the flavors bind together and sing. **STRAIN** into the Collins glass, aiming it down the side so it incorporates with the soda. Garnish.

SPICE TRADER SYRUP: PAGE 313 ✳ BOTTOM: PAGE 62 ✳ COLLINS SHAKE: PAGE 46

THE ETIQUETTE

Long before the Aperol spritz was on my radar, I wanted to use the Italian bitter liqueur to make a variation on the Airmail cocktail (rum, lime, honey, and prosecco). Aperol used to list a few ingredients on the front of the label—rhubarb, cinchona bark, and gentian—so working from there I thought a bittered rhubarb and raspberry Airmail sounded so good, especially with pisco. A safe play that filled a menu need for sparkling drinks. —TROY SIDLE

MISE EN PLACE

GLASS.....TULIP

ICE ....HAND-CRACKED CUBES

GARNISH...RASPBERRY

METHOD ...COLLINS SHAKE

SPEC

1.0 OZ......LA BOTIJA PISCO ACHOLADO

.50 OZ......LIME JUICE

.75 OZ......RASPBERRY SYRUP

2.0 OZ......SPARKLING WINE, TO BOTTOM

.125 OZ.....APEROL, TO FLOAT

IN A TULIP GLASS, CONTRIBUTE the sparkling wine and about 3 hand-cracked ice cubes. Set aside to chill. In a shaker tin, combine the raspberry syrup, lime, and pisco, plus 5 ice cubes. **COLLINS SHAKE.** Taste. The cocktail will be a little piquant with the lime and spirit. Since it will gain sweetness from the sparkling wine and Aperol down the road, this is a good thing! It should all settle together in the end. **STRAIN** into the tulip over the ice. If it looks a little short at this point, add a few more hand-cracked ice cubes to bring the line of the drink higher in the glass. Measure out the Aperol and lightly float it onto the surface of the drink. Garnish with a raspberry.

RASPBERRY SYRUP: PAGE 312 ✳ COLLINS SHAKE: PAGE 46 ✳
BOTTOM: PAGE 62 ✳ FLOAT: PAGE 81

RABBIT HOLE

CIRCA 2015

Strawberry and fernet are absolutely stunning bedfellows, so this was a love letter to all my friends who enjoy the combo as much as I do. Tumbling down this Rabbit Hole is a story of "moreishness," a drink so dry, quaffable, and bracing that you just want more and more. This is the rare cocktail I would order two of in a row. Because what does one do with a Rabbit Hole? You DOWN the Rabbit Hole. Or several. —TYLER FRY

MISE EN PLACE

GLASS . . . . . **DOUBLE OLD-FASHIONED**

ICE . . . . **CRUSHED**

GARNISH . . . **ORANGE WHEEL HALF,
STRAWBERRY HALF**

METHOD . . . **SWIZZLE**

SPEC

.75 OZ. . . . . . **LETHERBEE FERNET**

.75 OZ. . . . . . **FERNET-BRANCA**

.75 OZ. . . . . . **LEMON JUICE**

.75 OZ. . . . . . **STRAWBERRY SYRUP**

INTO YOUR DOF GLASS, JIGGER your strawberry syrup, lemon, and fernets. Add crushed ice to fill the glass about three-quarters of the way up and **SWIZZLE**. Take a quick taste, making sure to get the opening of the straw all the way down to the bottom of the glass where you'll get a good snapshot of how the drink is progressing. It should taste a little sweet and a little hot. Add more ice and swizzle again just briefly to combine. Top with crushed ice and garnish.

STRAWBERRY SYRUP: PAGE 312 ✳ SWIZZLE: PAGE 47 ✳ AROMA: PAGE 72

TRADEWINDS

CIRCA 2014

This recipe was inspired by Batavia arrack and how to complement its unique flavor with other ingredients. In the end, the rum and green Chartreuse dominate the flavor profile and are gently supported by the pineapple juice. There's a nice Balance and interplay between the flavors; each is present, but not overwhelming. —JOHN SMILLIE

MISE EN PLACE

GLASS.....DOUBLE OLD-FASHIONED

ICE ....CHUNK

GARNISH...PINEAPPLE LEAF

METHOD ...ROCKS SHAKE

SPEC

1.5 OZ......BATAVIA ARRACK

.75 OZ......LIME JUICE

1.0 OZ......PINEAPPLE JUICE

.25 OZ......DEMERARA SYRUP
        (OR TVH+)

.50 OZ......GREEN CHARTREUSE

ANGOSTURA BITTERS, TO FLOAT

IN THE LARGE SIDE OF a shaker tin, stack the Chartreuse and Demerara syrup, then add the pineapple, lime, and arrack. Add 5 ice cubes and **ROCKS SHAKE** until frost develops on the exterior of the tins. Taste. Batavia packs in a lot of proof, as does the Chartreuse, so you are looking for both of those to have softened almost totally in line with the sweetness of the pineapple. Shake an inch longer if you think it could use a little more dilution, but not so much that it treads into watery, since it'll be served on a chunk of ice. **DOUBLE STRAIN** into a DOF glass over an ice chunk. Garnish with a (cold) pineapple leaf and use a dropper to disseminate a thin line of Angostura evenly around the outer rim of the cocktail. Take a picture and promptly remove the pineapple leaf before you lose an eye.

DEMERARA SYRUP: PAGE 311 ✴ PINEAPPLES: PAGE 68 ✴
FLOAT: PAGE 81 ✴ GARNISH PLACEMENT: PAGE 301

DEVIL'S PLAYGROUND

CIRCA 2009

This was my first cocktail that made a menu at The Violet Hour. It's a bracing yet refreshing drink that was basically a riff on our version of a Dark and Stormy, which was one of the bar's popular cocktails at the time. Genever was new to the back bar then—I like the malty, spicy, kind of funky and earthy flavor it has, so I thought that was a good contrasting flavor to use as the base for a bright and citrusy cocktail. The gin and ginger are the dominant flavors, and I love the way the cassis makes the drink look kind of like a lava lamp when you pour it over the top. You want that little flair at the end to make the experience more exciting. **—HENRY PRENDERGAST**

MISE EN PLACE

GLASS . . . . . **COLLINS**

ICE . . . . **SHARD**

GARNISH . . . **LEMON FLAG**

METHOD . . . **COLLINS SHAKE**

SPEC

2.0 OZ . . . . . . **GENEVIEVE GENEVER-STYLE GIN**

.75 OZ . . . . . . **LEMON JUICE**

.25 OZ . . . . . . **SIMPLE SYRUP**

.25 OZ . . . . . . **GINGER SYRUP**

7 DROPS . . . **ANGOSTURA BITTERS**

9 DROPS . . . **ORANGE BITTERS**

.25 OZ . . . . . . **CRÈME DE CASSIS, TO FLOAT**

CLUB SODA, TO BOTTOM

POUR THE SODA INTO THE bottom of the Collins glass; set aside. Add the bitters, simple syrup, and ginger syrup to a shaker tin (don't overdo the ginger measure because its zingerone heat could get overwhelming). Then add the lemon juice and gin. Taste for Balance—you want a fine integration of the ginger and gin, where the spirit keeps its chewy oakiness but the ginger keeps its bright spice. Overall, it should also taste relatively dry, since you will be adding the crème de cassis as a float later. Add your ice shard to the Collins. Add 3 ice cubes to your shaker tin and **COLLINS SHAKE. DOUBLE STRAIN** to make sure there are no ice chips in attendance. Use a little theatrics to float the cassis on top. Garnish.

SIMPLE SYRUP: PAGE 311 ✳ GINGER SYRUP: PAGE 313 ✳
COLLINS SHAKE: PAGE 46 ✳ FLOAT: PAGE 81

WHICH CRAFT

CIRCA 2019

A great example of how we take classic cocktails and change them just enough to make them our own without breaking what makes the original template work. This drink is loosely a margarita, just a little bit drier with the addition of Strega—the fennel notes of the Italian bitter go with the botanical profile of the persimmon liqueur, the Peychaud's pulls out some vanilla from the reposado. The lime helps everything click together. —PAT RAY

MISE EN PLACE

GLASS.....COUPE

ICE ....NONE

GARNISH...NONE

METHOD ...COUPE SHAKE

SPEC

1.5 OZ......REPOSADO TEQUILA

.75 OZ......LIME JUICE

.25 OZ......STREGA

1.0 OZ......APOLOGUE PERSIMMON LIQUEUR

.50 OZ......SIMPLE SYRUP

1 DASH ....PEYCHAUD'S BITTERS

INTO YOUR SHAKER TIN, DASH the bitters first so you don't forget them. Then stack your Strega and your simple syrup to make sure you're not adding extra sweetness. Follow that with the Apologue, lime, and the tequila. Taste. Can you taste how the vanilla in the Peychaud's is working with the vanilla qualities in the tequila and the light fennel note in the agave spirit is Echoing the fennel flavor in the Strega? You should be able to taste that dynamic right away. Add 5 ice cubes. **COUPE SHAKE.** Taste for sweet/sour Balance. **DOUBLE STRAIN** into a coupe. Garnish-less, this cocktail is.

SIMPLE SYRUP: PAGE 311 ✳ STACKING: PAGE 36 ✳
COUPE SHAKE: PAGE 45 ✳ MARGARITA: PAGE 150

VICE & VIRTUE

CIRCA 2012

To make a stirred tequila cocktail that featured less of a leather armchair/"I know cigars" personality and more "bitter and fruit," I reached for gentian-based Bonal and apricot liqueur. Gentian is my jam. Having it present in the drink but not too forward in the profile makes this a fairly safe cocktail for most drinkers. The apricot and pecan fight with the gentian in the Bonal, the vermouth, and the Peychaud's in an entertaining way, while the Siete Leguas is a beautiful earthy canvas to let those two duke it out. —OWEN GIBLER

MISE EN PLACE

GLASS.....COUPE

ICE ......NONE

GARNISH...ORANGE PEEL, EXPRESSED
AND DISCARDED

METHOD ...COUPE STIR

SPEC

2.0 OZ......SIETE LEGUAS BLANCO
TEQUILA

.75 OZ......BONAL GENTIANE-QUINA

.25 OZ......COCCHI VERMOUTH
DI TORINO

.25– OZ.....ROTHMAN & WINTER
ORCHARD APRICOT LIQUEUR

1 DASH ....PEYCHAUD'S BITTERS

1 DASH ....BITTERCUBE BLACKSTRAP
BITTERS

SING IT WITH ME: CH-CH-CH-CHILL that coupe! In a mixing glass, add the bitters and apricot liqueur—*do not* overpour the liqueur. If you over- or underpour by even a quarter ounce, your measurements will be off. Add the vermouth, Bonal, and tequila, followed up with ice that will fill the glass three-quarters of the way. **COUPE STIR** to combine and loosen but not drown these ingredients. Taste. If you hear your inner voice asking, "Why would someone put three modifiers in this?" that means you need another dash of Peychaud's. **STRAIN**. To garnish, hold the orange peel about a foot above the drink and express the oils from that height, then discard the peel—there would be no reason to aim for subtlety in the build if you then rub orange oil all over the rim of the glass and blow out the aromas.

VIEUX CARRÉ: PAGE 35 ✳ GARNISH: PAGE 73

TEACHING BAD APPLES

CIRCA 2018

Teaching Bad Apples is meant to be enjoyed if you want a low-ABV drink before dinner, or if you've had a big meal and want a cocktail to help you digest. It's meant to be a training-wheels cocktail for people interested in bitter spirits like Campari and Zucca. A tall, frosty beverage with a lime wheel sticking out of the top makes it appear friendly, and the edges of the bitter ingredients soften with the help of the pineapple, lime, and honey. I've converted many vodka drinkers to the bitter side with this refresher. —JIM TROUTMAN

MISE EN PLACE

GLASS.....**COLLINS**

ICE ......**CRUSHED**

GARNISH...**LIME WHEEL**

METHOD ...**WHIP SHAKE, ROLL**

SPEC

1.0 OZ......**CAMPARI**

1.0 OZ......**ZUCCA RABARBARO**

.50 OZ......**LIME JUICE**

.50 OZ......**PINEAPPLE JUICE**

.50 OZ......**HONEY SYRUP**

2 DASHES ..**ANGOSTURA BITTERS**

I'D RECOMMEND GETTING ALL YOUR ducks in a row before you shake this one up: Get the crushed ice into your Collins glass and the lime wheel ready to garnish. Dash your bitters into your shaker tin, then donate the honey syrup. Stack the lime and pineapple juice, then flip your jigger and stack the Zucca and Campari. Taste, looking at your combo of Campari and Zucca and how it Balances against the pineapple and honey. The bitters will be dominant at this point because you haven't added any water content. Add 2 ounces of crushed ice to **WHIP SHAKE**. Taste; the harshest edges of the bitters should have mellowed a touch, but remember that most of the water content for this drink is going to come from the crushed ice it sits over in the glass, so this will be mighty sweet and bold at this point, and that is okay! **ROLL** the contents of the tin into the Collins, top with additional crushed ice if needed, and garnish.

HONEY SYRUP: PAGE 311 ✳ STACKING: PAGE 36 ✳ PINEAPPLES: PAGE 68

TONGUE & CHEEK

CIRCA 2009

Before starting at The Violet Hour, I hadn't considered the use of a vermouth in a shaken, citrus-driven drink. Then, having tasted a few cocktails that did this—like the Six Corner Sling (page 288)—I wanted to try it out myself. I have also always loved fruited whiskey smashes, so I wanted to combine the two ideas. The Carpano works incredibly well with strawberry; the strawberry and mint are also a pretty easy combo, as are whiskey and mint. The Angostura adds a bit of spice and bitterness. I love that this drink is a true crowd-pleaser but is also complex, so it can be revelatory for novices and connoisseurs alike! —JANE LOPES

MISE EN PLACE

GLASS.....COLLINS

ICE ....SHARD

GARNISH...1 MINT SPRIG

METHOD ...COLLINS SHAKE

SPEC

1.5 OZ......W.L. WELLER SPECIAL RESERVE BOURBON

.75 OZ......CARPANO ANTICA VERMOUTH

.75 OZ......LEMON JUICE

.75 OZ......SIMPLE SYRUP

1 DASH ....ANGOSTURA BITTERS

1 ....MINT SPRIG

1 ....STRAWBERRY HALF, TO MUDDLE

CLUB SODA, TO BOTTOM

MUDDLE THE STRAWBERRY AT THE bottom of the shaker tin. Add the simple syrup, lemon, sweet vermouth, bourbon, and bitters, plus 3 ice cubes. Prep your Collins glass with a mint sprig at the bottom, then add an ice shard and about an ounce of club soda and set aside to chill. **COLLINS SHAKE**. It should taste fresh, fruity, and Balanced, but not overly sweet or tart. If your strawberry is out of season, you can add a second strawberry half and muddle again or bump up the simple syrup to the same end. **STRAIN** into the Collins. Garnish.

SIMPLE SYRUP: PAGE 311 ✳ COLLINS SHAKE: PAGE 46 ✳ BOTTOM: PAGE 62

SMALL DIFFERENCES

CIRCA 2020

This recipe came together with the help of Toby and Pat Ray on my final day of bartender training. I wanted to create the kind of cocktail I would want to drink on a cold winter's night, so I looked to the template of the Vieux Carré for a framework. The main flavors are walnut, deeply baked raisin, and apples that have been sitting out for far too long (in a good way). It's truly an ensemble of flavors, as the rustic funk of the Armagnac plays nicely with the oxidized raisin notes of the Madeira. The apple brandy ties those flavors together, and the mist of walnut liqueur adds the final aromatic component. —NINO SCOCCOLA

MISE EN PLACE

GLASS . . . . . DOUBLE OLD-FASHIONED

ICE . . . . NONE

GARNISH . . . NUX ALPINA WALNUT
LIQUEUR

METHOD . . . COUPE STIR

SPEC

1.0 OZ . . . . . . DOMAINE TARIQUET
ARMAGNAC

1.0 OZ . . . . . . LAIRD'S BOTTLED-IN-BOND
APPLEJACK

1.0 OZ . . . . . . RARE WINE CO.
CHARLESTON SERCIAL
MADEIRA

.25 OZ . . . . . . DEMERARA SYRUP (OR
TVH+)

1 DASH . . . . ANGOSTURA BITTERS

1 DASH . . . . PEYCHAUD'S BITTERS

NUX ALPINA WALNUT LIQUEUR, TO RINSE

IF YOU HAVE AN ATOMIZER on hand to execute the rinsing of your chilled DOF glass with walnut liqueur, nice work. Do that. For the rest of you, chill the glass with ice, then toss the ice and splash a quarter ounce of walnut liqueur into the glass for the rinse. Walnut liqueur isn't proofy enough to be potent if added to the glass with ice cubes, you just want that light coating of moisture to get the liqueur to stick to the glass. In a mixing glass, combine both bitters, then the Demerara syrup, then the Madeira, applejack, and Armagnac. Fill the mixing glass three-quarters of the way full with ice and **COUPE STIR**. Taste as you stir, checking in to watch the progression of how the brawny brandies soften and embrace the velvety goodness of the Madeira. Stop stirring as soon as the drink

tastes like it's going to tip over the cliff of Balance into a gorge of watery swill. **STRAIN** into the DOF. Give the drink a quick smell and add a few more drops of walnut liqueur to make those aromatic qualities explode from the glass.

VIEUX CARRÉ: PAGE 35 ✳ DEMERARA SYRUP: PAGE 311 ✳
COUPE STIR: PAGE 46 ✳ RINSE: PAGE 83

RECIPE FLOURISHES: RECIPES

BARTENDING TENETS

LOOKING AT BARTENDING THROUGH DIFFERENT LENSES

Bartending is more than taking an order, moving liquid from one vessel to another, and putting your final product in front of a guest with a smile. Bartending should bring out the creativity of an architect and a storyteller, the physicality of a top-tier athlete as well as a brain surgeon, the scholarly endeavors of both a psychologist and historian, and the patience of a saint. One needs to exhibit all of these qualities under great pressure and under the scrutiny of a hundred impatient eyes.

When we opened The Violet Hour in 2007, we had a mission to make things so delicious that people would happily traipse outside their comfort zones. That's why we made the rules, why the decor looks the way it does, and why we launched with *six* gin cocktails, a brandy section, and one very non-vodka-y vodka cocktail on the menu. But the drinks and the ambiance were only part of the puzzle. The other part was to build an army of talented bartenders who could not only make delicious beverages materialize, but also rub their bellies and pat their heads at the same time, cleaning their stations while telling the twentieth person that we don't carry Grey Goose. Bartenders who worked hard both individually and as a team, an entertaining cadre of smart and savvy characters who would create a memorable experience for every thirsty guest who walked into our sultry living room.

Cooking is a marathon, and cocktails are figure skating. Nobody gives a fuck what you look like at the end of a marathon, but no matter how hard you're working at the bar, you need to give off happy-to-be-here Hospitality vibes during a shift. That's why of all the skills I think you need in this industry, grit is the most important. You fuck things up all the time, and things that you can't control swoop in and explode your night. Being able to shake off these large and small failures and want to try again, to be better next time, is the most important trait for folks to have if they want to make a go of this industry.

For this reason, we opened the bar armed with a number of underlying philosophies that would speak to the art of bartending. These are things we teach our bartenders on day one, to serve as the cobblestoned street beneath their feet for the rest of their time with us at the bar. Pillars that every bartender could return to again and again when questions arose about how to make a drink, or which way to advise a guest. These philosophies speak to who we are and what we aim to do with our beautiful bar, and we hold true to these tenets still today.

In the following pages, you'll discover our insider intel on what it means to be a proper bartender. We'll offer tips on how to open your mind to new flavor horizons, how to get super nerdy (in the best way) and develop your own personal style, how to find potential spiritual meaning in the everyday rituals of the profession, and how to ensure that you are offering the best Hospitality possible, whether you're a gainfully employed barkeep or an at-home cocktailian aiming to impress your next houseguest.

⇥ PERSONAL ⇤ STYLE

For the first few years of making cocktails, you're learning a little bit about a lot of things. This is your bachelor-of-liberal-arts time, when you taste everything and keep notes on what rum styles you prefer over others, how you hold your shoulders when you shake for best results, or how many shots of green Chartreuse you can do after a shift and still be 100% the next day.

It's a time of exploration and absorption of the many, many elements that go into becoming a technically proficient drinks maker. At a certain point, this becomes like riding a bike or tying your shoes. That wonderful moment is when your brain frees up to start pursuing the things that most interest you.

Part of becoming a bartender (or even an at-home drinks maker) is finding your personal style, approach, and specialty. I don't mean what color suspenders you wear or what your shaker face looks like, but how you express yourself—your inspirations and ideas and likes and dislikes—through your recipes. It could be a certain spirit or spirit category, or the science or history of cocktails. Or maybe you know the painful details of all amari ever created. Don't overthink it! It doesn't really matter *what* you are drawn to—what matters is that you find something and follow it to your heart's content.

I have looked in awe at folks who tease nuance out of copitas of rare mezcal; can blind taste a wine, naming not only country of origin but which side of the hill it was grown on; or immediately know the distiller from a sip of whiskey. To get to that point you have to specialize, specialize, specialize. Really dig deep until you can explain, WITH ENTHUSIASM AND NOT CONDESCENSION, what you have learned.

Even better if you figure out how to communicate your knowledge and passions to a five-year-old, or a drunk friend who has a hard time staying focused, in a way that makes sense and that lights curiosity in their eyes instead of boring them to tears. This is your master's and PhD phase of the study.

One of the coolest parts about finding your specialty is the empowerment that comes with knowing a volume's worth of detail on something. It can mean you are the go-to for obscure botanical knowledge at the bar, or that you go on to open your own program with a focus on that element. Everyone at The Violet Hour knows I am a sucker for sweet vanilla, so a lot of my drinks feature Licor 43 and Carpano Antica instead of dry curaçao or Dolin sweet vermouth. What interests me even more is how things combine. How to get the best out of an ingredient by putting it next to others that showcase it, and then using the proper technique to coax it all to serendipity. It's how to achieve gestalt: 1 + 1 = 3, but the "+" is technique.

In the early days, Michael Rubel's cocktails always seemed to include either whiskey or unaged spirits from Latin America. Andrew Mackey likes to sneak bitter things into pretty drinks. Hank's palate was always on the sweet side, but don't tell him I told you that or I'll get into trouble. Jane liked playing with salinity, while Robby's drinks were always very rock and roll, with high notes *and* low ones. David liked imported modifiers, Tyler layers flavors that you don't think will work but do, Stephen Cole thinks like a chef and uses well-placed bitters or ingredients like seasoning, and Kyle's drinks always seemed like he made them while stoned to bejesus, but not sure how that plays into bartending. The list could go on and on and on.

This whole thing might be painfully obvious to you already. Most of the time this entire journey is something that happens naturally. You simply gravitate toward an area and your innate curiosity does the rest. I'm just saying that if you consciously look at this process, you might get there faster, saving a few years of aimless wandering or struggle to try to find your place in this (bar) world. Literally, the worst outcome of looking consciously at bartending is that you accidentally learn a bunch of cool stuff.

At TVH, I found that personality was highly regarded. The technique, yes. Showmanship, yes. Skill, speed, precision, all imperative. But we were also encouraged to be ourselves, and that was meaningful and unique to the program.

—JANE LOPES, 2008–2011

RITUAL

I have always had the same opinion of organized religion that I do of vodka: mostly a scam, but very useful in certain situations, like foxholes or when you have come into a cache of fine caviar.

Most of the folks I've run into in the hospitality industry have little to do with it also. Maybe it's the late-night Saturday shifts that make That Sunday Service a tough row to hoe. I have met many very spiritual folks, just not many who tip their hats to the pope.

That changed when I met Father Bill, a Catholic priest who taught law at Notre Dame (the South Bend one, not the Paris one). He was a long-standing participant at Tales of the Cocktail and would also drive the two hours from South Bend to The Violet Hour for a cocktail on occasion. Always a stellar conversationalist with well-thought-out opinions that he could articulate well past midnight Mass, Father Bill and I have spent many a . . . contemplative evening . . . debating the presence of a holy power, but he also opened my eyes to the parallels between cocktail bartending, drinking, and, yes, religion.

While it will sound like sacrilege to some less-enlightened members of the cloth, the overlap is clear. As Father Bill so eloquently puts it, "The reasons you go to a bar are the same as why you go to church. When you want a community that is akin to yours. If I am a Catholic and I am visiting Prague, I still go to Sunday Mass, because even though it's in a different language, it's still the same thing. Maybe a friend of mine just died—I go to church for consolation. Or if a friend of mine just got engaged, I go to church to celebrate. Maybe I just need people around me because I just had bad news—these are all the same reasons why someone shows up at a bar and asks for a drink."

What are churches, if not places where a community gathers together to find common ground? What is the bartender, if not a priest? Someone to listen to the triumphs and woes, the confessions, if you will, of his guest? I think most of it boils down to how both realms offer their own rites and rituals.

Bartenders go through their own personal routines as they get ready for a shift. The quiet and meditative things that happen before the supplicants shuffle in looking for solace in a place that doesn't play Billy Joel. The lacing up of boots, apron set like an epitrachelion, flashlight, lighter, ballpoints, Sharpie, all in the proper pocket. Standing in front of a locker, a metal altar with heavy metal stickers and a list of all the whiskeys and the distillery provenance. A cup of La Colombe coffee and a Big Star taco: the sacrament.

Once the doors open, there are clear and obvious moments of repetition that help cement the routine, like the nod and smile, the welcoming gesture offered with a "sit anywhere you like." Later, the hollered "Good night!" as your guest traipses out into gloom. Some rituals are as small as capping an ashtray, wiping down the bar, and spinning down a bev nap. At TVH we have staff "meetings" called Attitude Adjustments, a cheeky shot placed strategically during the night, a communal moment where the water of life is lifted in honor of your coworkers, tapped on the bar, and "over the teeth and through the gums, watch out stomach, here it comes!" As close to grace as we get.

The making of a Sazerac or martini can be solemn and soulful. It starts with a call and response like a Catholic Mass. Gin? London dry. Vermouth? Equal parts. Twist? Of course. Stirred? Naturally. Then those first ice cubes clinking into a glass, the bottles raising and falling like petitioners at mass, the choral hymn of booze and bitters stirred, the rush of lemon filling the air like myrrh and sandalwood. A nod, a sip, a kind word exchanged. The relief of letting the day melt away like the cubes in the sink, turning back to the water, watching the knave, from the nave, turning water content into wine coolers.

I see no difference between the most religious, most spiritual endeavors and making and enjoying a cocktail. It's all just intended to bring some inner peace. I'm not saying get drunk to ease your worried mind—I'm saying that there can be a sense of peace by performing the alchemy of taking three things and turning them into one thing that is greater than the sum of its parts. It's not quite turning water to wine, but it's close. The act of kindness and service and creating something for someone with the express purpose of pleasing them and making their life better is a noble and hallowed endeavor.

I think, at the end of the day, it all comes down to comfort. Rituals are formed for comfort. Human beings like shit to stay the same. We like recognizable things and people and smells and tastes that say, without saying it, "Everything is going to be fine." Our love of safety gets expressed through repetition, in the known; the boring *same ol', same ol'* is why we want to go to the bar where, famously, "everybody knows your name," and your usual is slid perfectly down the mahogany into your hand. Way better than being out in the cold dark being hunted by tigers. A cheers, a sip, a smile.

⟩⟩ HOSPITALITY ⟨⟨

Hospitality is just paying undivided attention to the human condition, filling the immediate need while planning for the next, and remembering it for next time.

Hospitality, the industry, is a newish term for the world in which we bartenders function. It used to be called the service industry, but "service" is providing something concrete for someone else. You are really serviced only by your local body shop and carhops on roller skates, so I guess the change makes sense. *Hospitality* is something so much more. It's a feeling, a motivation, an underlying mentality and desire to take care of other people. It is the art of entertaining.

Many bartenders will tell you that Hospitality has to come from deep within your bones, and from there you develop ways to put it into practice. In some ways, yes, that is true. But I also believe the actual key to getting it right is as simple as handing your friend a beer just before they finish the one they're holding. It is this: anticipation. And in many ways, it absolutely can be taught and learned.

A very smart friend of mine once said to me, to paraphrase, "All working in the service industry is making lists, either on paper or in your head, and being able to revise them and prioritize those items on the fly." This is what I mean by anticipation. Making a list of things that need to get done and doing them in an order that prioritizes both the long term and immediate needs with common sense. This applies to everything from ordering the right booze to prep and service through breakdown. To master the art of anticipation behind the bar, we look at the theory in the same way we look at creating cocktails: from the ground up. We've broken this into three categories: mise en place, empathy, and personalization.

MISE EN PLACE

The term *mise en place* means "put in place" in French. Historians say it was Escoffier (the same guy who gave us the Mother Sauces) who applied the term to cooking after returning from the Franco-Prussian War. Chef realized that strict and tidy organization allows for efficient use of time. He also knew how not having too many irons in the fire that need one's full attention is of the utmost importance to a functional kitchen, just as it was in the military. You can't julienne carrots and sweat onions at the same time, because you will burn the onions. But you can cook down a stock and julienne carrots at the same time, as only one needs immediate attention.

The same applies to the bar. If you are making syrups and cutting garnishes while serving, you're fucked. I worked at a bar where part of the barbacks' job was to cut lemons and limes. They did this in the back on a wobbly stack of beer cases. At six p.m., right in the middle of happy hour. Instead of washing glasses and checking the restrooms, they were out of commission. SO stupid.

Mise is the mechanics of anticipation, because without forethought and organization, you will be running around gathering and prepping ingredients all night instead of assembling and serving them. Mise includes every little fucking thing, from your workstation to the ingredients you need for the night to making sure the room is set up in a way that'll be ergonomic for both the servers and thirsty patrons. Cutting garnishes, labeling and stocking, setting your station, lighting and putting out candles, setting the right music, making sure the tables are the right height.

Mise en Place starts with making a list and then prioritizing that list by the down time involved in the task. If a syrup needs two hours to steep, that's the first thing to do; you can pick mint right up to the minute before service. If things need to cool, those are done before juicing and lighting candles. Good mise is all about multitasking, some things heating up, some macerating, some being iced down all the while tackling the quick tasks that come together at the very end of set up.

These are the rituals of getting ready for the shift that are the same every day. Ones that give you the time and head space to gird yourself for a bumping shift. It should be a time where you are bringing order to a space and arranging things where they make sense and will be of most use. Like feng shui meets cockpit ergonomics. All this is useful whether you are setting up a bar, a party at your house, or even just a quick gathering of a couple of friends for a quick cocktail.

EMPATHY

The second part of anticipation happens in the heat of the moment, when you have people sitting in front of you. A lot of this is simply about making guests comfortable. We put the straw at six o'clock in the glass so it's right there facing them. We hand them hot mugs so *they* can grab the handle while we burn our fingers, an offering to the Hospitality gods. We ask them "Still or sparkling?" before they even have a chance to ask for water, and inquire about another round before their glass is totally empty. A guest should never have to ask for anything.

To nail this, you have to be present in the moment and see what they are going to need before they even realize they need it. Have your head up, scanning the room, making a mental list, instead of hunching over concentrating on the cocktail you are making. You can't be thinking about how you're going to visit a friend after shift or your days off just ahead. You have to get into the zone—that rarefied time and space where muscle memory has taken over and you're thinking three, five, eleven steps ahead. It feels (I would guess) like a musician who's played a song a thousand times: There are no chords, no chorus, bridge, chorus, just the song and the feeling. And this happens only when you have everything you need right at your fingertips. For that, you need to anticipate everything.

Do not make a big show of it! You cannot make the act of Hospitality about *you*. It's being able to make people feel comfortable without them knowing why they are so at ease. If you're outside with a friend and their beer is sitting on the table in the sun, put your hat down so it shades the bottle and keeps it cold longer. They will probably not even notice that, but their beer will be better. Anticipation makes Hospitality invisible.

PERSONALIZATION

You've got the basics down. Now we add the flourishes. This all comes down to paying attention to specific needs. Does cucumber make someone burp uncontrollably? Or do they hate ginger? Make a mental note of that and avoid those ingredients. Remember the name of your guest. Remember what they order so you can offer them something else in their wheelhouse when they return. Supercharge your empathy, listen carefully to what they're saying. Develop a rapport.

One of the things I always do on my first check-in with a guest after I've delivered them a cocktail is try to get more information about what they like in the drink, not just *if* they like the drink. Asking "Is your drink okay?" gets you fuck-all in terms of tactical intelligence that you can use to personalize their next round. But leading questions like "How's that ginger working out for ya?" or "Did you like the grapefruit garnish on that rum Old-Fashioned?" will give you an idea of your next step. If the ginger was great in the Dark and Stormy, then I'm thinking a ginger-laced Devil's Playground (page 228) could be the next logical play, and I'll mark that in my brain to recommend when the guest is ready. Thinking ahead to what you might offer next is a simple moment of showmanship that can make folks feel, as the kids say, "seen."

I'll give you another example: One night one of our bartenders was waiting on a couple, and they started talking about math and numbers. The guests, Dawn and Jacques, challenged him to make a cocktail relating to the Fibonacci sequence.* With some quick thinking, he came up with a cocktail that conformed to this structure. Dawn and Jacques enjoyed this interaction so much that they left a tip laid out in Fibonacci sequence: a single, a single, two dollars, three dollars, a five spot, a five and three singles, a ten spot and three singles, and a twenty and a single.

Small details matter, even if a guest isn't completely aware of them. Like napkins: We would always place a cocktail napkin in a diamond shape in front of the guest before the cocktail is handed to them. Almost without fail, guests could be very fidgety and would oftentimes move the napkin around. I remember being taught to always correct the orientation of the napkin back to the original diamond shape with the corner pointed at the guest, but to also do it slyly and not draw attention to it as to make the guest think they did anything wrong. Hospitality is ultimately about the small details.

—PATRICK SMITH, 2009–2019

That's some geeky cocktailing, but it speaks directly to the idea that when you make someone feel like they're part of the game, like they're in on the joke, you've won the ultimate prize in Hospitality.

---

* The Fibonacci sequence is where two numbers are added together to get the next in the sequence, so it goes 0, 1, 1, 2, 3, 5, 8, 13, 21, 34 . . .

HOSPITALITY

251

RECITES

RECIPES

Last round of recipes. Even if you were to just skip the whole lesson and mix up one of these twenty-five TVH originals, you'll still feel better off than you did before. But if you're following along with the training, direct your attention to the notions of Ritual and Personal Style as you mix these final drinks. When you do, remember the pillars of good Hospitality! Set up proper mise en place, put on some good tunes, light a candle or two, pray to the gods of good Balance, Texture, Temperature, and Aroma as you mix for yourself or others. Sometimes the bartender has given you a hint to how each drink represents their style or ritual in the introduction to the drink, so soak those in! Let their insights influence your opinion about the drink, argue with it, or suck it down with gusto. Honestly, just *think* about what you are reading and drinking and see how that makes the whole process more delightful.

CHICAGO FLIP

CIRCA 2007

A flip with broad shoulders. The tawny port is chock-full of dried stone fruit, fig, and nuttiness. The Licor 43 shines through to make this a guiltless pleasure. Bourbon is there to keep it from being too much like an Irish Cream. It's mighty rich, so I'm all for making one as a nightcap and splitting it with your favorite cuddle buddy.
—TOBY MALONEY

MISE EN PLACE

GLASS . . . . . COLLINS

ICE . . . . NONE

GARNISH . . . GRATED NUTMEG,
3 DROPS PIMENTO DRAM

METHOD . . . MIME SHAKE, COUPE SHAKE

SPEC

2.0 OZ . . . . . . BUFFALO TRACE BOURBON

.75 OZ . . . . . . TAYLOR FLADGATE 20-YEAR
TAWNY PORT

.75 OZ . . . . . LICOR 43

.25+ OZ . . . . SIMPLE SYRUP

1 . . . . WHOLE EGG

CRACK THE EGG AND PLOP it into your shaker tin. Stack the simple syrup (or use Demerara, if you wanna be decadent) and Licor 43, then jigger out the port and bourbon. Give this a thorough **MIME SHAKE**, making sure the egg incorporates with the other ingredients. Taste. If it's on the dry side, you can add a touch more simple syrup. Add 5 ice cubes and **COUPE SHAKE** viciously to whip air into the egg and lift it toward the heavens. **DOUBLE STRAIN** into your cocktail glass. Garnish, remembering that freshly grated nutmeg is decidedly better than ground nutmeg. And be sure to put the dropper for the pimento dram as close to the foam as possible, because you want the dram to stick there on the surface of the drink, not sink down into the drink because you threw it in with too much force.

SIMPLE SYRUP: PAGE 311 ✷ EGGS: PAGE 64 ✷
NUTMEG: PAGE 80 ✷ STACKING: PAGE 36

THE HUMMINGBIRD

CIRCA 2008

This was the first drink I conceptualized from start to finish that made a menu at The Violet Hour. As a newer bartender, I relied heavily on palate and intuition, looking at the tequila and chasing Complementary flavors from that point. The way the cherry comes into play with the lemon and tequila is refreshing, and the egg white dried everything out so it wasn't cloyingly sweet. —ROBBY HAYNES

MISE EN PLACE	
GLASS	COUPE
ICE	NONE
GARNISH	LEMON PEEL, EXPRESSED AND DISCARDED
METHOD	MIME SHAKE, COUPE SHAKE

SPEC	
1.75 OZ	BLANCO TEQUILA
.75 OZ	LEMON JUICE
.75 OZ	CHERRY HEERING
.50 OZ	SIMPLE SYRUP
9 DROPS	CHERRY BITTERS
1	EGG WHITE

DROP THE EGG WHITE INTO the tin. Add the bitters, simple syrup, cherry Heering, and tequila. **MIME SHAKE**. Taste. Do you need to add a tiny bit more simple syrup because the egg white has driven the drink too dry? Do that now. Give the tin 5 ice cubes. **COUPE SHAKE**. Start slow and work your way to a faster pace to get a big, beautiful, aerated and fluffy cocktail. **DOUBLE STRAIN** into a chilled coupe. Open the gate of your Hawthorne strainer a little and give it a more exaggerated up-and-down motion to get the last bits of foam out of the tin. For the garnish, really mow down the oils on top of the cocktail so the Aroma will be bright and citrusy and refreshing. Discard the lemon peel after expressing.

SIMPLE SYRUP: PAGE 311 ✳ MIME SHAKE: PAGE 65 ✳ GARNISH: PAGE 73

KEEPING UP WITH THE CARTHUSIANS

CIRCA 2018

With a name that nods to the show Keeping Up with the Kardashians, *this is an unabashed (and more sophisticated) variation on the Lemon Drop. It's super easy drinking—bright and citrusy, but with layers of depth and intrigue from the yellow Chartreuse, which is somewhat lighter and more easygoing than its green companion. The sage syrup helps bring out the herbaceousness in a pleasingly mild way.*
—ANEKA SAXON

MISE EN PLACE		SPEC	
GLASS	COUPE	2.0 OZ	VODKA
ICE	NONE	.75 OZ	LEMON JUICE
GARNISH	LEMON PIGTAIL	.25 OZ	YELLOW CHARTREUSE
METHOD	COUPE SHAKE	.50 OZ	SAGE SYRUP

EASY AND STRAIGHTFORWARD. STACK THE sage syrup with the Chartreuse, then add the lemon juice and vodka to a shaker tin with 5 cubes of ice and **COUPE SHAKE** to chill. Taste. Dilution is key; you're serving the drink up, so you want it to taste perfectly Balanced in terms of water content. Also look for how the sage syrup and the Chartreuse pair together—all those herbs should be coming through like a shining light at the end of a tunnel. If not, add a tiny bit more sage syrup so it pushes those elements to the forefront. **STRAIN** into a coupe. To garnish, use a channel knife to cut a long, tight spiral around the pole of the lemon, thin enough that you can coil it up into the shape of a winding pigtail. When you do this, hold the fruit over the drink so the lemon oils gracefully fall onto its surface. Insert the pigtail into the cocktail to serve as garnish.

SAGE SYRUP: PAGE 314 ✳ COUPE SHAKE: PAGE 45 ✳ GARNISH: PAGE 77

GUN SHOP SAZERAC

CIRCA 2010

Everybody has their own take on the classic New Orleans Sazerac. It's a drink that allows only for slight flourishes—maybe you add a different whiskey, or stir differently, do a little bit of this or a little bit of that. With the split of brandy and whiskey and a little Demerara for oomph, this is a way more viscous version of the drink, which makes it pleasing for people who aren't motivated by whiskey alone. Think of it as a fruity, accessible take on the classic. —KIRK ESTOPINAL

MISE EN PLACE

GLASS . . . . . DOUBLE OLD-FASHIONED

ICE . . . . NONE

GARNISH . . . LEMON PEEL, EXPRESSED
AND DISCARDED

METHOD . . . COUPE STIR

SPEC

1.0 OZ . . . . . . RUSSELL'S RESERVE 6-YEAR
RYE WHISKEY

1.0 OZ . . . . . MAISON SURRENNE COGNAC

.25 OZ . . . . . . DEMERARA SYRUP

23 DROPS . . PEYCHAUD'S BITTERS

.125 OZ . . . . . HERBSAINT LEGENDRE,
TO RINSE

IF YOU'VE EVER MADE A Sazerac before, you know this one starts with preparing your drinking vessel with a rinse of Herbsaint. If not, now you know! Put the Herbsaint (or another anise-flavored liqueur, ideally around 45% ABV) into your DOF glass with crushed ice and turn the vessel to coat the entire interior. Dump the ice out and set that aside. In a mixing glass, combine the bitters, Demerara syrup, Cognac, and rye with ice cubes climbing three-quarters of the way up the glass and **COUPE STIR**. Taste as you go, stopping stirring when the drink tastes pitch-perfect. The cocktail is served "down" in the glass, so it must taste 100% correct before you strain, because it won't gain more water like an Old-Fashioned over ice will, instead it'll warm, revealing any flaws in your technique. **STRAIN** into the prepared glass. Express the oils from the lemon peel over the top of the drink—high above the glass if you want only a hint of lemon. Discard the lemon peel and get on with your day.

DEMERARA SYRUP: PAGE 311 ✳ RINSE: PAGE 83 ✳ COUPE STIR: PAGE 46

NEGRONI TREDICI

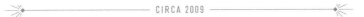

CIRCA 2009

Ahh, the days where you could just slightly tweak a cocktail and it would blow people's minds! Following in the storied tradition of the Little Italy cocktail (rye whiskey, sweet vermouth, Cynar), I wanted to create a rich, almost savory mash-up of that drink and the Negroni by bringing Cynar into the mix. I used a big, bold gin and subtle sweet vermouth so the drink would explode with botanicals while keeping earthy Cynar front and center. With a bracing sandpaper bitterness, it's a stoic version of the classic.
—TOBY MALONEY

MISE EN PLACE

GLASS . . . . . **COUPE**
ICE . . . . **NONE**
GARNISH . . . **LEMON PIGTAIL**
METHOD . . . **COUPE STIR**

SPEC

2.0 OZ . . . . . . **BEEFEATER GIN**
1.0 OZ . . . . . . **CARPANO ANTICA VERMOUTH**
.25 OZ . . . . . . **CAMPARI**
.25 OZ . . . . . . **CYNAR**
13 DROPS . . **ORANGE BITTERS**

FILL A MIXING GLASS THREE-QUARTERS of the way full with ice and add the bitters. If you are working with super-cold ice, slide the bitters down the inside of the glass instead of dashing them in—this will make sure they fully integrate into the cocktail instead of sticking to the ice cubes. Stack the Cynar and Campari in the small side of the jigger and pour the combination into the mixing glass. Add the vermouth, then the gin. **COUPE STIR**. Taste. It will be big and bold but should be delightfully drinkable at this point. **STRAIN** into a chilled coupe. Express the oils from the lemon pigtail right above the coupe, so you get a lot of oils on top of the drink. Wind up the lemon peel to look like a pigtail and hook it on the side of the glass so it isn't just floating around like a dead body in a kiddie pool.

STACKING: PAGE 36 * COUPE STIR: PAGE 46 * GARNISH: PAGE 77

POLKA DOT NEGRONI

CIRCA 2016

A crystalline summer Negroni, with Salers as the bittering agent instead of Campari. Salers, the French aperitif is fascinating to me, so earthy, with notes of dust motes— dry, like how it tasted when you got chalk dust in your mouth from cleaning the erasers because you were caught passing notes in civics class. From there, I needed a huge gin to bring in brawny proof and juniper—Junipero's strength is more bricklayer than CrossFit. Finally, Dolin Blanc brings the essence of summer picnics without the ants, or fragrant midnight walks in the country with just your pinkies entwined, to the glass. —TOBY MALONEY

MISE EN PLACE

GLASS.....NICK & NORA

ICE ....NONE

GARNISH...SKEWERED CHERRY; LEMON
           PEEL PIGTAIL

METHOD ...COUPE STIR

SPEC

1.5 OZ......SALERS

1.0 OZ......JUNIPERO GIN (OR OTHER
           NAVY-PROOF GIN)

1.0 OZ......DOLIN BLANC VERMOUTH

THIS IS PRETTY CLOSE TO the ABV of a regular Negroni, so you want this teetering on the edge of understirred so the high-proof gin can elevate the low-ABV ingredients. Sooooo, in a mixing glass, combine the vermouth, gin, and Salers. Ice the mixing glass with enough cubes to reach three-quarters of the way high. **COUPE STIR.** Taste after a dozen rotations or so to see where the water content is. Once all the cogs settle in together, you can **STRAIN** into a Nick & Nora. Drop the skewered "polka dot" (cherry) into the cocktail and hum "Itsy Bitsy Polka Dot Negroni" while you add an irresponsible amount of lemon oil to the top of the drink as you pull the pigtail from the fruit, spiraling from the pole to the equator, over the top of the drink with a channel knife. Length-wise, it's half a lemon's worth of peel. Discard the pigtail.

NEGRONI: PAGE 35 ✳ COUPE STIR: PAGE 46 ✳ GARNISH: PAGE 77

CROCODILE TEARS

CIRCA 2019

A delightfully smoky cocktail with a gentle kiss of herbaceousness, this recipe was inspired by the rise of mezcal in America. I had profound love for the bitter vegetal earthiness of Salers and wanted to make a white Negroni variation that would satisfy the palate of a mezcal lover. The Salers is crucial for adding the touch of bitterness that lets you truly call it a Negroni variation. The tequila and blanc vermouth act as the core notes that keep this cocktail from being off-Balance. Lastly, the green Chartreuse ties it all together with its array of spices and botanical flavors. —RUBÍ VILLAGOMEZ

MISE EN PLACE		SPEC	
GLASS	COUPE	1.0 OZ	LUNAZUL BLANCO TEQUILA
ICE	NONE	.50 OZ	MEZCAL UNIÓN UNO
GARNISH	GRAPEFRUIT SIDEWINDER	.50 OZ	GREEN CHARTREUSE
METHOD	COUPE STIR	1.0 OZ	DOLIN BLANC VERMOUTH
		.25 OZ	SALERS

CHILL YOUR COUPE. ADD A few ice cubes to a mixing glass to chill it a little before pouring in your vermouth, Chartreuse, mezcal, tequila, and Salers. Taste the drink to get a sense for how all those big green vegetal flavors are colliding. Add more ice to the mixing glass, so it sits three-quarters of the way full before you COUPE STIR, fast! Stop just before your cocktail is ready to serve. Taste. It should be very cold and boozy, but with every ingredient coexisting in soft harmony—no player jumping out higher than the others. STRAIN into the chilled coupe, garnish with the oils of the lavish grapefruit sidewinder, and place the peel on the rim.

NEGRONI: PAGE 35 ✳ COUPE STIR: PAGE 46 ✳ GARNISH: PAGE 77

HURRICANRANA

CIRCA 2014

The Flaming Heart (page 271) is one of my favorite TVH classics, a great call for anyone asking for a spicy margarita. With this drink I wanted to do something similar but more aggressive. With the green Chartreuse and the mezcal, it becomes something slightly savory, complex in its herbaceousness, and wonderfully smoky. —DAMIEN VANIER

MISE EN PLACE

GLASS.....COUPE

ICE ....NONE

GARNISH...CUCUMBER SLICE

METHOD ...COUPE SHAKE

SPEC

2.0 OZ......MEZCAL

.50 OZ.....COCCHI AMERICANO

.75 OZ......LIME JUICE

.125 OZ.....SIMPLE SYRUP

.50 OZ......GREEN CHARTREUSE

5 DROPS ...GREEN TABASCO

1 ....CUCUMBER SLICE, HALVED, TO MUDDLE

1 ....MINT SPRIG, TO MUDDLE

CAREFULLY LAUNCH 5 DROPS OF the Tabasco into the small side of a shaker tin. This hot sauce will create a vegetal bomb if there is too much competing with the green Chartreuse, so go light on both of those elements when you measure, because you can always add more later. Now grab your fruit and drop it in the same side of the tin and **MUDDLE** the cucumber just enough to break up the pieces and release some of the juice. Add the mint and just *move it around*—just a brush to release the oils. Measure and pour the green Chartreuse, simple syrup, lime juice, Cocchi Americano, and mezcal, in that order. Add 5 ice cubes and **COUPE SHAKE.** It might take a touch more effort because of all the flotsam and jetsam, and because you have a few high-proof spirits in play that demand more dilution. Taste. You should get enough savory spice from the hot sauce without setting your taste buds aflame; if you need more, add more. **DOUBLE STRAIN** into a chilled coupe and garnish with a cucumber slice at eleven o'clock.

SIMPLE SYRUP: PAGE 311 ✳ COUPE SHAKE: PAGE 45 ✳ FACES OF A CLOCK: PAGE 301

DANCE OF DRAGONS

CIRCA 2018

Because of my Italian heritage and penchant for all things bitter, I rarely submitted a cocktail without weaving in a potable bitter. This recipe is no exception. Built for tiki and amaro lovers alike, I worked to bring Big Summer Energy to a cocktail with undeniable holiday vibes. You get flavors of clove, honey, and fermented stone fruits that stand front and center against a subtle backdrop of bitter tree bark and almond.
—ROSALIA COSTELLO

MISE EN PLACE

GLASS.....COLLINS

ICE ....CRUSHED

GARNISH...MINT SPRIG, ORANGE
            PIGTAIL KNOT

METHOD ...SWIZZLE

SPEC

1.0 OZ......SMITH & CROSS
             JAMAICA RUM

1.0 OZ......AMARO DI ANGOSTURA

.75 OZ......LIME JUICE

.25 OZ......FALERNUM

.50 OZ......HONEY SYRUP

5 TO 6 .....MINT LEAVES

START WITH A COLLINS GLASS, preferably a fancy one from a local vintage store with a '60s-esque gold decal. Place 5 or 6 vivacious mint leaves in the bottom of the glass. Measure out your honey syrup, falernum, lime juice, amaro, and rum. Take a minute to let those ingredients mingle, then fill the glass three-quarters full with crushed ice. **SWIZZLE.** Top with more crushed ice. After giving the most carefully selected mint sprig a gentle spank against the back of your hand, insert it. To even further perfect the imbiber's olfactory experience, peel a long, thin pigtail from an orange (over the top of the drink so those oils don't just hang in midair nowhere near the cocktail) and tie that pigtail in a knot around the mint spring like you're tying up a birthday present for a crush you're hoping will notice your wrapping job.

HONEY SYRUP: PAGE 311 ✳ FALERNUM: PAGE 314 ✳
SWIZZLE: PAGE 47 ✳ GARNISH: PAGE 76

SO FAR, SO GOOD

When Letherbee gin hit the market, it was exciting because it was a modern gin made in a London dry style with a higher proof than normal; you didn't see that flex very often in 2015. Everybody was using it in these big stirred cocktails with an element of bitterness, so I wanted to try something different by making a drink that would be light but still strong, with some sweetness from the Dolin Blanc and the simple syrup.

—EDEN LAURIN

MISE EN PLACE		SPEC	
GLASS	CYCLONE	1.0 OZ	LETHERBEE GIN
ICE	CUBES	1.0 OZ	DOLIN BLANC VERMOUTH
GARNISH	ORANGE FLOWER WATER; SUGAR CUBE; ORANGE PEEL, EXPRESSED AND INSERTED	.50 OZ	LEMON JUICE
		.50 OZ	CHERRY HEERING
		.50 OZ	SIMPLE SYRUP
METHOD	ROCKS SHAKE	SPARKLING WINE, TO BOTTOM	

IN A SHAKER TIN, STACK the simple syrup and cherry Heering, then add the lemon juice. Then stack the gin and vermouth. If you don't have Letherbee, use a bombastic London dry in its stead. Put ice cubes in your cyclone glass so they chill the vessel. Add an ounce of bubbles to the glass, then set aside. Prepare your garnish: Douse your sugar cube in orange flower water and pull your orange peel. Back to the shaker tin: add 5 cubes and **ROCKS SHAKE**, then taste. Knowing that the drink will meet a dry sparkling wine at the end, and how it will be served on ice, does it taste sweet enough? Adjust, then **STRAIN** the contents of the tin into your prepped glass. To garnish: express and insert the orange peel. Put the sugar cube in the bowl of the barspoon and saturate the cube with the orange flower water. Pour off any excess orange flower water so it's not dripping wet. Gently place the sugar cube on top of the cocktail with the spoon.

SIMPLE SYRUP: PAGE 311 ✳ BOTTOM: PAGE 62 ✳
NARRATIVE ARC: PAGE 193 ✳ ORANGE FLOWER WATER: PAGE 37

FLAMING HEART

CIRCA 2010

For so long I agonized over how to get "spicy" into cocktails. Making a syrup from jalapeños or any dried pepper was fraught with peril because you never knew how hot it would turn out. So, we started using green Tabasco because I liked the flavor, and since you can measure the amount used in a drink precisely, it also provided a consistent and reliable amount of spiciness to the cocktail. The green pepper notes of the hot sauce pull out similar ones in the tequila, while the vanilla of the Licor 43 bridges the gap between the heat and the sweet pineapple juice. —TOBY MALONEY

MISE EN PLACE

GLASS.....DOUBLE OLD-FASHIONED

ICE ....CUBES

GARNISH...LIME WHEEL

METHOD ...ROCKS SHAKE

SPEC

2.0 OZ......LUNAZUL BLANCO TEQUILA

.75 OZ......LIME JUICE

.50 OZ......PINEAPPLE JUICE

.25 OZ......SIMPLE SYRUP

.50 OZ......LICOR 43

9 DROPS ...FEE BROTHERS OLD FASHION AROMATIC BITTERS

9 DROPS ...GREEN TABASCO

IN A SHAKER TIN, COMBINE the Tabasco and bitters. Stack the Licor 43 and simple syrup, ensuring precision in your sweeteners. Then donate the pineapple and lime juices, finishing up with the tequila. Taste. Analyze the effect of the hot sauce and the quality of your pineapple juice. Sugar cancels out the effects of capsicum, so how sweet the pineapple is will be inversely proportional to how spicy this drink is. Add 5 ice cubes and **ROCKS SHAKE**. Taste. The blast of coldness from the ice will have muted the spice element to a degree; if you need to add a drop or two more hot sauce to get a nice spicy quality out of the drink, do it! **STRAIN** into a DOF glass over ice cubes. Garnish.

SIMPLE SYRUP: PAGE 311 ✳ PINEAPPLES: PAGE 68 ✳
STACKING: PAGE 36 ✳ ROCKS SHAKE: PAGE 46

RIKI TIKI TAVI

CIRCA 2019

This cocktail came about one night when we were throwing ideas at each other and decided that it would be fun to make a variation on the Flaming Heart (page 271) with a fall/winter twist using Scotch and pineapple rum. The drink takes the ideas of "tiki" and "campfire" and gives you the satisfaction of a fun summer drink with an appropriate amount of smoke and spice for some guilt-free tropical times when it's dead cold out. Fruity, flirty, smoky, and spiced, we were going to call it the Stiggins' Julep after the rum, but Toby vetoed that and I blurted out "Riki TIKI Tavi," because it's a tiki drink with the bite of a mongoose. It was meant as a joke but it just stuck.
—MAX BECKMAN AND RUBÍ VILLAGOMEZ

MISE EN PLACE

GLASS . . . . . JULEP TIN

ICE . . . . CRUSHED

GARNISH . . . GRATED CINNAMON,
MINT SPRIG

METHOD . . . SWIZZLE

SPEC

1 OZ. . . . . . . PLANTATION STIGGINS'
FANCY PINEAPPLE RUM

1 OZ. . . . . . . BLENDED SCOTCH WHISKY

.25– OZ . . . . . ST. GEORGE SPICED
PEAR LIQUEUR

.50– OZ . . . . . FALERNUM

1 DASH . . . . ANGOSTURA BITTERS

2 DASHES . . BITTERCUBE ORANGE
BITTERS

INTO YOUR JULEP TIN, DASH your bitters. Stack the falernum and pear liqueur—otherwise, you tread close to the line of oversweetening. Stack the Scotch and rum. Add crushed ice to fill the tin three-quarters of the way and **SWIZZLE**. Taste. How is the Balance between the fruitiness of the pineapple and smoky Scotch? You are going for a nice round mouthfeel because the cinnamon and mint are both sharp, so if your Texture is wonky and if the pineapple isn't coming through, you might need to add .125-ounce pour of pear liqueur to boost those qualities. Swizzle again, then top with more crushed ice and garnish.

FALERNUM: PAGE 314 ✳ STACKING: PAGE 36 ✳
SWIZZLE: PAGE 47 ✳ CINNAMON: PAGE 80

PART AND PARCEL

CIRCA 2008

*One of the first vodka drinks we had on the menu at TVH was the Vodka Cobbler—the raspberry and blackberry seeds would constantly get stuck in the strainer so everybody hated making it. I wanted to invent a vodka drink that would be easier to build, but also popular so nobody would order the cobbler anymore. St-Germain was brand-new at the time, and that stuff is like catnip to vodka drinkers, so I decided to use that and make a simple Hemingway Daiquiri variation. —*TROY SIDLE

MISE EN PLACE

GLASS.....COUPE

ICE.......NONE

GARNISH...NONE

METHOD ...COUPE SHAKE

SPEC

2.0 OZ......VODKA

.75 OZ......ST-GERMAIN ELDERFLOWER LIQUEUR

.25 OZ......LIME JUICE

.75 OZ......GRAPEFRUIT JUICE

.50 OZ......SIMPLE SYRUP

5 DROPS ...BITTERMENS HOPPED GRAPEFRUIT BITTERS

CHILL THAT COUPE. IN YOUR shaker tin, combine the bitters (the hopped grapefruit brings a world of complexity to this), simple syrup, lime juice, grapefruit juice, St-Germain, and vodka. Pop 5 ice cubes into your shaker and COUPE SHAKE to get the chill and dilution down to drinkable. Taste—if the grapefruit juice and the bitters are shouting above the other flavors too loudly, add another .125 ounce of lime juice to take that volume down and help click the citrus together with the sweeteners. STRAIN into your chilled coupe.

VODKA COBBLER: PAGE 143 ✳ SIMPLE SYRUP: PAGE 311 ✳
BULLIES: PAGE 37 ✳ COUPE SHAKE: PAGE 45

ENORMOUS ROLLING MAUL

CIRCA 2012

This is an Old-Fashioned riff with dark chocolate and tobacco notes in the rum Juxtaposing the bright bitter orange of the marmalade. The drastic Juxtaposition of the rum, marmalade, Peychaud's, and lemon (orange would have been the easy choice) makes this a real barn burner. If there is any way you can go buy a bottle of Santa Teresa 1796, do it. —TOBY MALONEY

MISE EN PLACE

GLASS.....ROCKS

ICE ....CHUNK

GARNISH...17 DROPS BITTERCUBE
ORANGE BITTERS;
LEMON PEEL, EXPRESSED
AND INSERTED

METHOD ...CHUNK STIR

SPEC

2.0 OZ......SANTA TERESA 1796 RUM

.25+ OZ.....ORANGE MARMALADE
SYRUP

9 DROPS ...PEYCHAUD'S BITTERS

ADD THE BITTERS TO YOUR mixing glass, dropping them down the side so they commingle with the body of the cocktail immediately. Measure and donate the syrup and the rum. Taste. Adjust if needed. Add ice to the mixing glass, enough to fill it up three-quarters of the way. **CHUNK STIR** with tranquility. The marmalade syrup is tricky because the bitterness can seem to cover up the sweetness of the drink, so pay extra attention to the Texture of the cocktail when tasting. If it's not thick and rich and wonderful, you can add more syrup, one tiny bit at a time so you don't overdo it. **STRAIN.** Garnish; express the oils of a lemon peel over the top of the drink and insert the peel, then carefully drop the bitters over the surface of the drink, making sure to space them out evenly so they will play nicely with the lemon oil for as long as possible.

ORANGE MARMALADE SYRUP: PAGE 314 ✳ CHUNK STIR: PAGE 47 ✳ FLOAT: PAGE 81

THE ANTIDOTE

CIRCA 2016

Around 2016 I was coming into my stride as a bartender, getting really good at taking a classic cocktail template and changing it without breaking it. This was a tequila version of the Penicillin with amaro—a summertime version of the Scotch drink with a little more depth. The name made perfect sense for a Penicillin riff, but I also liked conceptually that people were asking me for "The Antidote." —PAT RAY

MISE EN PLACE

GLASS . . . . . DOUBLE OLD-FASHIONED

ICE . . . . CRUSHED

GARNISH . . . STRAWBERRY HALF

METHOD . . . WHIP SHAKE, ROLL

SPEC

1.5 OZ . . . . . . BLANCO TEQUILA

.50 OZ . . . . . ZUCCA RABARBARO

.75 OZ . . . . . LIME JUICE

.25+ OZ . . . . HONEY SYRUP

.50 OZ . . . . . GINGER SYRUP

1 . . . . STRAWBERRY, HALVED,
TO MUDDLE

FILL YOUR DOF GLASS WITH crushed ice to chill. In your shaker tin, **MUDDLE** the strawberry lightly, then add the ginger syrup, honey syrup, lime, Zucca, and tequila. Taste. You're working with two syrups here, so if it's too sweet, you could always try auditioning a dash of Ango. **WHIP SHAKE** with about an ounce of crushed ice. Check your DOF for dilution—throw your Hawthorne over the top and strain out excess liquid before you **ROLL** the cocktail into the glass. If the liquid isn't flowing seamlessly, you can agitate the ice a little with a straw so the liquid can sneak all the way down into the bottom of the crushed ice. Cut your strawberry so that it will sit on the rim with the entire inside face of the strawberry angled toward the nose of the person sipping the drink—this way you get the most Aroma as you drink. Garnish.

GINGER SYRUP: PAGE 313 ✳ HONEY SYRUP: PAGE 311 ✳ WHIP SHAKE: PAGE 46

BARTENDING TENETS: RECIPES

277

SWISS KISS

An ode to Lemon, my Bernese mountain dog (the breed has a white spot on the back of their neck that's called the Swiss Kiss), this recipe was inspired by alpine Aromas and flavors and lands somewhere in between a Corpse Reviver No. 2 and a Gin Smash. Usually, alpine flavors manifest in cocktails in the form of Chartreuse, but this is a more subtle take with génépy and a slight float of absinthe, which makes it a pretty approachable way to get into the style. It's certainly not a drink for everyone, but I think it's a decent introduction to a gin cocktail. —ZAC SORENSEN

MISE EN PLACE

GLASS . . . . . DOUBLE OLD-FASHIONED

ICE . . . . CHUNK

GARNISH . . . MINT SPRIG

METHOD . . . ROCKS SHAKE

SPEC

1.5 OZ . . . . . . LETHERBEE GIN

.50 OZ . . . . . . DOLIN GÉNÉPY LE CHAMOIS

.75 OZ . . . . . . LEMON JUICE

.50+ OZ . . . . . SIMPLE SYRUP

11 DROPS . . PEYCHAUD'S BITTERS

.125– OZ. ABSINTHE, TO FLOAT

ADD UP THE PROOF OF your ingredients so you can estimate how long to shake this drink. Combine the bitters, syrup, génépy, lemon juice, and gin (in that order) in your shaker tin. Taste. The génépy can be a bully, so pay attention to how strong that flavor is at this moment. It should soften a little after the shake. Give it 5 ice cubes and **ROCKS SHAKE**. Taste again. Have all the components melded together so it tastes seamless, or is it still clashing? If it's the latter, you should shake a bit longer to add more dilution until the components shimmy into place. **STRAIN** into a DOF glass over an ice chunk. Measure out your absinthe into a jigger to make sure you don't overdo it—start with .125 ounce floated on top and give the drink a smell. Is the absinthe prominent enough? If not, add a bit more. Garnish with your mint sprig, making sure to express the oils atop the absinthe first.

SIMPLE SYRUP: PAGE 311 ✳ ROCKS SHAKE: PAGE 46 ✳
FLOAT: PAGE 81 ✳ SPANKED MINT: PAGE 78

THE NEW RAHM

CIRCA 2014

Rahm Emanuel, the former mayor of Chicago, used to come into The Violet Hour every once in a while, and he'd always order a beer—usually a hoppy West Coast IPA. I took it upon myself to convert him to cocktails with a drink that had similarly wild, fruity, tannic, and bitter qualities. Salers has a bitter gentian element to mimic the hops, and those IPAs can be fruity as well, so strawberry aligns with that aspect. The drink was revolutionary at the time because it had very little alcohol and we hadn't yet waltzed into this new era where low-ABV drinks are as popular as high-ABV drinks. It's a nice pocket drink to have for folks who like beer and want something that won't knock them on their butts. —AUBREY HOWARD

MISE EN PLACE

GLASS . . . . . COLLINS

ICE . . . . ICE CUBES

GARNISH . . . MINT SPRIG,
           ANGOSTURA BITTERS

METHOD . . . COLLINS SHAKE

SPEC

1.5 OZ . . . . . . SALERS

1.5 OZ . . . . . . COCCHI AMERICANO

.50 OZ . . . . . LEMON JUICE

.50 OZ . . . . . SIMPLE SYRUP

3 . . . . STRAWBERRIES, TO MUDDLE

1 . . . . MINT SPRIG, TO MUDDLE

CLUB SODA, TO BOTTOM

ADD ICE CUBES AND SODA to your Collins glass to chill. Add the sprig of mint to your shaker tin, brushing it up and down the sides to wake up the oils. Add strawberries and **MUDDLE**. Add the simple syrup, lemon, Cocchi, and Salers. Throw in 3 ice cubes and **COLLINS SHAKE**. Taste. The bitterness from the Salers should have softened and merged together with the sweetness of the Cocchi. If not, add a touch more simple syrup. **STRAIN** into the Collins. When using mint as a garnish like this, adding an aromatic element like Angostura creates a totally different bouquet—one that is more complex than a traditional mint garnish. Express the oils of the mint with glee before adding a few drops of Ango to the leaves.

SIMPLE SYRUP: PAGE 311 ✳ BOTTOM: PAGE 62 ✳ COLLINS SHAKE: PAGE 46

OUT OF THE AIRLOCK

CIRCA 2016

I like to think of this drink as where the Sazerac meets the boulevardier—a stirred whiskey cocktail that would be fitting for drinking when it's hot outside. With Cocchi Americano in play instead of sweet vermouth, it's lighter in body and character than either of those classics, but that's what you'd want to drink when it's warm out. I think anyone familiar with classic New Orleans cocktails would find it super enjoyable.
—ZAC SORENSEN

MISE EN PLACE

GLASS.....DOUBLE OLD-FASHIONED

ICE ....NONE

GARNISH...ORANGE PEEL, LIGHTLY
            EXPRESSED AND
            DISCARDED

METHOD ...COUPE STIR

SPEC

2.0 OZ......WILD TURKEY
            101 RYE WHISKEY

.75 OZ......COCCHI AMERICANO

.50 OZ......CAMPARI

.125 OZ.....DEMERARA SYRUP

2 DASHES ..PEYCHAUD'S BITTERS

HERBSAINT, TO RINSE

PREPARE YOUR DOF GLASS à la Sazerac by adding some crushed ice and rinsing it with the Herbsaint. Dump out the ice and give it a sniff—the rinse in this cocktail is supposed to be a delicate addition, not something that will overwhelm the other flavors, so resist the urge to add more at this point. You should be able to smell the Herbsaint without having so much that it tickles your nose into a sneeze. In a mixing glass, combine the bitters, Demerara syrup, Campari, Cocchi, and rye. Add ice so the mixing glass is about three-quarters of the way full and **COUPE STIR**. Taste. Has the Campari softened into the rye so neither one stands out above the other? If not, stir a little longer. **STRAIN** into the prepared DOF. Express the oils from the orange peel over the cocktail, holding the peel relatively high over the drink because your rinse was also modest, then discard. The faint Aroma of the orange oil and Herbsaint blending together should be simply divine.

DEMERARA SYRUP: PAGE 311 ✳ RINSE: PAGE 83 ✳ COUPE STIR: PAGE 46

THE WICKER PARK SOUR

CIRCA 2011

Somebody once told me Malört tastes like a burning Band-Aid at the bottom of a dumpster. Malört is like wormwood hell, but I like it! It works really well in cocktails when used the right way. To take it from the shoot-it-down-quick world into the cocktail world, I used a full ounce—a legitimate amount—to make this weird and surprising drink. The grapefruit juice and honey soften that classic Malört finish and help lessen its presence a little—it's definitely more drinkable than it looks, especially if you like bitter things. —ANDREW MACKEY

MISE EN PLACE

GLASS . . . . . COUPE

ICE . . . . NONE

GARNISH . . . 3 DROPS PEYCHAUD'S
BITTERS

METHOD . . . MIME SHAKE,
COUPE SHAKE

SPEC

1.0 OZ . . . . . . JEPPSON'S MALÖRT

1.0 OZ . . . . . . TABERNERO PISCO ITALIA

.75 OZ . . . . . . LEMON JUICE

.50 OZ . . . . . GRAPEFRUIT JUICE

.25 OZ . . . . . . SIMPLE SYRUP

.50 OZ . . . . . HONEY SYRUP

1 DASH . . . . ANGOSTURA BITTERS

1 . . . . EGG WHITE

CHILL YOUR COUPE. IN THE large side of your shaker tin, combine the bitters, simple syrup, honey syrup, lemon and grapefruit juices, pisco, and Malört. Slide the egg whites into the small side of the tin. **MIME SHAKE.** Taste and give it a beat before analyzing the interplay of the Malört and the bitterness of the grapefruit juice. They just go together, right? Add 5 ice cubes and **COUPE SHAKE. DOUBLE STRAIN** the cocktail into the chilled coupe—using the double strain technique here will ensure you don't get any rogue pieces of eggshell or ice chips in the drink (though you should have checked for shell before, so this is juuuust a reminder not to skip that step). Garnish with the Peychaud's, which should stick pleasingly to the foamy bed of egg whites.

HONEY SYRUP: PAGE 311 ✳ SIMPLE SYRUP: PAGE 311 ✳
EGGS: PAGE 64 ✳ BITTERS ON EGG WHITE: PAGE 79

DAYWALKER

CIRCA 2019

I've been asked so many times to make a dirty martini when working a shift, but that drink isn't quite for me, so I thought I'd try to make a variation without using olive brine (and since we don't stock olives anyway). What eventually evolved was something pretty different from where I began. With dominant flavors of caraway, bergamot, gentian, cinchona, and bitter grapefruit peel, it is surprisingly accessible as an after-work sipper on an "I needed this today" kinda day. —ABE VUCEKOVICH

MISE EN PLACE

GLASS . . . . . COUPE

ICE . . . . NONE

GARNISH . . . LEMON PIGTAIL

METHOD . . . COUPE STIR

SPEC

1.5 OZ . . . . . . AALBORG TAFFEL AKVAVIT

.50 OZ . . . . . . ITALICUS BERGAMOT LIQUEUR

.50 OZ . . . . . . DOLIN DRY VERMOUTH

.50 OZ . . . . . . BONAL GENTIANE-QUINA

2 DASHES . . GRAPEFRUIT BITTERS

CHILL YOUR COUPE. MEASURE THE bitters, Bonal, vermouth, Italicus, and aquavit into your mixing glass. Taste. With three sweet ingredients in this drink, make sure you have struck a fine Balance between sugary notes and the herbaceous spice-heavy dryness of the aquavit. Add ice cubes to the mixing glass, enough to fill it up three-quarters of the way full, and **COUPE STIR**. Taste along the way and stop stirring when the drink tastes like it's about to topple into something watery. **STRAIN** into the chilled coupe. Garnish; the lemon oils from the pigtail that leap from the fruit as you cut the ribbon of peel over the top of the drink should bring a great bump of clean citrusy brightness to the experience. Hang the pigtail over the edge of the glass at eleven o'clock and sip away.

STACKING: PAGE 36 ✳ COUPE STIR: PAGE 46 ✳ GARNISH: PAGE 77

EEYORE'S REQUIEM

CIRCA 2009

This is quintessentially a TVH drink because it's taking a standard Mother Drink—the Negroni—and reengineering it for a new audience. In this case, it's a six-touch cocktail that cranks the complexity, bitterness, and Texture of the original all the way up to 11. Is it overly complicated? Maybe. But is it so delicious that you bounce up and down like Tigger when you drink it? Completely and totally, yes, yes, it is. I probably should have named it "Caulfield's Requiem," but then it would have to have been a rye drink.

—TOBY MALONEY

MISE EN PLACE

GLASS . . . . . COUPE

ICE . . . . NONE

GARNISH . . . ORANGE PIGTAIL

METHOD . . . COUPE STIR

SPEC

1.5 OZ . . . . . . CAMPARI

1.0 OZ . . . . . . DOLIN BLANC VERMOUTH

.50 OZ . . . . . . JUNIPERO GIN
            (OR NAVY-PROOF GIN)

.25 OZ . . . . . . CYNAR

.25– OZ . . . . . FERNET-BRANCA

1 DASH . . . . ANGOSTURA ORANGE
            BITTERS

1 DASH . . . . REGANS' ORANGE BITTERS

CHILL YOUR COUPE. COMBINE THE bitters, Fernet, Cynar, vermouth, gin, and Campari in a mixing glass. Wrestle enough ice cubes to fill the glass three-quarters of the way full and **COUPE STIR**. Taste early and often, like how we vote here in Chicago. The Texture should start to round out, with the Fernet swooping in with a sting of menthol that cuts just slightly. Stop stirring the second the drink starts to lose its rich sweetness. **STRAIN** into your chilled coupe and garnish. When you pull and organize your pigtail, make sure you hold the citrus near the top of the drink so it sprays enough oil over the surface, then hang the pigtail on the glass and revel in how the drink explodes with flavor.

NEGRONI: PAGE 35 ✳ STACKING: PAGE 36 ✳
COUPE STIR: PAGE 46 ✳ GARNISH: PAGE 76

GLAZED & INFUSED

CIRCA 2018

When the Finnish brand Kyrö entered the Chicago market, I made several classic cocktails—namely, a martini, a Martinez, and a Negroni—with their gins to see how they would play with other ingredients. This ended up being a mash-up of the three, with a cool Balance between bright flavors and darker ones. Kyrö's flagship gin (formerly called Napue) tastes like summer, but the oak-cask-aged version has more fall and winter flavors, so that dynamic brings a lot of interest to the drink.

—MAX BECKMAN

MISE EN PLACE

GLASS.....**COUPE**

ICE.......**NONE**

GARNISH...**ORANGE DISK, FLAMED**

METHOD ...**COUPE STIR**

SPEC

1.0 OZ......**KYRÖ GIN (NAPUE)**

.50 OZ......**KYRÖ DARK GIN**

.50 OZ......**CARDAMARO**

.25 OZ......**CYNAR**

.75 OZ......**DOLIN BLANC VERMOUTH**

3 DASHES ..**BITTERCUBE ORANGE BITTERS**

1 DASH ....**PEYCHAUD'S BITTERS**

CHILL YOUR COUPE. SLIDE THE Peychaud's and orange bitters down the side of a mixing glass. Add the vermouth. Stack the Cynar and the Cardamaro to make sure you don't overpour either. Stack the two gins for the same reason—the Napue comes in at 46.3% ABV and the dark is 42.6% ABV, so while the combo is on the high side for distillates, it's Balanced out by having an equal ratio of low-ABV aromatized components in the mix, too. Ice that mixing glass with enough cubes to fill 'er up three-quarters of the way. **COUPE STIR.** Taste. The gins, vermouth, and two amari should start to come together nicely. Taste again, looking for water content; the quicksilver edge of the gin needs to soften and melt into the cocktail seamlessly. Keep stirring if you aren't quite there yet. **STRAIN** into your chilled coupe. Garnish with the flamed orange disk.

STACKING: PAGE 36 ✳ COUPE STIR: PAGE 46 ✳ FLAMED ORANGE DISK: PAGE 75

SIX CORNER SLING

CIRCA 2008

As a bridge to guide a drinker from the whiskey sour to the Sazerac, or to dabble in the world of whiskey and vermouth, this recipe is refreshing yet complex, with an herbaceous quality that balances the lemon juice and whiskey. Of all the cocktails I've created, the way the ingredients play together in this cocktail evoke the greatest sense of wonder. You have this idea of what this cocktail should taste like, but somehow it has this magical, unrecognizable flavor that keeps you coming back for another sip. —IRA KOPLOWITZ

MISE EN PLACE

GLASS . . . . . **COLLINS**

ICE . . . . **SHARD**

GARNISH . . . **LEMON NOTCH,
        ORANGE NOTCH**

METHOD . . . **COLLINS SHAKE**

SPEC

1.5 OZ . . . . . . **OLD OVERHOLT STRAIGHT
        RYE WHISKEY**

.75 OZ . . . . . **PUNT E MES**

.75 OZ . . . . . **LEMON JUICE**

.75 OZ . . . . . **SIMPLE SYRUP**

7 DROPS . . . **BITTERCUBE BOLIVAR
        BITTERS**

7 DROPS . . . **BITTERCUBE ORANGE
        BITTERS**

1 OZ . . . . **SODA WATER, TO BOTTOM**

.125 OZ . . . . . **HEIRLOOM GÉNÉPY,
        TO FLOAT**

FILL A COLLINS GLASS WITH THE ICE SHARD and soda to chill. This cocktail has nuanced flavor, so the proportions HAVE to be exact! Add the bitters, simple syrup, lemon juice, Punt e Mes, and rye whiskey to the large side of your shaker tin, in that order. Add 3 ice cubes then **COLLINS SHAKE**. Taste to make sure you have added enough dilution. **DOUBLE STRAIN** into your prepared Collins. Float the génépy. To garnish, express the oils from the citrus peels over the cocktail, one at a time. Insert the peels next to one another in the glass, squeezing the notch over the edge so they stay extended out of the glass.

SIMPLE SYRUP: PAGE 311 ✳ COLLINS SHAKE: PAGE 46 ✳ GARNISH: PAGE 76

FROM THE NORTH WIND BLOWS

CIRCA 2014

This dessert cocktail was inspired by the glassware. When I first started bartending, I thought it would be super cool to fill a tulip-style glass entirely with liquid. Most of the drinks served in that vessel were on crushed ice, so I wanted to play with people's expectations by doing something different. The Cognac and vermouth together create a nice sweetness that plays to the dessert drink idea, and while it's served cold, it has all the feelings of sipping an adult hot chocolate cozied up next to a fire.
—SPENCER RUTLEDGE

MISE EN PLACE

GLASS.....TULIP OR HURRICANE

ICE ....NONE

GARNISH...GRATED NUTMEG

METHOD ...MIME SHAKE,
             COLLINS SHAKE

SPEC

2.0 OZ......PIERRE FERRAND
             1840 COGNAC

.75 OZ......DEL PROFESSORE
             ROSSO VERMOUTH

.50+ OZ.....DEMERARA SYRUP

1 DASH ....ANGOSTURA BITTERS

1 ....WHOLE EGG

4 OZ.......RED RYE ALE, TO BOTTOM

CHILL YOUR TULIP GLASS, THEN add the beer. Plop your egg into the small side of your shaker tin. To the large side of the tin, add the bitters first, then the Demerara syrup, vermouth, and Cognac. **MIME SHAKE** for a quick few seconds. Add 3 ice cubes and **COLLINS SHAKE** again to frost the contents of the tin. Taste: the cocktail should be on the big and boozy side, since it will dilute with the kiss of red rye ale when it mingles with the beer in the glass. **DOUBLE STRAIN** into your prepared glass and grate a flourish of nutmeg over the top for aromatic delight.

DEMERARA SYRUP: PAGE 311 ✳ COLLINS SHAKE: PAGE 46 ✳
BOTTOM: PAGE 62 ✳ EGGS: PAGE 64 ✳ NUTMEG: PAGE 80

COPPER DAGGER

CIRCA 2008

When I workshopped this drink, I was exploring the idea of using amari and other nontraditional spirits as a base for a recipe, instead of something like whiskey, gin, or rum. Averna was my favorite thing at the time—to this day, it still reminds me of all the good flavors in Coca-Cola, like lavender and citrus. The rum creates a Balanced base and St-Germain took it into a really Curious territory. I love the way the cinnamon from the bitters really comes through in the Aroma. —IRA KOPLOWITZ

MISE EN PLACE

GLASS . . . . . NICK & NORA
             WITH SIDECAR
ICE . . . . NONE
GARNISH . . . 7 DROPS BITTERCUBE
             BLACKSTRAP BITTERS
METHOD . . . MIME SHAKE,
             COUPE SHAKE

SPEC

1.75 OZ . . . . . AMARO AVERNA
.25 OZ . . . . . . PLANTATION O.F.T.D. RUM
.75 OZ . . . . . . LEMON JUICE
.25 OZ . . . . . . ST-GERMAIN ELDERFLOWER
              LIQUEUR
.75 OZ . . . . . . SIMPLE SYRUP
1 DROP . . . . BITTERCUBE BLACKSTRAP
              BITTERS
1 . . . . EGG WHITE

SEPARATE YOUR EGG INTO THE small side of the shaker tin. To the large side of the tin, add the bitters. Stack your simple syrup and St-Germain, add to the shaker, then jigger your lemon juice and toss it in the shaker. Stack your amaro and rum and add to the shaker. **MIME SHAKE**, then add 5 cubes of stoic and uniform ice and **COUPE SHAKE**. Taste, looking for the way the dark rum, deep amaro, and floral St-Germain Juxtapose each other, causing a bit of dissonance. This is a good thing. **DOUBLE STRAIN** into a Nick & Nora, pouring the excess cocktail from the tin into a sidecar. Garnish with bitters, adding 4 drops to the cocktail and 3 to the sidecar.

SIMPLE SYRUP: PAGE 311 ✳ EGGS: PAGE 64 ✳
STACKING: PAGE 36 ✳ FLOAT: PAGE 81

PART FIVE

CREATIVE PROCESS

INVENTING A RECIPE FROM START TO FINISH

People always say a liberal arts degree is for kids who don't know what they want to do with their lives, but I see it as an education where you learn how to see the world not just in black and white, or through a microscope, but in vivid Technicolor from the space station. The liberal arts realm covers a well-rounded host of disciplines from economics and history to political science, philosophy, English, foreign languages, sociology, psychology, and the arts. It's an education where you are learning to think critically about *many different disciplines* instead of specializing in a single one. Only through this can you see the interconnectivity of it all.

By now, you know that the way we train our bartenders at The Violet Hour is very similar. Elsewhere in the book, I have made passing mention of the concept of gestalt—something that is made of many parts and yet is somehow *more than* or *different* from the combination of its parts. It is often expressed in the mathematical equation $1 + 1 = 3$. Gestalt is the heart and soul of the program we've built at TVH.

Gestalt works in reference to the cocktail itself and how many ingredients make up a drink, yes, but by now you should realize it's also about the *way* you invent and assemble that drink, too. The backstory, the Intentions, the ways you build complexity, and the ratios and methodologies you use take those components from disparate things to something whole. You need to understand *every little fucking thing* about the tools at your disposal, to pay attention to how things combine and how each thing affects the others.

It's obvious things, like how 80 proof rum and 151 proof rum will give you different daiquiris because this will lead to you changing the spec or shaking longer. It's looking for the sugar in lime juice and the citrus aspect in Campari so you can adjust your other ingredients so everything Balances. You have to be aware of contrast and simpatico, and how to jump and jive and ADJUST in the heat of the moment to create something beautiful. There comes a time that you will make these decisions with mere intuition; you'll toss an extra ice cube into the shaker because you have a cask-strength whiskey, or bring down the dashes of bitters in the split second after you pick up the bottle because you know it's low and 3 dashes are too much. This takes thousands and thousands of hours and fabricated drinks to do. That's why it's so much fun. Every part is intrinsically connected to every other part: This is the creative process of bartending and mixing drinks.

And don't forget that the creative process isn't just those hours that you are at the bar, making dealer's choices on the fly or workshopping cocktails for the menu. You need to be flexing those creative muscles all the time, reading and writing, discussing literature and the taco truck you ate at last week. Creativity comes from analyzing why things work or don't work for you. Being a curmudgeon or a pretentious ass isn't the same as critical thinking; blowing your friend's minds with your *enthusiastic* description of an espadín mezcal is way cooler. Putting together flavors and colors and textures is our job, and it's not that different from that of a painter or a sculptor. So you need to be out there experiencing, sucking the bone marrow, foie gras, and Jell-O shots out of life.

In the spirit of all that, we're concluding the book with a few broad strokes. First, a more streamlined example of how to start inventing a drink, with an examination of the workshopping process we follow at the bar. Next, we scrutinize one of the bar's most famous cocktails, the Juliet & Romeo, to see how every lesson in this book comes together to intertwine in a single recipe.

DRAFTING
AND
POLISHING
A RECIPE

Creating original cocktails, if you haven't had dozens of hours of practice already, can feel like rolling a boulder up a hill or trudging through the mud of horse muck after a torrential summer downpour. It's hard, putting pencil to paper for the first time and hoping something ingenious pops out. When most bartenders start out, there is a lot of staring at the blank pages of a notebook, figuring out exactly where to begin.

Hopefully the lessons we've laid out in the previous chapters of this book have made the starting line a little less intimidating, but it's worth mentioning here, during the final curtain call, that no writer starts out with a Pulitzer Prize. It's going to take practice to go from shaking your first Daiquiri to inventing the next Old Cuban. Thomas Edison didn't roll out of bed one morning and invent the lightbulb! He worked hard to get there, stole other people's ideas to rejigger them as his own, and you will have to do that with your cocktail practice as well. There will be many, many tins of muddled liquids assembled with good intent but ultimately tossed into the depths of the kitchen sink, because they don't click the way you think they will. And all of that is natural and normal. Don't beat yourself up about it! Pull up your bootstraps, leave your worst concoctions in the rear view, and keep your sights set on what you can improve during the next round.

There is only so much we can teach you in a book, but in a final attempt to help you inch a little closer to success, we're going to leave you with a few guides, guidelines, and tips. Once more, into the breach!

GET YOUR IDEA
ON PAPER

First, we start with the who/what/when/where/why, the style you have in mind, how the drink will be served, and what flourishes you imagine might make sense to include. Write down answers to these questions in pencil so you can fiddle with the ideas and measurements later if you need to.

What is your Inspiration?

What is the Intention? Who is the audience and what is the context?

What is the base ingredient?

What ingredients will sing alongside the base?

Will the drink be shaken or stirred (i.e., made with citrus or just booze)?

Will it be served up or on the rocks?

What Mother Drink template will you use?

What aromatic wizardry will you utilize to bring the whole thing together?

SKETCH OUT A SPEC

Now start fleshing out your spec using the recipe form we give bartenders. Again, harness the power of a steadfast no. 2 pencil so you can erase and rewrite specs as your instincts guide you toward measurements that will have the right Balance, complexity, and intrigue.

DRINK NAME

REASON FOR NAME, INSPIRATION FOR COCKTAIL: _____

_____

DATE

MISE EN PLACE

GLASS TYPE: _____

ICE TYPE: _____

GARNISH TYPE: _____

SPEC

____ OZ. _____
MAIN SPIRIT

____ OZ. _____
ANCILLARY SPIRIT

____ OZ. _____
FORTIFIED WINE/AMARI/LIQUEUR

____ OZ. _____
JUICE (LEMON OR LIME)

____ OZ. _____
*LENGTHENING JUICE
(GRAPEFRUIT, PINEAPPLE)*

____ OZ. _____
FLAVORED SYRUP

____ OZ. _____
SIMPLE/DEMERARA SYRUP

____ DASH _____
BITTERS (IF INCORPORATED)

_____
FRUIT, HERB

_____
EGG (WHITE, YOLK, WHOLE)

RINSE: _____
LIQUOR

BOTTOM: _____
SODA/CHAMPAGNE/BEER

FLOAT: _____
LIQUOR OR BITTERS

LACE: _____
SYRUP OR LIQUEUR

METHOD: _____
STIR/SHAKE/ROLL/BUILD

BRIEF DESCRIPTION OF METHOD: _____

_____

WORKSHOP

After a recipe has been drafted, it's time to workshop the drink from rough draft to final manuscript. At the bar, we do this as a staff exercise so everyone can be involved in determining what cocktails land on the menu. The process racks up a surprising number of hours. I tried to ballpark it once, and it was shocking.

Because we launch four menus a year, bartenders are almost constantly either dreaming up an idea for their next submission, tweaking one that's in the works, or participating in a final menu tasting to prepare their notes for serving the final drink. There is SO much that goes into this ephemeral thing that lasts but three months.

This is how it works: Bartenders polish their cocktails solo first, then submit them for the first workshop, where each drink is presented on its own merits. In these sessions, the author of the cocktail will give a little explanation of the idea behind the name (Inspiration), the style of the drink, the theme it speaks to, and the intended type of drinker on the cocktail's receiving end (Intention). Then everyone tastes it. There are most definitely some jitters to be felt when your creation is all of a sudden being tested by a murderers' row of amazing palates. We stick to constructive criticism, but even a discreet head tilt can mean a lot if certain folk do it. We talk about the Balance, the Texture, the water content, and the Aroma. Then we set it aside for a while, keep tasting drinks, and go back to it 5 minutes later to see if it held up over time (Narrative Arc).

Some cocktails that enter the room are just spot-on, and we love it when that happens. But for the most part we are editing during these sessions. I have always believed that less is more when putting together a chic ensemble, composing a dish, or creating a cocktail, and in light of that, we have found that the way to fix most drinks is to take something out, not add something. The culprit will usually stick out like a sore thumb.

Eventually we land on twenty-five to thirty drinks that are all great, all worthy of going on the menu. But we have only twenty slots to fill. So we do a "Kill Your Darlings" round, slashing and burning with the fervor of a newspaper editor on a hot deadline. It's heartbreaking to see something you worked really hard on, something delicious and righteous, not make the cut through no fault of your own. There is a lot of "fuck, that drink was killer, be sure to submit it next season . . ." kind of talk.

At the end of the process, we get all the drinks lined up and we look to see if there are too many served on chunks of ice, or too many tall crushed ice drinks, or if everything is pink or orange, or if every drink has mint as a garnish. We do little tweaks so every drink will be identifiable if it is whisked by on a tray. Sometimes we will have to take a cocktail and rework it to fit in another glass, and that will mean different ice or adding soda, so then the spec has to be jiggled. That's stage one.

A few days later, the whole staff (and often staff from other bars and restaurants in our One Off family) get together to taste the whole menu, all twenty drinks, so we can look at each drink individually and also within the context of the entire menu. Each bartender presents their drink with its full story again, then we discuss how to describe the drink, how to sell it, and what might be a good suggestion for drinks that would come before or after. The staff gets so many "What should I try next?" questions from guests that they need to find threads and journeys through two, three, and four cocktails and be able to explain how the cocktails relate and also why they should be drunk in a certain order. That's why we do this round in one sitting.

My favorite TVH tradition is the process of tasting a new menu as a team—being able to coexist in the same room at the same time as all of those brilliant, lovely coworkers, learning everyone's quirks and ticks and penchants, and being immersed in cocktail education while imbibing everyone's seasonal creativities.

—ROSALIA COSTELLO,
2014–2019

Do you know the saying "If you want to know the truth about something, ask a toddler"? For my money, if you need an unvarnished opinion, ask a hospitality worker who's day-drinking for free with a huge group of friends. About seven cocktails in, the wheels start coming off the bus and I have to start herding the cats with my drill sergeant voice. I'm parched and raspy by drink number twenty, but by that point, I have a picture of how the easy-breezy gin cocktail in slot three of the shaken side has a lot in common with the brown and bitter cocktail in slot nine of the stirred side, and what the vibe of the entire menu feels like.

This process is so important for the staff at The Violet Hour because it involves everyone. Even the folks working the door and the servers! We get to see the individual cocktails and the whole menu through the eyes and palates of a few dozen folks with very different tastes. Some have been at the bar for over a decade. Others might be joining for the first time. This is how we develop a menu that will have a wide variety of both accessible and adventurous cocktails.

This process can be tough if you're a home bartender, but you should try to get your cocktail creations in the hands of people who are willing to both pat you on the back and stab you in the front with honesty. The cool thing is you will never stop learning and getting better at creating drinks. There isn't one day that it's like, "Welp,

I'm good enough, I'm done." Every day, month, and year will make you better, but luckily, you will never be perfect, and that makes it worthwhile.

For those playing along at home who don't have a captive audience to test their creations on: no fear! Build the drink and ask yourself some questions to determine what might need to be adjusted.

How is the Balance of the drink? Too sweet?
Too acidic? Just right?

———

How is the Texture? If it's too thin, bump up the sweetener
a touch to get it back in line.

———

Do the style and personality of the drink fit the
glassware and ice?

———

Does the drink have enough complexity, or would it benefit
from an Echo, Complement, or Juxtaposition?

———

Is it too complex? Subtract an ingredient from your
recipe and try again.

———

Does the Narrative Arc evolve in a way that's pleasing,
or does it need to be adjusted?

———

Get someone else to taste your drink and ask them the
same questions! Present it to them the way we do at
TVH workshopping events.

———

*Don't forget the finishing touch on your cocktail. Citrus garnish and pineapple
leaves should be placed at 11 o'clock if the imbiber is right handed, or 1 o'clock
if left handed. Mint and straws go at 6 o'clock.*